Grounded in ancient wisdom and the newest scientific evidence, this book provides a host of tools for those suffering from depression. Strosahl and Robinson invite us to take a wholly new view of what depression is, and how to deal skillfully with it through strategies born of acceptance and self-compassion. Their book shows the pathways into and out of depression and gives us a vital map to see clearly where genuine peace and freedom lie.

—Mark Williams, professor of clinical psychology and
Wellcome Principal Research Fellow at the University of Oxford

Bill Knaus has hit the bullseye! From a horde of scientific studies and his own extensive experience, he has distilled an accessible, easily assimilated, pragmatic, and schematic approach to dealing with 'parasite' anxieties. Readers can work through this program in small bites to gradually advance their control over their destructive anxieties."

—Joseph Gerstein, MD, FACP, Harvard Medical School

The Mindfulness & Acceptance Workbook for Depression

Using Acceptance & Commitment Therapy to Move Through Depression & Create a Life Worth Living

KIRK D. STROSAHL, PH.D.
PATRICIA J. ROBINSON, PH.D.

New Harbinger Publications, Inc.

Publisher's Note

Distributed in Canada by Raincoast Books

Copyright © 2008 by Kirk Strosahl and Patricia Robinson
New Harbinger Publications, Inc.
5674 Shattuck Avenue
Oakland, CA 94609
www.newharbinger.com

Cover design by Amy Shoup
Interior illustrations by Sara Christian
Text design by Michele Waters-Kermes;
Acquired by Catharine Sutker
Edited by Jasmine Star
CD audio produced by Troy DuFrene

Library of Congress Cataloging-in-Publication Data

Strosahl, Kirk, 1950-
  The mindfulness and acceptance workbook for depression : using acceptance and commitment therapy to move through depression and create a life worth living / Kirk D. Strosahl and Patricia J. Robinson.
    p. cm.
  Includes bibliographical references.
  ISBN-13: 978-1-57224-548-8 (pbk. : alk. paper)
  ISBN-10: 1-57224-548-4 (pbk. : alk. paper) 1. Depression, Mental. 2.
Acceptance and commitment therapy. I. Robinson, Patricia J. II. Title.
  RC537.S845 2008
  616.85'270651--dc22
                    2008011919

FSC
Mixed Sources
Product group from well-managed
forests and other controlled sources

Cert no. SW-COC-002283
www.fsc.org
© 1996 Forest Stewardship Council

10   09   08

10   9   8   7   6   5   4   3   2

To my dearest lifelong friend, Gregory E. Campbell, who taught me a great deal about what it means to be accepting, mindful, and committed to living. The world was made a better place because you were in it. You left it far too early, my friend. And to my mom, Joyce V. Strosahl, my lifelong friend, confidant, supporter, and advisor.

—KS

To my mom, Wanda Johnson, my dad, Ennis Robinson, my mother-in-law, Joyce V. Strosahl, and my father-in-law, John Strosahl. Thank you for being my friends and teachers. And to Greg Campbell, with the hope that this book will inspire moments of peace, like that of the color of golden corn that you painted and shared with the world.

—PR

To our daughter, Joanna May Robinson, for all of her dedication and hard work, and her sense of humor. She helped us write a more readable book and one that made sense. To all of the people we have served, past and present, in honor of their bold journeys out of depression and into chosen lives. To Regan, Ezra, Frances, Joanna, Ashley, Amanda, James, Elspeth, McCullough, Alex, Jackson, A.J., Ellie, and Logan—we hope you are always learning to hold your story lines lightly while you pursue your dreams! And to Jasmine Star, a fantastic editor who made this book much better than it was before she started, all with good humor, insight, compassion, and energy.

—KS and PR

Contents

Dear Reader:

Welcome to New Harbinger Publications. New Harbinger is dedicated to publishing books based on acceptance and commitment therapy (ACT) and its application to specific areas. New Harbinger has a long-standing reputation as a publisher of quality, well-researched books for general and professional audiences.

As part of New Harbinger's commitment to publishing sound, scientific, clinically based research, Steven C. Hayes, Ph.D., Georg H. Eifert, Ph.D., and John P. Forsyth, Ph.D., oversee all prospective ACT books for the Acceptance and Commitment Therapy Series. As ACT Series editors, we review all ACT books published by New Harbinger, comment on proposals and offer guidance as needed, and use a gentle hand in making suggestions regarding content, depth, and scope of each book. We strive to ensure that any claims that are unsubstantiated or clearly ACT inconsistent are flagged for the authors so they can revise these sections to ensure that the work meets our criteria.

Books in the Acceptance and Commitment Therapy Series:

- Have an adequate scientific base

- Are theoretically coherent—they fit with the ACT model and underlying behavioral principles as they have evolved at the time of writing

- Avoid jargon and unnecessary entanglement with proprietary methods, leaving ACT work open and available

- Keep the focus always on what is good for you, the reader

- Support the further development of the field

- Provide information in a way that is of practical use

These guidelines reflect the values of the broader ACT community to ensure that you will receive information that can truly be helpful and that can alleviate your suffering.

Depression is one of the most common and most destructive psychological problems human beings can face. It can seemingly take away love, relationships, work, and even life itself. Depression is a challenge that can bring heroes to their knees.

You are holding a volume that takes all of that in, stands up, and presents a powerful alternative. Humble and yet bold, *The Mindfulness and Acceptance Workbook for Depression* is written by Kirk Strosahl and Patti Robinson. Kirk and Patti were first exposed to ACT in 1986 and quickly became central to the work in its earliest days. Kirk and Patti began to explore its clinical applications and became leading innovators, therapists, and trainers in the ACT community. Kirk was a coauthor on the original volume on ACT in 1999. Skilled clinicians with an ability to get to the essence of issues, Kirk and Patti have made ACT far more accessible and have infused it with their humanity and wisdom. This book reflects the highest values of caring and we recommend it wholeheartedly.

Sincerely,
Steven C. Hayes, Ph.D., John P. Forsyth, Ph.D., and Georg H. Eifert, Ph.D.

Foreword:
Trading Illusions for Actions

Depression is not just a feeling. Depression is an action.

That simple insight will strike with a force as you read this book. It is an insight worth preparing for because as it dawns, it initially contains both good news and bad news. The bad news is that the human mind will often turn it into yet another source for blame: "If depression is an action, then I should not be doing it, but apparently I am, so it must be my fault." No surprise there. Judging and blaming is what our minds often do, particularly when we are depressed. But the actions that lead to depression—the actions that in a deep sense *are* depression—are nothing to be blamed for. After all, the human mind is far, far too tricky for anyone to untangle from it without help. Depression is not the *fault* of the depressed.

The empowering news inside this same insight is even more powerful and more sustaining than the illusion of helplessness or the habits of self-blame. As you read this book you will see that there is a concrete, active path forward. You are not a victim of your life. You are not doomed to endless suffering.

As you understand the actions that have kept you entangled, you will begin to see that there is another way. The alternative is not beyond you. It is available, with help to see it, right here, right now.

In this remarkable book, the husband-and-wife team of Kirk Strosahl and Patti Robinson lay down an innovative, creative, and effective pathway out of depression and into your life. The book is like turning on a light inside darkened rooms of suffering. With the light comes greater understanding of what is in those rooms, where you are, and what has been in your way. It becomes easier to see how to navigate and how to come out into the warmth and freedom of a life without walls, directed toward your values.

From the first few pages of this book until the very last, the light of awareness that it casts is almost tangible. You can sense the gentleness, strength, and humanity of the human beings, two of my dearest friends, who have written this book. These authors are humble, centered, compassionate, and wise. They've been there. They are ready to walk you, step by step, through the actions that have created trouble and the actions needed to let go of depressed habits of mind. If you have patience with the process, self-compassion for the pain you are in, and a willingness to face the difficulties and fears of taking a fundamentally different pathway forward, this book can change your life.

I can say that without fear of contradiction, because the scientific evidence showing that the processes this book targets are central to depression has grown exponentially over the last decade. We now know a great deal about how cognitive entanglement works and how to help people become disentangled through mindfulness. We now know a lot about how avoidance of experience works, and how acceptance can dampen down the war within. And we know a lot about how openness to experience can help you get in touch with your values and to begin to create a life with your moment-to-moment actions that resonates more with your deepest yearnings for meaning, wholeness, and connection with others.

You do not need to trust me or trust these authors for the benefits of this book to be felt. You do not need to believe anything or be convinced of anything. What you need is the willingness to look without blinking—to see what is true in your experience. As you try the methods in this book, your own experience will be your best teacher.

Depression is not just a feeling. Depression is an action. The "word machine" in between our ears may indeed fear what that means, but for human beings the message is hopeful, vital, and valid. You do not need to wait for life. It has begun and it is yours to *live*.

If you are ready to open up to that possibility, turn the page and begin.

—Steven C. Hayes
University of Nevada

A New Perspective on Depression

Our doubts are traitors, and make us lose the good we oft might win,
by fearing to attempt. —William Shakespeare

Depression is one of the most common emotional health issues in contemporary society. It's hard to turn on the TV without seeing some type of advertisement for a new drug, over-the-counter supplement, or other purported cure for depression. Newspaper stories explain the tragedy of a suicide by describing the victim's struggle with depression. Indeed, the media and other cultural institutions teach us to see depression as a monster—an illness that's passed from one family member to another. We read stories of scientists using high-tech brain scanning equipment and see pictures of human brains with and without depression. We read other stories about scientists confidently predicting that we are just around the corner from discovering the gene that controls depression. In other words, the popular view of depression is that it is an abnormal state of mind, a biological illness that must be vanquished by treatment.

We also get emotional appeals about what life is like when depression is treated successfully. We see or hear that the formerly depressed person is now in a state of bliss, that his or her relationships have been restored and new ones formed. We see advertisements where a person who used to sit dejectedly with head in hands now walks gleefully with children, spouse, or pets and seems to be absolutely carefree. Indeed, the message is that in order to get your life under control, you must first get rid of your depression. All you have to do to acquire this state of bliss is get your doctor to put you on the drug that is being advertised.

A DIFFERENT PERSPECTIVE

This book offers you an opportunity to understand your depression and what to do about it in an entirely different light—that depression is the result of living a life that is out of balance in some important way. Depression never springs out of an otherwise healthy, vital, purposeful life. Depression is not an aberration, a fluke, or an accident of nature. It is a logical result of what you're putting into your life. Your depression is telling you something that you need to listen to. It's a signal that you need to spring into action and address the aspects of your life that are out of balance.

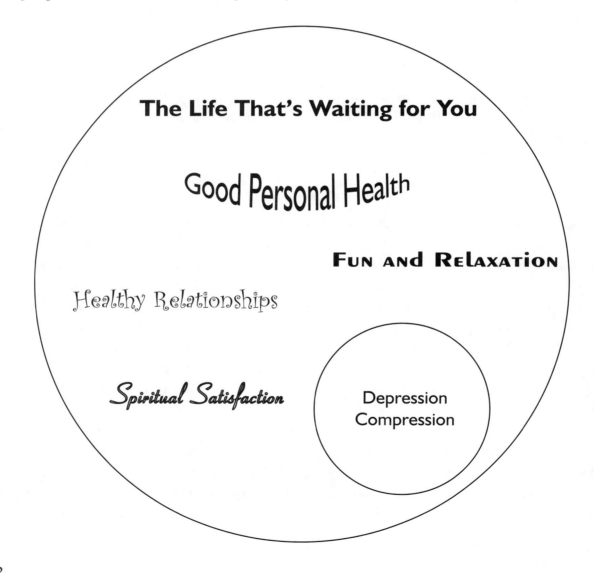

What If Controlling Depression Isn't the Goal?

If your depression is a signal, what is it telling you? The answer differs from person to person, but the general message is that you're acting in ways that are steadily pulling you away from the things in life that you value. Compared to what is possible for you, your participation in life is shrinking. Most people assume that depression causes them to withdraw from life activities, and therefore believe the goal is to eliminate their depression in order to get on with life. Unfortunately, this commonsense approach simply doesn't produce the desired results. Paradoxically, well-intentioned attempts to suppress or eliminate depressing thoughts, memories, and emotions often intensify these experiences. In other words, the very things you do to control your depression may increase it. The result is that you fall into the habit of constricting your activities, feelings, thoughts, and memories in the service of being less depressed, only to find that you're more depressed. This narrows your life down to a small fraction of what it can be.

What If the Goal Is to Feel What You Feel and Pursue a Life Worth Living?

Most people want the same things in life: good health; loving relationships; meaningful work experiences; and positive recreational, spiritual, and leisure activities. This is a vital life—a life worth living—and pursuing it is not a feel-good exercise, with one pleasant event leading to another. Rather, it is a commitment to living, in which you willingly experience your feelings and thoughts, both wanted and unwanted, and do what is valuable or meaningful to you.

Unfortunately, many of the messages from contemporary society offer little support for this approach to living. The biggest obstacles on the road to a life worth living are created and reinforced by our social training. The human capacity to think and feel creates an opportunity to improve many aspects of the external world, but it also makes us susceptible to being programmed with rules for living that suck the vitality out of our day-to-day experiences and, in the extreme, lead to depression.

This book offers strategies that will help you define what you want your life to be about, accept the inevitable ups and downs that life has to offer, and keep your eye on the prize. This might sound overly simplistic and even unrealistic at some level, but it's effective because it addresses a paradox that underlies being stuck in depression: The harder you try to suppress or control depression, the more depressed you get. The more you avoid situations that might produce depression, the more these situations languish and fester. When you fall into this trap, you create an even greater sense of not being in control of your destiny.

SOME BACKGROUND ON ACCEPTANCE AND COMMITMENT THERAPY

Acceptance and commitment therapy (ACT; pronounced like the word "act") grew out of the cognitive behavioral therapy movement in the late 1980s. ACT was developed from a program of basic research that examined the role of language and thoughts in suffering. ACT has been applied to all kinds of problems, ranging from chronic pain to anxiety to quitting smoking. In clinical studies, ACT has proven to be a good treatment for depression, and it seems to continue producing benefits well after treatment is completed (Zettle and Rains 1989; Zettle and Hayes 1987).

ACT Fosters Mindfulness and Acceptance in Daily Living

ACT is based on the assumption that most unwanted internal experiences cannot be eliminated or controlled, so they must be accepted. An example is emotion. Most emotions are learned and automatically triggered responses to specific situations, interactions, or events. Since we're programmed to emit emotional responses almost from the moment of birth, there's no way to keep them from occurring in response to stressful or unpleasant situations. However, by using mindfulness and acceptance strategies, you can step back from your instantaneous emotions, rather than be consumed by them. Similarly, unpleasant thoughts, memories, and some physical sensations are based in learning, occur automatically, and cannot be willfully snuffed out of existence. When you learn to accept, rather than struggle with, aspects of your inner world over which you have no control, you can invest your time and energy in things you *can* control.

ACT Focuses on Valued Actions

One aspect of living that is under your immediate control is your daily behavior and how consistent it is with what you believe in. A unique feature of ACT is the heavy emphasis it places on values-based living. By helping people explore their personal values, ACT provides a compass heading toward living a meaningful life. Over the years, we've found that it's much easier to accept painful aspects of life when you have a sense of direction that dignifies what you are experiencing.

The Goal of ACT: Psychological Flexibility

The purpose of the ACT approach to depression is to help you develop greater flexibility in your approach to life. In ACT, being flexible means sticking with things that are healthy even though they may not feel good, and stopping things that are unhealthy even though they might serve a purpose at the time (and might even feel good!). This ability to persist when persistence is useful and desist when what you're doing isn't working, is perhaps the single most important skill needed in the confusing times we live in. Flexibility means that you have a sense of direction and meaning in life, that you accept the myriad challenges associated with living, and that you're able to act in ways that are consistent with your values. Further, you can do all of these things even while experiencing distressing thoughts, feelings, memories, and sensations.

A Mantra: Accept, Choose, and Take Action

Another way of thinking about ACT is as a prescription for healthy living:

A for Accept

C for Choose

T for Take action

"Accept, choose, and take action." Say this aloud several times now and really take it to heart. It may be helpful to you as you read and practice ACT strategies over the coming weeks. Write it on several pieces of paper and tape them to your refrigerator, your vanity mirror, your toilet seat, the edge of your computer screen, and wherever else you'll see it often. We want these three simple concepts to become your daily mantra. Say it to yourself twenty times a day or more! Sometimes we're accused of functioning more like cheerleaders than therapists, but heck, if cheerleading helps a person build a life worth living, we're down with it!

HOW THIS BOOK IS ORGANIZED

This book is organized into three major sections to help you in your journey toward health and well-being. Part 1 is called "Create a Context for Change." As you start your journey, you need to understand what your depression experiences are, how they affect your current life, and the ways that depression might be preventing you (or protecting you) from dealing with personal problems you need to deal with. This will allow you to understand how your depression operates, both between your ears and in the outer world.

Part 2, "Step Out of Depression and Into a Vital Life," is designed to help you clarify what you want your life to be about and then remove the obstacles, some of them self-imposed, that get in the way of living that life. You'll need to learn some skills that will help you accept unpleasant realities, step back from them so they don't consume you, and then act in ways that promote better results for you. This part of your journey will sometimes be confusing, and involve thinking and behaving in ways opposite to those you might have used in the past. If you stick with it—and you can!—you'll begin to see the paradox that underlies depression, and be able to do something about it.

Part 3, "Make a Commitment to Vitality," will help you develop a plan for making your new strategies for valued living into habits that will inoculate you from having to deal with depression again. This is actually the most important part of this self-help program, because depression is sneaky and can creep up on you again in the future. If you learn to create forces in your life that support your new ways of behaving, you can protect yourself from a relapse. We'll teach you strategies for identifying early warning signs that you might be slipping, and help you develop a set of behaviors you can use to halt the descent into depression. We'll also offer guidance on forming a network of social supports that you can use to keep you on track.

HOW TO USE THIS BOOK

Like many people, you may be interested in a self-help book because of a desire to learn how to control your depression without bothering others or incurring the cost of professional help. This strategy can succeed to the extent that you stick with this program, so we've designed it to make this easier for you. Each chapter in this book has the same basic organization: We introduce one or two important ACT concepts and illustrate these with stories of people who have struggled with depression. These real-life case histories are drawn from our work as psychologists over the last twenty-five years. We offer a wide variety of examples to ensure that some of them remind you of your own situation. Each chapter includes exercises to help you develop your awareness of a particular issue and to practice skills that will help you be succeed. We summarize key points to remember at the end of each chapter.

Some people will read this book quickly, while others may only read a chapter per week. It's less important to be good at every strategy we discuss than to be good at using a few key strategies that fit your personal style. It's okay to jump around in the book, focusing on chapters that appeal to your interests and needs at the time. If you become adept in just a few ACT strategies, we are confident that you'll notice an immediate effect on your quality of life.

The ideas and activities we offer are sometimes just common sense, sometimes subtle, and sometimes confusing. Don't get discouraged if some concepts are harder to grasp than others. The nature of the depression beast is such that ACT has to battle it using strategies that sometimes seem counterintuitive. Our advice is to stick with this approach for at least two months to give it a chance to work for you. In one clinical study, most patients reported major improvements in mood and life satisfaction within the first month of working with these powerful concepts (Robinson 1996).

To help you use this program over time, we've developed the enclosed CD to support the strategies and activities described in this book. There are two basic libraries on the CD: One contains the worksheets for many of the exercises in this workbook. The other contains audio-recordings of certain acceptance and mindfulness exercises. If you can, use the audio-recordings for those exercises because they provide more specific guidance than is possible when you have to first read the exercise and then close your eyes and do the visualization. Look for the following icons in the text:

 This icon tells you that you can download a blank copy of the worksheet from the CD.

 This icon tells you that we've recorded this exercise to help you get into it.

RALLY YOUR SOCIAL SUPPORT

You're more likely to complete this program if you receive support from someone else. If social support is a major issue for you, you might want to go ahead and take a look at chapter 16, which offers a lot of guidance in this regard. One strategy that will be useful right now is to mention what you're trying to do to a friend, an intimate partner, a physician, a sibling, or someone else who can hold your feet to the fire. Making a commitment to try something different in front of someone else is a powerful way to support your success. You can do the same with your family doctor. Mention that you're trying to overcome depression and want to use this program. Ask your doctor to check in with you about how you're doing with the program at each medical visit. If you're working with a therapist, it would be a good idea to take this book with you to your next appointment and go over the structure of the program together. Then, you can come up with a plan for integrating various sections of the book into the therapy process, perhaps using some of the chapters in part 2 as homework that you will complete between sessions.

A LITTLE STORY

There is an ancient Buddhist tale that might help you find the boldness to commit to reading this book and following through with its program. It's a story that speaks to having the courage to give life your best shot, despite the inevitable process of change that we all must learn to accept.

> *A young monk walks many miles, hoping to gather enlightenment from a renowned Zen master. When the student enters the master's chamber, the master is sitting on the floor drinking from a cup. The master explains to the student that the cup is very precious. The student agrees, and the master asks, "Why do you think this cup is so precious?" The student suggests it is the color and size of the cup and the slender quality of its handle. The master agrees that all of these aspects make it an attractive cup, but these are not its most precious*

properties. The student becomes confused and asks the master to answer his own question. The master sighs. "It is most precious because it is already broken and it has already held so many cups of tea."

Your life has a beginning and an end, with everything in between being an exercise in uncertainty and change. As the old saying goes, "The only constant in life is change." This is the nature of pursuing your dream of a life worth living. The journey is perfectly made to teach you what you need to know, if you will only accept that everything is destined to change. Is this a reason to avoid starting the journey? We think not, especially as change is inevitable either way! We hope you agree, and we challenge you to keep reading.

Create a Context for Change

The unexamined life is not worth living. —Plato

The first principle to follow in stepping out of your depression and back into your life is to understand that you can only start from where you are, not from where you would like to be. To solve a complicated problem like depression, you must understand how you got into it in the first place. This requires you to take an honest look at several factors known to contribute to depression. In part 1 of this book, we'll introduce you to a new way of thinking about depression and teach you to recognize the key elements of the depression trap: avoidance of painful issues, attachment to unworkable ideas about how to live life, and ignoring the results of some of your coping efforts. Together, these elements lock you into a vicious cycle that you can easily escape once you learn to recognize it. You'll complete several self-inventories to identify how depression is affecting your life, and you'll come to understand the forces that are driving you into the small and restricted living space we refer to as "depression compression."

Once you understand how depression works, you'll be in an excellent position to do something about it. This is the focus of part 2. Right now the key is to learn to think about your depression in a new way and then get an accurate picture of the factors that are propelling you in unintended directions. This might be difficult at times because the truth doesn't always feel good, but the truth actually will set you free! So read each chapter carefully and try to complete all the self-inventory exercises. Don't beat yourself up, just collect the results and get ready to step out of your depression.

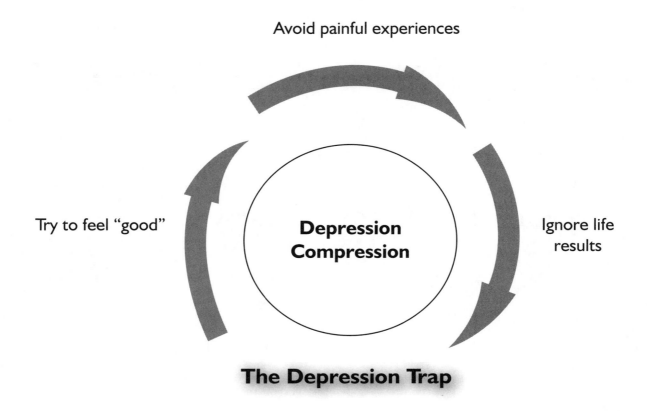

Here's a worksheet to help you keep track of your confidence in your grasp of the material presented in each chapter. After reading each chapter, come back to this worksheet and rate your confidence level on a scale of 1 to 10, where 1 indicates that you need more help and 10 indicates that you've totally got it. Take your time with these initial chapters because they require you to get outside the box and rethink how depression is functioning for you, and against you, in your life right now. If you give yourself a chance to complete part 1, we promise that you'll understand depression in a new way that will give you a fresh start on creating the kind of life you want to live.

PART 1 CONFIDENCE WORKSHEET

Need More Help			Not Confident			Confident			Got It!	
1	2	3	4	5	6	7	8	9	10	

	Chapter	Confidence Level
1	See Depression for What It Is	
2	Recognize Pathways Into and Out of Depression	
3	Take Inventory of Depression and Its Impact on Your Life	
4	Recognize the Depression Trap	
5	Understand Your Mind, Trust Your Experience	

Debriefing. If your confidence rating is 5 or less for any chapter, you might want to reread those sections of the chapter that were confusing to you. If that doesn't work, you might want to share the chapter with a friend or supporter and see if putting your heads together helps to clear the air. Enlisting this type of support often helps deepen your understanding and can inspire you to keep working your way through the program. It takes patience to make changes in your life. Be kind to yourself when you feel frustrated with the results you're getting.

CHAPTER 1

See Depression for What It Is

One of the saddest lessons of history is this: If we've been bamboozled long enough, we tend to reject any evidence of the bamboozle. The bamboozle has captured us. Once you give a charlatan power over you, you almost never get it back. —Carl Sagan

If you're looking at this self-help book, it's likely that you're struggling with serious issues in your life that you haven't been able to fix. You may be in a bad relationship, maybe even an abusive one. Maybe your job is at a dead end and you haven't mustered the courage to move on to something else because of the risks involved. You may simply be demoralized by the demands of life and the ongoing stress of it all. Perhaps you're trying to care for an aging parent while raising your children and pursuing a career. Perhaps you're having trouble with one or more of your children and can't find the right way to approach it. Or you might not be approaching it at all because you don't like conflict. You may be struggling with health problems that can't be solved, like chronic pain or a chronic disease like diabetes.

Perhaps you're fighting a secret or not so secret addiction to alcohol, drugs, sex, or food—habits that help you escape from and numb personal pain in the short term, but lead to more depression in the long run. It may be that you're so busy reliving your past that you've forgotten how to live in the present, or worse, you're letting your past dictate how you're willing to live in the present. You may simply be living by the numbers, hoping that life will cut you a better deal if you follow all the rules. You might even be experiencing a lot of success in your life at the surface level, earning a good salary and having a nice home and lots of "toys," but feel unhappy and out of sorts anyway.

At first glance, none of these scenarios seems way out of the ordinary. These types of personal challenges are the bread and butter of everyday living. People fall in and out of love, get divorced, change or lose jobs, and grapple with unwanted events like illness and the death of loved ones. People often cope with stress in ways that don't work that well. There are almost 24 million people dependent on alcohol and other drugs in the United States alone (Grant et al. 2004), roughly 8.6 percent of the entire population. The pervasiveness of these types of problems corresponds to the substantial lifetime risk of depression: approximately 25 percent for women and 20 percent for men (Kessler et al. 2005). This means that one in four women will experience depression, and one in five men. If you're reading this book in a bookstore or a waiting room with twenty people in it, look around and guess which five people are or have been struggling with depression, or will do so in the future. Do these numbers suggest that something is amiss in our basic human training? Is depression the common cold of modern living? If so, what's the pathogen responsible for this epidemic of suffering?

The purpose of this chapter is to help you identify and understand what depression is and how it works, and to help dispel some myths about depression that could lead you into a blind alley. If you're going to focus your energy on getting on top of your depression, we want to help you zero in on the strategies that will give you the biggest bang for your buck. You'll learn to recognize symptoms of depression and understand their positive and negative impacts in your life. When you begin to understand the way depression affects your life, you can take a slow, deep breath of fresh air and see new options for addressing your challenging circumstances.

THE ACT PERSPECTIVE

Acceptance and commitment therapy (ACT) offers a new view of depression, suggesting that there's something in the water supply of your social upbringing that sets you up for depression, particularly when you face challenging life situations. Perhaps you've been trained to believe that the goal in such situations is to be strong and not allow yourself to feel any pain. Worse yet, maybe you've learned that having negative emotions such as sadness, guilt, anger, or fear is a sign that you aren't healthy. This type of message puts you at odds with the way you feel in situation after situation. Perhaps you've fallen into the habit of avoiding troublesome situations in your life in the hope that they'll just go away and then you'll feel better again.

But depression doesn't arise in a vacuum, and the fact that it's present in your life is a signal that something isn't working quite right. Consider this: Perhaps avoiding problems in your marriage, family, job, or health doesn't make the problem go away, and actually makes the situation worse. If you don't address important problems in an intimate relationship, you may feel less connected to your partner and start to drift away. As things get worse, your depression will deepen and you may begin to avoid other problems, like the fact that you're feeling less and less intimate with your partner. Likewise, if your job is unfulfilling and your approach is to not think about the fact that your work is losing its meaning, avoidance of the problem can just make your work less interesting and eventually drag down your sense of accomplishment. Or if you have a risky health habit like smoking, drinking too much, or being too reliant on drugs, simply turning your back on the problem doesn't make it less risky. In all of these situations, somewhere in your mind you remain aware that you aren't dealing with a problem that is detracting from your sense of who you are. Even if it's unintentional, falling into a pattern of avoiding unpleasant or painful feelings and the situations that trigger them is a major cause of depression.

Think about the life circumstances that surround your experience of depression. Then consider this information from an eagle's-eye view, in which you take many steps back and ask yourself the following questions: If your depression is telling you something about your current life situation, what is the message? Is it possible that depression is protecting you from having to feel the emotional pain you would otherwise endure if you turned around and faced the music? Is it possible that the very behaviors you use to keep your mood in check are actually increasing your depression? For a moment, simply consider this possibility.

The first step in the journey to a vital life is to begin asking unusual questions that often produce confusing answers. However, confusion would be a good sign just now, because the very things you think might help your situation could, in fact, be doing just the opposite. For example, even though you might protect yourself from a conflict with your partner by not discussing dissatisfactions with the relationship, this just allows the problems in the relationship to grow and fester. This will increase your depression, not decrease it. With depression, there are all kinds of strange loops like this to deal with, and it can become very confusing.

MEANINGS OF THE WORD "DEPRESSION"

"Depression" is an interesting word that has multiple meanings. Let's take a look at some of the ways it's used in everyday language:

- **Sadness:** A state of unhappiness and hopelessness

- **Psychiatric disorder:** A disorder characterized by symptoms such as feelings of hopelessness and dejection, poor concentration, lack of energy, disturbed sleep or appetite, self-critical thinking, and sometimes suicidal tendencies

- **Economic slump:** A period in which an economy is greatly affected by unemployment, low output, inflation, and widespread poverty

- **Reduced activity:** A lowering of activity, quality, vitality, or force

- **Hollow:** A geographical formation that's lower than the surface area surrounding it

- **Low pressure area:** An area of low barometric pressure that often brings rain

Like the range of meanings for the word, the experience of depression varies significantly from person to person. However, there are common aspects that form the basis for our definition of depression. We think of depression as a period of life constriction, much like being in a low pressure area in one's life. Life constriction means that you aren't succeeding in making your life what you would like it to be; your life isn't producing the sense of vitality, purpose, and meaning that you hoped it would. As you expend more and more of your energy dealing with the symptoms of depression, you have less and less energy to devote to other areas of your life. As a result, your life pursuits begin to shrink in scope and become compressed. Compared to the options that are actually available to you, your pursuits become increasingly restricted in number and scope. This is what we call "depression compression."

Humans behave differently when living in depression compression. Depressed people complain not only of sadness, but also of a sense of numbness and detachment. Pursuing fundamental activities of living in many realms, such as relationships, health, work, and play, seems less important, less necessary. It's as if you're hiking blindfolded; even though you keep moving your feet, you can't see your destination and therefore have no sense of direction. You also can't see the obstacles, and thus they go undetected and ignored, and all too easily become stumbling blocks. Amanda's situation serves as a good illustration of living in depression compression.

■ Amanda's Story

Amanda, a twenty-seven-year-old unmarried bank executive, has struggled with depression since early adolescence. She was overweight even as a child and was often teased by kids at school. In high school, she was a good student but didn't have many friends and never dated. She felt ashamed of the way she looked and pushed away boys who expressed an interest in her. She described her high school years as awful and painful to the core. She felt that other students talked about her behind her back and made fun of her weight.

In college, she tended to steer away from social settings and continued to gain weight. Her efforts to create a sense of comfort and pleasure centered on cooking and eating, and she tipped the scales at over two hundred pounds by the time she was twenty-five. She met a man in a cooking class, and they dated for six months and eventually had intimate relations. Amanda was devastated when he abruptly terminated the relationship soon after their intimacy started. She felt she'd made herself vulnerable and that she'd been exploited. She was sure he had been turned off by how she looked naked, and she vowed to never be hurt by a man again.

She continued to gain weight, and physical activity became increasingly uncomfortable for her. At age twenty-seven, she was diagnosed with diabetes and her depression spiraled out of control. She overdosed on medication one night, hoping to go to sleep forever, and woke up in the emergency room. The ER physician prescribed an antidepressant, which Amanda took for several months after a follow-up visit with her family doctor. Although she noticed some improvements in her energy and her sleep, she still felt depressed and continued to avoid social activities except those required by her work.

DEPRESSIVE EXPERIENCES

Amanda's situation is fairly typical of people who are prone to depression. She did have a real problem with her weight, as many people do in modern society. However, she became preoccupied with her physical appearance and overly identified with an image of herself as ugly and unlovable. Then she began behaving in ways that conformed to her image of herself. She avoided people, and so people began to avoid her. She began to use overeating, another avoidance strategy, to nullify her negative feelings about herself. This led to weight gain and eventually diabetes. She turned away from one of her main life values: to have a life partner and a family. Instead, she anticipated a bad ending to any close relationship and focused her efforts on making sure she wouldn't be rejected. Finally, when she learned she was diabetic, she engaged in the ultimate form of avoidance: trying to kill herself.

While there are as many circumstances that lead to depression as there are people who become depressed, there are similarities in how depression is experienced. The number one thing to remember about depression is that it's a downward spiral in which experiences in one realm of living create a domino effect that results in a decline in other areas. As Amanda's case shows, there are five main ways that most people experience the downward spiral of depression: feelings, sensations, thoughts, memories, and behaviors.

Feelings

Depression often involves chronic sadness, anger, and irritability, but in a more blunted and free-floating fashion than we usually experience emotions. Sometimes feelings seem to come out of the blue, particularly crying spells when there seems to be nothing to cry about. Depression also involves a sense of emotional numbness and constriction. When a depressed person experiences positive emotions, they are often muted. This is referred to as *anhedonia*, which literally means "the inability to experience pleasure." When negative emotions are in play, they seem to arise quickly and with great force. This emotional battering drains the person of energy on a daily basis. Amanda described her depression like this: "I feel like I'm trying to live in a dark room where things seem to move around me like shadows."

Sensations

Depression also produces a variety of unpleasant physical symptoms, such as abdominal pain, chest pain, headaches, or various other pains and bodily discomforts. Breathing patterns may be shallow, resulting in less oxygen in the blood, so concentration and focus may be a problem. Tension may increase, and this can cause more restlessness, particularly at night. Fatigue is common, resulting in less desire to engage in physical activities and more problems with muscle aches and pains. In addition, depression is associated with increased risk of illness and disease, suggesting that it impacts the immune system in various ways. Depressed people tend to view themselves as unhealthy in the physical sense of the word. In Amanda's case, she often went to the doctor with complaints ranging from an upset stomach to painful menstruation. When asked about her physical health, she said she hadn't felt healthy in years.

Thoughts

We human beings tend to have slightly more negative thoughts than positive thoughts, even when we're not depressed. Of course, the ratio of negative to positive slants even more toward the negative in a depressed state. Depressed thinking is characterized by a black-and-white flavor, and perfectionistic, self-critical thoughts are common, such as "I'm a loser," "I'm unlovable," or "I'm damaged goods." Thinking is often focused on past setbacks and disappointments; guilt and feelings of shame are common. In a depressed state, people spend an excessive amount of time reviewing past mistakes, blaming themselves for letting others down, and imagining negative outcomes in the future. Another thinking pattern in depression is to ruminate about being depressed in the first place, repeatedly experiencing thoughts like "What's wrong with me?" or "Why can't I be happy some of the time, like other people?" This just feeds the depression cycle. Amanda was a poster child for the problem of rumination. When she wasn't thinking about her physical appearance, she was focusing on past rejections and preparing for more in the future.

Memories

Depressed people spend a lot of time remembering events, particularly those that trigger depressed feelings. As we'll explain in chapter 10, research on memory in depression suggests it is skewed in a negative direction. For example, depressed people tend to recall negative events more easily than they do positive events. Additionally, their memory for life events is more vague and general in nature. This tendency toward imprecise memories can trigger a vicious cycle of distorted thinking. In Amanda's case, she ruminated over memories of the cruel things her father had said to her as a child and selectively remembered the most negative events of her years in school. Eventually she came to label her entire childhood as traumatic.

Behaviors

Depression both affects daily behavior patterns and is affected by them. Depressed people may engage in excessive amounts of certain behaviors, such as eating, sleeping, or consuming alcohol, and neglect behaviors like exercise, leisure pursuits, or spending time with friends or family. They tend to spend more time "in their heads" and therefore shy away from others and from activities that demand physical action and sustained attention. This is because much of depressed behavior is dedicated to preserving what scarce energy is left. Not engaging in positive behaviors due to lack of energy is a core problem, because it increases depression. As a person becomes less active, the body naturally produces less energy in a negative feedback loop. In Amanda's case, she didn't do any exercise and increasingly avoided social situations. Ultimately, as her social and physical activity level bottomed out, her mood worsened and she didn't have the energy needed to participate in activities that could improve her mood.

MYTHS ABOUT DEPRESSION

Because it is such a common problem, depression is frequently discussed on TV and the radio and in newspapers, magazines, and self-help books. The tendency in the media is to take the best sound bites about a subject, and in the case of depression, this has created quite a few misconceptions about what depression is and what it isn't. Amanda's example highlights many of the more common myths that surround depression and, in particular, how it develops and how it can be undone. Since these myths may create an inaccurate picture of depression and lead you to follow strategies that aren't likely to work, let's go ahead and take a look at them.

Myth 1: Depression Is Abnormal

The literal meaning of the word "abnormal" is "out of the ordinary." Thus, to be abnormal something must occur only rarely. However, we know from clinical research that approximately 10 percent of the U.S. population suffers from some sort of depression every year (Kessler et al. 2005). Here is an even more surprising statistic: The annual rate of any mental disorder or an addiction to drugs or alcohol is 27 percent, and the lifetime occurrence is nearly 50 percent (Kessler et al. 2005). This means that over the course of a lifetime, almost half of the U.S. population will develop a significant emotional health problem. In fact, the vast majority of normal people do report short periods of depression.

It's hard to argue that something like depression is abnormal when so many people experience it at some point. This is like calling the common cold an abnormal occurrence. Having a cold doesn't feel good, but it certainly isn't abnormal. When you recall Amanda's life situation preceding her descent into depression, did it seem all that unusual to you? The circumstances she confronted seem like the bread and butter of everyday living. Every person has things they don't like about themselves, almost everyone has been rejected in a relationship, and almost anyone would be scared if they heard they had diabetes. We'd be hard-pressed to identify anything about Amanda's life that's way out of the ordinary.

A different way to think about depression is that it actually plays a pivotal role in healthy living. It signals that your life is not working well. If you can accept this way of thinking about depression, it will be that much easier to stop blaming yourself and get on with the business of changing things that need to be changed and can be changed. If Amanda could accept that she was depressed and not beat herself up about it, she'd be in a position to channel her blaming energy into change energy.

Myth 2: Depression Is an Inevitable Response to Life Stress

We know from research that life stress is a trigger for depression at least half the time (Schotte et al. 2006). In fact, one highly publicized study found that at least 25 percent of all cases of clinical depression are really more likely a reaction to some form of loss or personal setback (Wakefield et al. 2007). What this suggests is that depression is often intertwined with negative life events. However, such setbacks are part and parcel of being alive, and when unfortunate events unfold, it's natural to feel bad. This isn't unhealthy. It's the attempt to suppress them or escape from negative feelings that causes problems. This was certainly true in Amanda's case. Her increasing isolation and weight gain were unconscious attempts to control her growing sense of vulnerability around others. When combined with the sudden diagnosis of diabetes, this dangerous pattern of escape from feelings (through overeating) and withdrawal (avoiding social opportunities) pulled her into depression compression.

The problem with this myth, that depression is an inevitable response to life stress, is that many people experience life stresses, some devastating, but don't go on to suffer from depression. This probably has to do with the models we observe as children, as this is how we learn to cope with stress. For example, if a parent responds to stress by withdrawing from family meals and avoiding meaningful conversations, there's a good chance the children will try similar coping strategies as adults.

Another factor is the direct instruction we receive about how to manage our feelings and actions in stressful situations. We all hear admonishments or rules like "Laugh and the world laughs with you; cry and you cry alone" or "Don't cry or I'll give you something to cry about." We differ in the extent to which we take these rules to be literal truths and try to use them to address the problems of living. As you'll learn, when rules dominate how you respond to life stress, they often constrict your actions, making it more difficult to be pragmatic and flexible in your approach to complicated life problems. In Amanda's case, she responded to stress by following rules that required her to withdraw from others in order to protect herself, such as "Nobody likes fat people, so I should just stay home where I'm safe from their critical looks and unkind remarks." The more Amanda withdrew, the more isolated she felt, and the more her energy was consumed by her struggle with depression. In effect, she was set up to collapse into depression compression when the right event came along, and it did.

Myth 3: Depression Is About Experiencing Emotions

Amanda's situation demonstrates another important myth about depression. Depression is often thought of as an active state of feeling bad, yet a lot of Amanda's behaviors were designed to protect her from negative feelings, such as loss, rejection, and shame. Her depression was as much about *not* feeling as it was about feeling. While one of the hallmark symptoms of depression is free-floating sadness, irritability, and shame, depression is also an experience of numbness and detachment. Depressed people complain of feeling alone in a room full of people. They experience a state of apathy and disinterest in social activities, often to the point of avoiding these situations. These aspects of the depression experience suggest that it may help us *avoid* feelings.

Sadness is part of the human condition, just like our other basic emotions, and when allowed to, it flows in and out of our awareness throughout the day. There are many things in life that *should* trigger sadness, such as learning that a good friend has cancer, being treated unfairly by your boss, or being spoken to unkindly by a loved one. But when you're depressed, sadness, anger, and tearfulness seem to appear out of the blue. They seem to be disconnected from the real world and often aren't the feelings you'd expect to have in response to the situation. In this sense, these free-floating emotional events are what you get when you avoid experiencing your emotions in a more direct and grounded way. Because the situations that produce sadness aren't being addressed, sadness becomes dislodged and starts hunting for a home. Even a minor event can become a lightning rod for these dislodged feelings. Depression is the emotional result of turning away from and refusing to directly experience unwanted feelings, thoughts, images, or memories.

Amanda spent enormous amounts of time and energy trying to avoid situations that would push her buttons. She consciously avoided interpersonal situations where she might meet men who were single and interested in her. Instead of enjoying spending time with men, she stayed on guard for any indications of interest on the other person's part. When her buttons were pushed, she didn't like the way she felt and would retreat into her world of isolation and eating to help quell her feelings. Sadly, these attempts to control how she felt backfired even in the safety of her seclusion. At home, she cried for no particular reason and at work she snapped at her coworkers at the slightest provocation. If Amanda could turn around and face her biggest fears, she would start to feel healthy again. It isn't that her issues in life would suddenly disappear. Rather, she could choose to stop running from them. She could choose to stay in situations that produced these unpleasant reactions and learn how to accept them. This wouldn't eliminate her reactions or make them pleasant, but it would allow her to form the social connections that she so badly wanted.

Myth 4: Depression Is a Biological Illness

That depression is a biological illness is perhaps the most widespread misconception about depression, as it has been actively promoted by the pharmaceutical industry, various consumer advocacy groups, and the medical professions. Each of these groups has something to gain by promoting the notion that depression is an illness. For the pharmaceutical industry, this converts into billions of dollars in drug sales. For consumer advocacy groups, calling something an illness absolves the "ill" person from responsibility for the problem and presumably reduces the stigma of having a mental health problem. For medical professionals, this simplifies the treatment approach to depression, allowing doctors to prescribe a medication and avoid all of the complexities of asking people to change behaviors that might be triggering their depression.

We can say with confidence that the scientific evidence does not support defining depression as a biological disease. That's why the World Health Organization, the global body responsible for defining and describing disease states, doesn't currently recognize depression as a disease. Of course, all human behavior ultimately comes down to a matter of biology, but it isn't at all clear that changes in brain chemistry cause depression, nor is it clear that such changes produce the mood, thinking, and behavioral problems associated with depression. It's just as reasonable to propose that it works the other way around—that depression causes changes in brain chemistry. In other words, when you begin to think, feel, and behave in a way that results in depression, you change your brain chemistry. The take-home message is that the idea that depression is a biological disease or an illness is simply an opinion about what depression is, not what science says it is.

So what is the best way to think about the condition of depression? Most experts agree that depression involves an interaction of thoughts, feelings, and behaviors that can ultimately affect, or be affected by, basic biological processes. This perspective is often referred to as the biopsychosocial model of depression (Schotte et al. 2006). In this approach, biology is but one of many factors that must be considered. At least equally important are the impacts of life stress, coping style, previous learning, thinking style, behavior, and social and cultural factors. In other words, depression is far more complex in how it develops and is resolved than we're commonly led to believe.

Amanda's case highlights this complexity of the factors involved in depression. For her, one of the biggest factors was how she'd learned to cope with her issues since childhood. Most of her strategies were designed to help her avoid problematic situations and feelings. Her thinking style was to be on guard for any situation that might involve rejection or humiliation. Her coping style was to isolate herself and use eating to help control her feelings. Because she tended to isolate herself, she didn't have many social supports to call on. Ultimately, the intervention that turned her life in a positive direction was more lifestyle oriented than biological. Things began to improve when she committed herself to an ACT campaign and began to adopt behaviors that produced better results.

Myth 5: Medication Is the Best Treatment for Depression

For at least two decades, there has been conclusive evidence that cognitive behavioral therapy is just as effective as medication in the treatment of depression. Interestingly, many studies suggest that cognitive behavioral therapy is actually more effective over time in terms of preventing future episodes of depression (Paykel 2006). This is important because depression tends to be a recurrent problem. Many people who experience depression have a pattern of recovering and then relapsing again. Often, this pattern continues throughout a person's life. Any approach that reduces the chances of being depressed again is definitely worth exploring.

Despite the clear-cut, long-term advantage of learning self-management strategies for ending depression and avoiding recurrence, the media continue to barrage us with messages suggesting that the key to treating depression is to take medication. Several things happened in the late 1980s and throughout the 1990s to fuel this misconception. First, many new antidepressant medications were introduced into the marketplace, and drug companies aggressively marketed these new medications to physicians and other health care professionals. Since most of these medications have fewer negative side effects at the start of treatment than older medications, primary care providers felt more comfortable prescribing them. Later, when bans against advertising to the public were lifted, drug companies marketed antidepressant medications directly to consumers. Today's ads make an emotional appeal suggesting that a normal life isn't possible unless the consumer uses the medication. At the same time, these ads tend to underplay the risks and limitations of using such medicines and often imply that no other changes are necessary to achieve a satisfying life; just take the medication as prescribed and the drug will do it for you.

These marketing activities have had a profound effect on the diagnosis and treatment of mental disorders in the United States. More people than ever are being diagnosed with depression, and more people than ever are being prescribed medications for depression. Fewer people are receiving therapy because antidepressant drugs are so readily available. At the same time, financing for mental health treatment has been severely curtailed due to the strategies of managed care. These strategies generally make it harder for people to get the mental health treatment they need. During the 1990s, the reduction in U.S. health expenditures for mental health services was roughly equivalent to the increase in expenditures on antidepressant medications.

A final misconception is that medicines work faster than therapy to reduce depression. There is, in fact, growing evidence that cognitive and behavioral interventions may produce very rapid improvements in depression (Kelly, Roberts, and Ciesla 2005). In fact, cognitive behavioral treatments like ACT may produce benefits faster than medications (Mynors-Wallis et al. 2000), and without the troubling side effects.

This leaves us with a very important question, which you are no doubt asking if you're taking antidepressants or considering taking them: "What role does the medication play in my recovery, and what role do the concepts and strategies in this book play?" Our answer (admittedly biased!) is a simple one: Even if you've benefited from antidepressants, it's still wise to practice the strategies we teach in this book. They could help you avoid depression in the future. If you're currently taking antidepressants, think about it this way: Medications might help reduce some of your symptoms, like overwhelming fatigue, loss of energy, lack of sleep, and problems with concentration, which can keep you from making positive changes in your life. Antidepressants can't make these changes for you; only you can do that. The skills and strategies suggested in this book can serve as a kind of map for when, where, and how to make these life changes. In other words, taking antidepressants (if you're inclined to do so) and learning the approaches in this book can complement each other. You could also elect to try the approaches we describe before making a decision about whether to try an antidepressant. You might find that you don't need to go that route if you really follow through with this program.

In Amanda's case, she did take an antidepressant for several months and found it only somewhat helpful. This is not unusual; people who take antidepressants often get some benefits but continue to experience various symptoms. In Amanda's case, she simply had too many depressive behaviors that the medicine couldn't help with. They might help her sleep better and have more energy, but she still had to change her behavior before she could succeed in areas of life that were important to her. She had to enter situations she was avoiding, and no medication could do that for her. This is the bottom line with antidepressants: They can help take the edge off various symptoms, but it's up to the person to make needed lifestyle changes. When Amanda understood more about what she could do to improve her mood, she began to experience very rapid positive changes in her outlook on life.

Myth 6: Depression Is Something You Have

It's tempting to talk about "having" depression like we talk about having a common cold. Saying you have a cold suggests that the cold has afflicted you through no fault of your own. And indeed, it's almost impossible to protect yourself from getting a cold because there are so many ways to be exposed to infectious organisms, and they're invisibly small. People often talk about depression similarly, as though it descends on them from out of the blue. This implies that there's no relationship between the person's life situation, their coping responses, and the development of depression. If this were true, the depressed person wouldn't be responsible in any way for the depression, just like a person with a cold isn't responsible. This, of course, is why the biological and genetic explanations of depression are so popular. They create the impression that you're a victim of depression and therefore not responsible for it.

There are two major problems with this idea. First, we know that people who develop depression start engaging in actions that feed into depression long before they develop the mood symptoms of depression. It can be difficult for the person to see the long-term impact of these behavior shifts, which seem like the right thing to do at the time. So it isn't as though people choose to behave in ways that they know will produce depression. In the flow of daily existence, these choices just happen, and they seem innocent and well-intentioned at the time. In Amanda's case, she developed a habit of avoiding situations that pushed her buttons long before she slipped into depression. You could say that her style of living made her vulnerable to depression.

A better way of explaining how depression develops is that it is the result of two types of avoidance: avoiding potentially unpleasant feelings, and avoiding the situations that trigger these feelings. When you do this enough, you get depressed. The idea that behaviors produce depression is new to a lot of people, but there is a commonsense aspect to this idea. We want to encourage you to see this for what it is: an attempt to give you a new way to think about depression. This is not designed to make you blame yourself for being depressed; it's designed to help you see that there is a way out of depression and that the way out is under your immediate control!

The second problem with the notion that depression is something you *have* is that it can lead you into the role of being sick. When you're sick, you may become especially passive and wait for your condition to improve on its own or for someone to come along and cure you. Depression seldom works this way. As you engage in more passive behaviors, such as avoidance, isolation, and withdrawal, your depression deepens. So depression doesn't really work like the common cold. Taking two aspirin every four hours, drinking lots of water, and getting lots of rest won't cure depression, and in fact, no medication can cure you if you continue to engage in actions that feed your depression. This is what Amanda discovered, and when she did, she was able to reverse her downward spiral by deliberately planning to approach, rather than avoid, the situations that were blocking her drive toward vitality, purpose, and meaning.

TRADING ILLUSIONS FOR ACTIONS

Once you understand depression for what it is, rather than what it seems to be, you're in an excellent position to begin to do something about it. What depression seems to be is a set of mental, emotional, and physical symptoms that can be overwhelming if you try to take them on individually. In reality, depression is a set of experiences that tells you something is out of balance in your approach to living. Depression is never an accident of nature; it is perfectly designed to tell you something important about how your life is going. Rather than rejecting your depression as a blight, you can learn to accept where you are at in your life and view depression as a natural consequence of living in a very complicated age. Right here, right now, you can stop beating up on yourself for being depressed and treat yourself with compassion instead. You can redirect your energy toward solving the dilemmas that have you stuck right now. There is a solution to this problem at your fingertips, and in the remainder of this book we'll show you how to turn your situation around.

■ *Amanda's Journey Toward a Vital Life*

At age twenty-seven, Amanda decided that she'd had enough of the type of life she was living, and started to use the ACT approach. Her first step was to stop blaming herself for feeling depressed and to stop using depression as a reason for not engaging her life. She accepted that what she was doing wasn't working and that the very strategies she was using to try to control her depression were actually making it worse. Even though she was depressed, she recognized that what she really wanted most in life was a partnership with a special person who would accept her for who she was and who would be a good parent and companion. She made a commitment to start dating again and practice letting go of her preoccupation with her physical appearance.

She also decided to do thirty minutes of fast walking a day so she could improve her overall health, and she committed to eating healthy meals on a regular basis and to stopping snacking when she felt nervous, stressed, or depressed. This was difficult because she'd been thinking and behaving in this way for so long that it was almost automatic. She had to learn how to allow her negative thoughts and emotions to come without being consumed by them. Early on, a couple of dates went badly when she got lost in her negative self-talk, but with time she found that her old, self-critical thoughts had less of an impact on her. Her next step was to face her fear that men were out to exploit her. She made a conscious commitment to go on two dates a month and to actively work to accept the fact that she had been hurt and that she could take her time in deciding about the type of man she'd like to marry.

About six months after she started her ACT campaign, Amanda met a man who was also overweight, and they felt comfortable together from the beginning. Predictably, she was afraid of being rejected, but she learned that he, too, thought of himself as unlovable and unattractive, and they were able to laugh about their common fear. In addition, Amanda noticed that her new walking and healthy-eating habits improved her sleep and her overall mood. Her diabetes, which had been out of control due to inactivity and snacking on junk food, started to moderate, and this made Amanda more optimistic about her future. One day she woke up and realized that she felt more content with life than she had in many years. She still felt vulnerable with her boyfriend and had thoughts about being fat and unlovable, but she didn't take them so seriously. Amanda was on the path toward a vital, purposeful life!

Secrets to ACT On

☞ Depression is not abnormal. Nearly a quarter of all people will experience depression at some time in their lives.

☞ Depression is something you do, not something you have. It's based in your behavior patterns, something that you can focus on correcting.

☞ Depression is not an automatic result of life stress or life difficulties. It arises from how you cope with these difficulties.

☞ Depression is as much about not feeling as it is about feeling. Depression is often experienced as a state of numbness, detachment, and disconnection with vital pursuits.

☞ Depression is a signal that your life is out of balance; it's a call to action and as such can help you live a better life.

The Coach Says

Illusions are persistent, and if it were easy to peel away the layers of the onion of depression, you would have done it long ago. Trying to look beyond your current perspective takes a great deal of courage; we are here with you as you lift the familiar veil and peek out at the possibilities.

Sneak Preview

In the next chapter, we'll tell you about paths into and out of depression. We'll introduce you to the two major culprits that produce depression, and show you how three basic response styles can help you develop the psychological flexibility needed to move through depression and reclaim your life.

CHAPTER 2

Recognize Pathways Into and Out of Depression

Life is like riding a bicycle. You don't fall off unless you plan to stop pedaling.
—Claude Pepper

As mentioned, depression never springs out of a vacuum. It is a result of how a person responds to an array of triggering events that life has to offer. Thus, it is important for you understand how depression compression starts and what maintains or worsens it. This chapter will explain how depression develops and what changes will be required to live life more vitally. We introduce the notion of siren songs that woo us off of the road we want to take in living our lives. We'll also introduce you to the three dimensions of psychological flexibility and show you how they can reduce your vulnerability to depression.

PATHWAYS INTO DEPRESSION: TRIGGERING EVENTS

It is widely accepted that most people experience some symptoms of depression every now and then. A term often used for these short-term feelings is *dysphoria*. Nearly everyone goes through periods of dysphoria, in which negative thoughts, feelings, images, or physical sensations are present. Vulnerability to depression is probably the result of culturally promoted rules about how to deal with emotionally challenging situations and the dysphoria they can produce. We'll explore this idea in detail later in the book. For now, let's just say that the purpose of coping behaviors such as physical or mental withdrawal in response to a stressful event is to allow you to rest and restore your energy. The problem is, some of us don't emerge from the fog after a reasonable period of downtime. We don't get back into the flow of life, with its many ups and downs. We stop pursuing a life that has vitality, purpose, and meaning.

To understand how depression might work in your life, you need to appreciate how depression gets started and how it's maintained over time. Given how overwhelmingly negative it feels to be depressed, the processes that trigger depression and keep it going must be powerful indeed. As a first step, let's examine the role that triggering events play. A *triggering event* might be thought of as an event, situation, or interaction that produces a strong initial surge of dysphoria. The amazingly high rate of depression in modern life suggests that there are numerous ways to trigger a person into depression compression. Let's look at three common triggers: loss, traumatic stress, and health problems.

Dealing with Loss

Sometimes people experience a loss or disappointment and fail to emerge from their grief. Instead of letting grief heal their wounds, they allow it to warp into an avoidance process. In this process, a person may live a quiet life, focused on maintaining a minimal amount of engagement or investment in work and play activities. The new life plan is to avoid making any attachments that might result in another future loss. This was the path that Maria unwittingly took.

■ *Maria's Story*

Since childhood, Maria aspired to be a mother. She married at twenty and conceived a child in the second year of her marriage. She and her husband were ecstatic. The pregnancy went well, and Maria gave birth to a beautiful baby girl, Martha. Her first few weeks of life gave Maria the most joyous moments of her entire life. Then Maria awoke one morning to find Martha dead in her crib. Maria wailed and sobbed, and when her tears stopped she fell into a deep silence. Her husband and extended family offered a great deal of support to her, but she didn't recover.

Years after the loss, she continued to avoid everything except the basics required for living. She worked but didn't enjoy her job or her coworkers. She cooked, but she had little interest in her husband's life or needs. She didn't read or have any hobbies; she just watched television and waited for bedtime. She slept poorly and often ate several times during the long hours of the night. She gained weight and was annoyed by suggestions from her husband and doctor that she should exercise, go to a grief group, or take some sort of action to turn her situation around. Maria wanted to stop thinking that she'd neglected Martha the night she died. She wanted to be left alone and never have to care about anyone as much as she'd cared for Martha.

Coping with Trauma

Life offers many challenges, and these often come into your life without being invited. Overwhelming challenges, particularly during your childhood and teenage years, may increase the likelihood of depression in adulthood. This is particularly likely if you develop strategies to help you avoid the pain of remembering and reduce the likelihood of exposure to future traumas. These avoidance strategies, such as overworking and problematic drinking, are common in today's world, and the cost is often poor relationships as well as health problems. Anna's story typifies this pathway to depression.

■ *Anna's Story*

Anna was the first person in her family to go to college. She was bright and hardworking, and completed her undergraduate studies in three years by going to school during the summers. She went into graduate school without taking even a short break. However, relationships were difficult for her due to a long history of trauma. Her parents divorced when she was a child, and her mother died when she was ten. When she was a teenager, her grandfather was murdered. And during her freshman year in college, she was a victim of date rape. Anna coped with her shock and trauma by minimizing social outings and avoiding dating. She worked long hours in her job as a child welfare worker and sent money to her father, who was an alcoholic. She rationalized that she would like to socialize and have female friends but didn't have time between her work and her studies. At night, she surfed the Internet and drank tequila. She set a limit of five shots, and this is what she drank every night before bed. Her sleep was disturbed by nightmares, she worried about a pain she felt in her chest when she awoke, and tension in her shoulders and neck annoyed her throughout the day. Anna just wanted to keep the bad memories and her sense of aloneness under control.

Reacting to Health Problems

Another common pathway into depression involves falling into patterns of behavior that lead to poor health. There's a common saying that health isn't much, but nothing else is worth much without it. Several problematic assumptions about health can lead people down this pathway. Many people believe that health comes naturally, that there is no real need to work to preserve it, and that doctors can find ways to eliminate health problems if they occur. A culture that fails to help its citizens develop the intention, courage, and skills to preserve personal health is bound to experience a runaway train of preventable health problems.

Behaviors such as smoking, drinking, taking drugs, overeating or eating poorly, and not exercising enough put people in jeopardy of serious health problems, both directly and indirectly. These risky behaviors are directly related to heart, lung, kidney, and liver disease and other chronic illnesses. Once established, an unhealthy lifestyle is difficult to change and the long-term results pervade all aspects of life. The absence of positive health behaviors, such as exercise, eating healthfully, and managing stress positively also puts people at risk for developing chronic illnesses. In this case, the person isn't trying to get sick but is in harm's way because the body's natural defenses are being weakened by the absence of healthy, protective behaviors. This was the situation for Joe, who used overeating to suppress a variety of negative feelings.

■ *Joe's Story*

Joe had always struggled with his eating. He simply loved food too much, particularly high-fat foods. The best moments in his childhood revolved around eating, cooking, and music. He met a delightful woman in his senior year of college and lost some weight to please her. They got married, and within the first year of their marriage, Joe gained fifty pounds. His wife was critical of his eating habits, particularly his eating ice cream by the carton at night after dinner. Eventually she had an affair, and Joe fought off devastating feelings of rejection by moving to a separate bedroom, eating even more at night, and listening to music alone.

When his doctor diagnosed high blood pressure and high cholesterol, Joe felt defective and told no one. He made excuses for not attending church and avoided family gatherings except on big holidays. He preferred to stay home where he could watch movies, listen to music, and enjoy his favorite foods. Joe didn't want to feel the pain of being rejected by his wife, and he didn't want to hear any more bad news from his doctor. He didn't want to have the worries he had about his body, which seemed to be failing him.

PATHWAYS INTO DEPRESSION: CONTROL YOUR MOOD, LOSE CONTROL OF YOUR LIFE

In each of these examples, there is a familiar theme we see in people who are struggling with depression. Depression is the result of sacrificing participation in life for a sense of control over distressing emotions, thoughts, or memories. Maria, Anna, and Joe each developed a style of living that was geared to avoiding painful personal problems. To avoid dealing with painful feelings, thoughts, or memories, each of them withdrew and settled for a less meaningful life. Their values regarding health, relationships, work, and play took a backseat as avoidance drove more and more of their daily choices. However, as their lives became less vital, their difficult feelings didn't evaporate; instead, their depression deepened.

Their stories demonstrate that depression doesn't occur by accident. Depressed behaviors produce very predictable results, even though you aren't trying to get those results. That is the paradox of depression. You engage in a behavior that you believe will help you feel better, and instead it makes you feel worse. For example, when you avoid spending time with friends because you're too depressed, they'll eventually stop reaching out to you. This will allow you to spend more time by yourself, and you may believe this will help your depression by preserving your energy. However, the less activity you engage in, the less motivated you feel to do things. You'll start to feel lonely and wonder if your friends have forgotten about you. This sense of isolation will make you feel even more depressed.

Every behavior in this cycle has its own logic and is done for a purpose. This doesn't mean you're trying to make yourself depressed. To the contrary, you're trying to do just the opposite. Unfortunately, the logic of depression doesn't quite hold together. Going back to the stories of Maria, Anna, and Joe, we can look at the purpose of their coping responses with an eye toward appreciating how depression logic tricked them into even deeper depression.

Maria spent most of her time at home cooking, eating, watching television, and lying in bed. She sought safety in the sameness of a highly constricted day-to-day routine and never confronted her painful feelings of loss and vulnerability. When her husband encouraged her to exercise or seek professional help, she said nothing and left the room, allowing her to avoid direct conflict.

Anna never complained; she also never told anyone about her traumas. When she talked to her father, she only mentioned her accomplishments so as not to risk his criticisms. By limiting her social contact and the topics of conversation, she sought to reduce her vulnerability and her exposure to painful memories, and she drank to reduce her physical and emotional pain.

To minimize the risk of failure, Joe backed out on agreements to do various activities with his wife and to follow his doctor's advice. He avoided social gatherings and follow-up appointments to avoid criticism, and he came up with excuses for avoiding exercise so he could justify his negative behaviors rather than deal with them.

For each of these people, the pathway into depression involved turning away from distressing personal or interpersonal issues rather than confronting them. This is done to protect the person from feeling painful emotions, thoughts, memories, or physical sensations. However, as you've learned, the paradox of depression—and of avoidance in general—is that personal or interpersonal issues worsen because of the avoidance, causing distressing emotions, thoughts, memories, and physical symptoms to increase. At a certain point, the person becomes trapped in a toxic cycle of avoidance, more unsolved issues, and worsening personal pain—and a general sense that there's no way out.

Because of the overwhelming burden of depression symptoms, the prospect of trying to address and resolve personal issues seems like a hopeless task. The frustration of not being in a position to approach and solve a painful situation results in unpredictable experiences of anger and irritability, a surprising but frequent symptom of depression. On the other hand, avoidance, isolation, and withdrawal only serve to amplify the pain of the situation. Knowing that the emotional pain is going to come anyway leads to a sense of anxiety, another emotion that often accompanies depression. The resulting emotional overload leads to the only remaining option: to slip into a stance of numbness, apathy, and indifference. However, this too is yet another form of turning away from the painful and seemingly unsolvable problems at hand.

Most depressed people know that avoiding personal problems doesn't help their situation. At some level, they know that tiptoeing around painful thoughts, feelings, or memories doesn't really solve anything. So why is it that intelligent, insightful people can know in their hearts that a particular strategy isn't helping, but still use it anyway? One of the unique features of ACT is that it helps to identify and substantiate two basic processes that lie at the heart of this paradox.

PATHWAYS INTO DEPRESSION: TWO SIREN SONGS

In the classic Greek epic *The Odyssey*, Odysseus and his small group of soldiers set out at the conclusion of the Trojan War to return to their families in Greece. They must traverse the treacherous north coast of the Aegean Sea in a small wooden boat, and along the way they endure unimaginable perils and hardship. At one point in the journey, they have to sail through a narrow passage. Hidden in the rocks above the shore are sirens, female sea deities who sing beautiful songs to attract travelers, put them in a spell, and lure them to their destruction on the rocks below. Not only are their songs lovely, their lyrics speak to the deepest longings of the listener. Aware of the power of the sirens' songs, Odysseus orders his men to cover their ears, tie him to the mast, and not release him under any circumstances, no matter what he says or does. While he knows the sirens' song is an illusion, he is so captivated by it that he begs his companions to release him. Only Odysseus's intention—his orders to his men in advance—prevents Odysseus's ship from being dashed on the rocks.

This story provides a metaphor for understanding the power of the processes that lure us into depression. One siren song is that protecting ourselves from negative feelings, memories, thoughts, or sensations will preserve our well-being, and that the best way to prevent these negative internal experiences from occurring is to avoid situations that could trigger them. This is the siren song of avoidance. Another siren song is buying your thoughts—believing that they represent reality. This is just like falling for the fictions and false promises in the songs of the mythical sirens. This is the siren song of fusion. As we'll show you, in depression you're tricked into following these siren songs even though you're trying your best to live your life fully and completely. These songs are powerful, and we hear them daily, regardless of whether depression is an issue. Whether a person slides into depression compression upon hearing their seductive song relates to both awareness and intention—the same factors that allowed Odysseus to travel past them and continue on his homeward journey.

The First Siren Song: Emotional Avoidance

Think of the first siren song, *emotional avoidance*, as the tendency to avoid making direct contact with distressing thoughts or images, unpleasant emotions, painful memories, distressing physical sensations, and the situations that trigger them. Emotional avoidance is a rather automatic response, meaning that you might be only minimally aware that you're engaging in an avoidance move at the time you engage in it. When you look back on the situation, you might be able to describe your behavior in avoidance terms, but that doesn't guarantee that you'll use a different response the next time a similar situation rolls around. The extent to which you're reluctant to make direct contact with this type of unpleasantness is probably the extent to which you will struggle with depression. In chapter 3, we'll address the issue of emotional avoidance and its impact on depression in much more detail. We'll also help you identify which issues in your life are causing you the most pain, as they're the ones you're likely to be avoiding.

The Second Siren Song: Fusion

Think of *fusion* as identifying with your negative thoughts, images, emotions, memories, and physical sensations in such a way as to make them into threats to your health and vitality. When you evaluate thoughts, feelings, and memories as dangerous, you'll be prone to try to eliminate these unpleasant intruders from your life. Unfortunately, the more you follow this strategy, the more depressed you get. In chapter 5, we'll examine the issue of fusion in your life. One form of fusion that's especially dangerous is being bound by specific rules about what constitutes health and happiness in life and how you must achieve it. You'll discover that you've been programmed to respond automatically to these rules, even though the road to health and happiness differs substantially from what your cultural training suggests.

As the diagram on the next page demonstrates, the problems of emotional avoidance and fusion interact in a vicious feedback loop. They make it difficult to accept unwanted thoughts, feelings, memories, images, or physical sensations produced by emotionally challenging situations.

PATHWAYS INTO DEPRESSION: HIDDEN BENEFITS

Depression serves a number of other highly useful functions that we normally don't recognize until they're pointed out. For one, depression is a socially acceptable reason for not engaging in health-promoting behaviors, such as having fun, investing in work, pursuing fulfilling relationships, and caring for one's body and mind day in and day out. In essence, depression is both the result and the cause of behaviors that allow a person to avoid an unpleasant life situation. Depending on the context, it can function to stymie healthy responses ("I couldn't confront my husband about his drinking because it

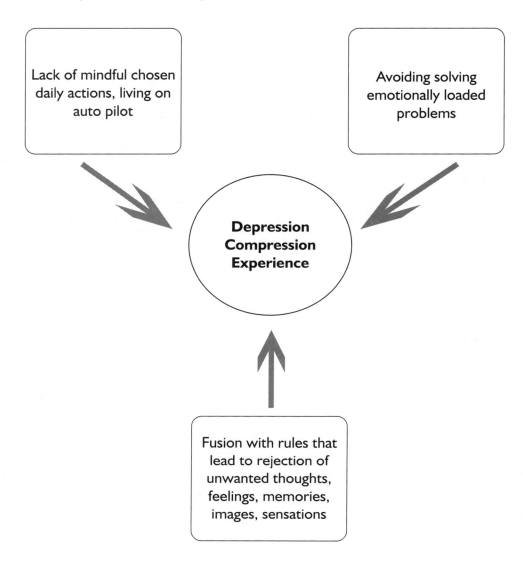

would worsen my depression") or it can be used as a reason why the depressed person can't engage in positive behavior ("I was so tired that I couldn't go to the movie with my wife").

If you consider Amanda, from the previous chapter, you can see all of the elements necessary to produce depression and to keep it going over time: Amanda doesn't want to experience the feelings of rejection or humiliation that might come from dating (the siren song of emotional avoidance), so she avoids meeting men altogether in the name of protecting herself from being hurt again. She believes that feelings of rejection or loss are threats to her health and well-being and must be avoided at any cost (the siren song of fusion). But the more she isolates herself from social connections, the lonelier she gets, and as she gets lonelier, her depression worsens. This makes her believe she's even less able to deal with the risks of rejection or humiliation (fusion again). She tries to control her depression by eating, but this causes her to gain weight and feel even less secure about her self-worth.

All of this is logical in its own way, but it isn't working for Amanda. She follows the siren songs of emotional avoidance and fusion, unknowingly paying the price by losing vitality, meaning, and purpose in her life. In the ACT approach, we view depression as the result of this type of well-organized but unintentional set of avoidance behaviors. This means that depression isn't something Amanda *has*, it's something she *does*. To be clear, Amanda isn't trying to be depressed; she's actually trying to not be depressed. However, as she tries to achieve one thing (control her depression), she gets unintended results (depression that is out of control). Only by changing her tactics—accepting her unwanted thoughts, feelings, memories, and images and making an intentional, values-based choice to socially reconnect—was she able to move through her depression and reclaim her sense of vitality.

PATHWAYS OUT OF DEPRESSION: THREE ROADS TO VITALITY

If the way into the depression compression experience involves avoidance, withdrawal, and attachment to self-defeating rules about how to preserve health and well-being, the way out must entail approach, involvement, detachment from unworkable rules, and making intentional choices concerning life situations that trigger sadness or anger. In ACT, we use the term "response style" to refer to the typical response you make when confronted with challenging circumstances. Think of a response style as a tendency to act in a certain way over time and in varying situations. In the ACT model, there are three basic response styles that, collectively, determine your level of psychological flexibility: acceptance versus rejection of unwanted internal experiences; living intentionally versus living on autopilot, and approaching versus avoiding difficult situations. By changing your response style in these three dimensions, you can expand your vital living space and release yourself from depression compression.

Acceptance vs. Rejection of Unwanted Internal Experiences

All humans have an unending cascade of thoughts, emotions, memories, images, and physical sensations, all of which are experienced privately. However, people vary widely in how they respond to these experiences. One of the most basic differences in how people respond has to do with whether they accept or seek to avoid unwanted internal experience. While avoidance works sometimes, such as when you jerk your hand away from a hot burner, habitual avoidance of painful emotions and thoughts exacts a heavy toll on a person's quality of life. Taking an accepting stance reduces the need to control, avoid, or numb uncomfortable feelings and allows you to move forward in chosen directions.

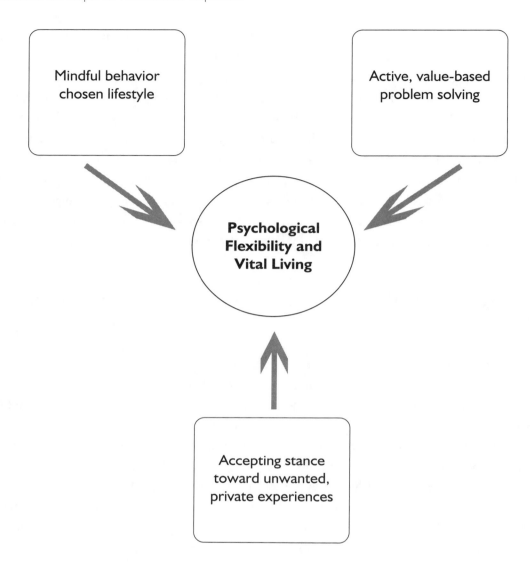

Let's say you want a new job and you find a possibility. You send in your information, and you're called in for an interview. With each step, you may quite naturally experience some anxiety and apprehension. You may have some tightness in your chest when you think about the upcoming interview, and you may notice thoughts like "What if I get so uptight that I screw up the interview?" If your response style is one of avoidance, you can easily get caught up in trying to control these unpleasant internal events, which diverts your energy and attention from actually succeeding in the interview. If your response style is one of acceptance, you can simply notice the feelings and thoughts that come up around your vulnerability and continue to invest your energy in moving forward with your plan.

Living Intentionally vs. Living on Autopilot

Do you often feel like you're on a treadmill and your efforts aren't paying off? Our evolution as a species that uses language seems to predispose many of us for an automatic, rule-driven approach to daily existence. We learn that we just need to hang tough, get that car and mortgage, and things will fall into place. However, increasing numbers of people are waking up in their thirties or forties and concluding that their rules about how to approach life have failed them.

While training in being tuned in to the present moment appears to help people pay closer attention to their experience and make more intentional choices, this type of awareness is seldom valued or taught in Western culture. As a result, your daily routine may not include a time for reflecting on choices you've made and how they worked for you. An intentional approach to lifestyle, guided by your experience and the actual results of your choices (rather than rules) tends to bring you into closer contact with your personal values. The more you practice this approach, the more you can resist being pulled into the illusions supported by common cultural rules ("Eat this food, wear these clothes, take this pill, and so on, and your life will be…"). Cultivating a more mindful approach to your own experience also supports your ability to view others more kindly. For example, you may find that you're less likely to judge a friend who has done something that hurts you. You may even become aware of things you did unintentionally that contributed to the problem.

We think of the opposite end of this response style as living on autopilot. The overall speed of life today is much faster than in previous generations, and we have far fewer connections to the physical world around us. We're pulled along by forces and devices that seem to help but may actually make us less aware—things like cell phones, global positioning devices, and cruise control. Many people prone to living on autopilot note that life seems to be going faster and faster, and they're often fixated on keeping up the pace. The more you live on autopilot, the more your behavior comes under the control of social rules and expectations. You do things because that's how they're done, rather than based on how well they work to promote your sense of vital living. In this style of responding, if a friend says something hurtful you may rely on rules about friendship to resolve the issue efficiently, telling yourself something like "Real friends don't do this, therefore, this person isn't a real friend." People with automatic, rule-based response styles are prone to depression because they lose touch with day-to-day experiences that could guide them toward more vital choices and actions.

Approaching vs. Avoiding Difficult Situations

We've already devoted some discussion to the topic of choosing to approach difficult situations with increased personal energy versus withdrawing, getting passive, and focusing on your suffering. People who are approach oriented tend take the bull by the horns and initiate activity with the intent of solving a problem. They aren't overly focused on negative feelings, thoughts, or uncertainties about the situation. For example, an approach-oriented person would tend to seek out a friend who had said something hurtful and try to move through the problem, even though the conversation might get tense at times. Although there's no guarantee that this would restore the relationship, an approach-oriented person would do it anyway.

People who are more avoidance oriented tend to withdraw from situations that are emotionally challenging. They tend to believe in letting the situation take care of itself, rather than messing with it and possibly making it worse. For example, you might decide not to talk with a friend who had hurt you, based on the belief that another bad interaction might end the friendship altogether. Or you might think the only solution is to wait for your friend to apologize. This assumes that your friend is actually aware that you feel hurt, which may not be the case. As discussed, avoidance can feed the cycle of depression because many challenging life situations will only get worse if you sit back and wait for them to get better on their own. This type of passivity also increases your sense of being out of control and contributes to a variety of negative emotions, such as frustration, anger, and rejection, when these strategies don't work.

PSYCHOLOGICAL FLEXIBILITY

When we state that the goal of ACT is to create greater psychological flexibility, we are saying that ACT teaches you to be more accepting of your experience, to be more mindful and intentional in your daily living, and to take action to resolve difficult life situations rather than avoid them. These three dimensions of vitality don't exist in isolation; they tend to interact and support one another. For example, the more accepting you become of your unwanted internal experiences, the easier it is for you to stay in the moment and live a mindful, intentional life. The more mindfully you approach your daily life, the more likely you are to detect problems and approach them with compassion. The more you approach problems in spite of the presence of unwanted thoughts, feelings, or other internal experiences, the more you learn to accept the stuff of your internal experience for what it is—just your stuff. All of this contributes to development of psychological flexibility and increases your ability to pursue a valued lifestyle.

You have what it takes to address the aspects of your life that are fueling your depression, but to do so, you have to be willing to turn around and face the music. There really isn't any other way to deal with life problems, because very few of them go away on their own. If you're willing to confront the issues that cause you personal distress, you'll be able to move through your depression and into a life worth living. This is how Maria, Anna, and Joe succeeded in transforming their lives.

■ *Maria's Journey Toward a Vital Life*

Maria finally came to grips with the fact that she'd avoided grieving the loss of her baby. Yes, she had cried a lot, but she didn't allow herself to accept all the thoughts and memories that came along with the tears. This was one reason she had never agreed to go to a grief support group and why she went through her daily routines like a robot. She fused with the thought that she was somehow responsible for Martha's death, which was too painful to bear. She was trying to live her life very quietly to avoid this thought and the guilt and grief it produced.

Eventually, Maria realized that her fear of experiencing these feelings and reactions was shrinking her life, her love, and her health. She had always wanted to be a devoted mother and wife, and she saw that avoiding her grief was robbing her of her marriage. She made a commitment to go to a grief support group at a local church. She was surprised to learn that almost everyone there had many of the same emotional reactions she had been running from. For the first time, she talked openly of her guilt over her daughter's death. Maria also committed to walking with her husband daily, and this led to talks about their relationship and how they could improve it. Maria noticed that she felt less dominated by her grief and guilt-related thoughts. They were still there, but she was able to focus on other aspects of her life. She spent more time cooking, and the quality of her diet improved. With the daily exercise, she began to lose weight, and her interest in sex returned. She was on the pathway out of depression.

■ *Anna's Journey Toward a Vital Life*

Anna talked to her doctor and admitted to her drinking problem and her avoidance of social situations. He helped her see that living a tightly controlled life probably helped her avoid memories of her traumas but at the cost of a more full life. Her doctor also said that the pain in her back and neck was related to stress, trauma, and poor sleep. He gave her a handout on stretching exercises to do before bed and suggested that she consult with a health psychologist. In consultation with the psychologist, Anna came up with a plan for cutting down on her drinking and for doing more social activities after work. She called a friend she hadn't seen in over a year and invited her to go to a movie. They had a great time, and several weeks later her friend introduced her to a number of new people at a dinner party.

Anna noticed that she felt better physically after cutting back on her drinking. Her sleep improved, and even though she still had occasional nightmares about the rape, she coped with them better. She committed herself to dating again, even though she expected to have a lot of fear and anxiety. It wasn't long before she was involved with someone, and sure enough, there was a lot of fear and anxiety along for the ride. Anna accepted that this was something she needed to go through even though it didn't feel good. She also started encouraging her father to see his doctor about his problems with alcohol. Thanks to her new skills, Anna was on the pathway out of depression.

■ *Joe's Journey Toward a Vital Life*

Joe got tired of the way he felt when he bailed out of his social commitments. He knew he wasn't living up to his values when he ducked out of family get-togethers and other social activities. He accepted that his tendency to ignore his health was part of his general pattern of avoiding things that were difficult for him. He had never really discussed the affair with his wife or expressed to her how hurt he was. He had always been afraid that she would leave him if he brought up the subject. He finally recognized that his refusal to come clean and confront her with his feelings was the biggest danger to their marriage. By not discussing what was going on inside, he wasn't supporting the honesty and openness he wanted in a relationship.

He committed to broaching the subject over dinner one night. Although it initially caused a lot of emotional anguish for both of them, it made a difference in their ability to talk. The cold, stony silence began to transform into some give-and-take. He also committed to working on his health, including eating better and walking daily. Joe's mood began to pick up, and he realized that he did have the ability to face and solve his problems. Joe was on the pathway out of depression.

PATHWAYS OUT OF DEPRESSION: DARE TO IMAGINE

When you slide more deeply into depression compression, you tend to feel utterly overwhelmed by the intensity of the experience. You feel numb, sad, irritable, and anxious. The near-constant barrage of negative thoughts and images about yourself, your relationships, and your past and future makes it difficult to concentrate, so you may forget things, even important things like paying bills or keeping appointments. You may feel tired and yet be unable to sleep. In this state, it's easy to think that the main goal is to get on top of your symptoms, meaning get rid of them so you can feel happy and have a good life.

We want to give you a different way of thinking about goals or directions you want to pursue. From the ACT perspective, getting on top of your depression is more a means to an end than the main focus. The end we have in mind is to help you create a life worth living, one in which you are doing life-enhancing things that support your values. Depression is important because it acts as a barrier to doing this. If you find a way to control or eliminate your depression yet don't make any fundamental changes in your life, we will not have succeeded in our primary mission.

EXERCISE: IMAGINE A BETTER FUTURE

This exercise will give you a glimpse of what you'd be doing in your life right now if depression symptoms weren't a barrier in your path. Imagine that your depression miraculously disappeared overnight and is no longer a factor in your life. In each of the areas listed below, write one important thing you would be doing in your life if the barrier of depression evaporated while you slept.

A Better Future

In my pursuit of personal health (including exercise, spirituality, diet, and alcohol or drug use), I would

_____

_____

In my relationships (partner, family members, friends), I would

_____

_____

In my work activities (including as a homemaker, volunteer, or student), I would

_____

_____

In my leisure life (including play, hobbies, recreation, creative pursuits), I would

_____

_____

Debriefing. Don't worry. We aren't going to ask you to do all of these things—just yet. For now, just pat yourself on the back for being willing to consider a future where your life is working better.

Today's Dreams Can Become Tomorrow's Reality!

Store your responses to the preceding exercise in a place where you can come back and review them from time to time, perhaps in a drawer in your bedside table. Whenever you see this list, think about your progress as a result of working with this book and whether you're getting closer to realizing any of these visions for your life. If you start to address emotionally difficult personal issues and situations, you can radically transform your life. It takes commitment, time, and accepting that you won't always feel good. But we guarantee you that this is something you can do!

Secrets to ACT On

☞ The triggering events for depression are as numerous and varied as the people who experience depression.

☞ Trying to gain control over your mood has the unintended effect of causing you to lose control over your life.

☞ The two siren songs that create depression are emotional avoidance and fusion with unworkable rules about controlling unwanted internal experiences.

☞ The pathways out of depression require psychological flexibility in the areas of accepting unwanted internal events, developing a mindful and intentional approach to daily living, and engaging in actions designed to solve problems rather than to avoid them.

The Coach Says

If you decide to turn around and face difficult personal and interpersonal problems in your life, you can quickly regain your sense of health and vitality. You have what it takes to get back on the horse that threw you. Let's get on with it and reverse the downward spiral of depression!

Sneak Preview

In the next chapter, you'll make an inventory of your depression behaviors in major areas of your life. We'll help you identify what you've done to try to control your depression, evaluate how these strategies have worked over time, and understand how your depression might be protecting you. We'll also introduce you to a core paradox about depression that will help you see it in a completely different light.

Take Inventory of Depression and
Its Impact on Your Life

CHAPTER 3

Take Inventory of Depression and Its Impact on Your Life

For a long time it had seemed to me that life was about to begin—real life. But there was always some obstacle in the way, something to be gotten through first, some unfinished business, time still to be served, a debt to be paid. Then life would begin. At last it dawned on me that these obstacles were my life. —Alfred D. Souza

Now that you understand how depression develops and stays around, we can get under way on your journey toward a better life. This step involves taking inventory of what depression does *for* you and what depression has done *to* you. As we explained in the previous chapter, depression does have a purpose, and when you begin to think about depression as something you do rather than something you have, it becomes important to assess which behaviors are driving you into depression and keeping you there. In this chapter, we'll help you understand which areas of your life are most impacted by depression behaviors. You'll identify the strategies you've used to cope with your depression and assess how they've worked for you. We'll also examine the ways that depression may be shielding you from having to deal with difficult life situations. Try to approach these exercises like a scientist studying a complex problem: be honest and objective, and above all, don't start beating yourself up. This is not an exercise in self-criticism; it's an attempt to figure out what behaviors are helping you live the kind of life you want and which aren't.

INVENTORY: DEPRESSIVE BEHAVIORS IN FOUR AREAS OF LIVING

One way to look at the array of behaviors that create and maintain symptoms of depression is to group them into life areas. The four areas we're most interested in are health, relationships, work, and play. We'll revisit these important areas of living often as you work through this program. In fact, we'll help you develop specific goals in each of these areas and teach you how to pursue them. We'll start by asking you to look at how your depression behaviors may be making their appearance in each arena.

EXERCISE: INVENTORY OF HEALTH, RELATIONSHIP, WORK, AND PLAY BEHAVIORS

Because we'll ask you to do this exercise again later in the book, you may wish to make copies of this blank worksheet so you'll always have a fresh copy. (Alternatively, you can print out fresh copies from the CD.) Write today's date on the worksheet before you begin, then take a few minutes to review the behaviors in the following checklists. Check off each behavior that you tend to engage in, then tally up the number of behaviors you checked in each list to generate four scores, one for each of the life areas. In addition, each item is coded according to the type of response style it represents:

A = Acceptance versus rejection of unwanted internal experiences

M = Mindful behavior versus living on autopilot

PS = Problem solving by approaching difficult situations versus avoidance

At the end of each checklist, you'll add up how many items you endorsed for each of these response styles.

Inventory of Health Behaviors

PS		I don't exercise on a regular basis, mainly because I have little energy and don't feel motivated.
A		I spend a lot of time trying to put negative thoughts, images, emotions, or memories out of my mind.
PS		I set goals for improving my health, such as doing more exercise or cutting down on smoking, but I tend to give up after a while.

A		I tend to drink alcohol, take drugs, or smoke cigarettes to help me control my feelings.
M		I seldom engage in any type of spiritual practice (church, yoga, prayer, meditation, journaling, and so on).
A		In my spare time, I spend a lot of time watching TV, reading, or cleaning, which helps distract me from how I'm feeling.
M		I find it hard to use healthy behaviors (such as walking, deep breathing, or mental imagery) to help me relax and slow down during the day.
A		I spend a lot of time analyzing why I'm depressed and trying to figure out how to feel good.
M		I don't have a bedtime routine that allows me to relax, review my day, and prepare for restful sleep.
M		I find that I spend a lot of my free time daydreaming.
PS		I use eating to help me feel better even though I could accomplish the same thing by being more active.
Total: _____		Subtotals: A: _____ M: _____ PS: _____

Inventory of Relationship Behaviors

PS		I try not to bother friends and relatives with my wants and needs because I don't want to burden them.
PS		I tend to isolate myself from friends or family because I don't want to get into disagreements or conflicts with them.
A		I avoid my friends because I think they don't really want to see me.
M		I spend a lot of time thinking about unpleasant things people did to me in the past.
PS		I spend a lot of time and energy taking care of other peoples' needs and tend to neglect what I want.
M		Much of the time, I find it hard to just be present with my intimate partner, children, or other people I'm close to.
A		I control what I let other people know about me to make sure they don't reject or ridicule me.
A		I often snap at people and then withdraw into my shell to avoid dealing with them.
M		I spend a lot of time thinking about how I've let others down in the past.
A		I tell people what they want to hear just to get them to stop interacting with me.
PS		I avoid acting on a problem if it might involve conflict with my partner, children, parents, or other people I'm close to.
Total: _____		Subtotals: A: _____ M: _____ PS: _____

Inventory of Work Behaviors

A		I avoid putting myself in a position where I might fail at something at work, even if it means I won't advance in my job.
PS		I've missed quite a bit of work or school because I feel too depressed to go.
A		When someone criticizes my work, I find it very difficult to continue trying.
M		I don't really like what I'm doing for a living, but I haven't done much to change things.
PS		I've failed to finish projects at work or school because I procrastinate too long.
M		I spend a lot of time at work or school daydreaming rather than focusing on the task at hand.
A		The more important a project or assignment is, the more likely I am to get stalled out doing it.
M		It seems like I'm just going through the motions at school or at work.
PS		When I have a conflict with a teacher or supervisor, I try to let it blow over without saying anything about it.
A		I would never ask for a raise or an increase in responsibility if I thought the answer was going to be no.
PS		I feel I'm not being challenged by or growing in my job or at school, but I haven't made much effort to change what I'm doing.
Total: _____		Subtotals: A: _____ M: _____ PS: _____

Inventory of Play Behaviors

PS		I seldom engage in relaxing or fun activities; I just don't feel like it.
M		I find it very hard to enjoy myself in solo activities.
A		I tend to avoid relaxing activities because I actually feel worse when I notice that I'm not enjoying myself.
M		I get frustrated when I have free time on my hands because I get distracted and don't do anything.
M		I would rather stay home than go to a park and play because I don't know how to relax in playful situations.
PS		I will often decide not to take a walk or do something fun so that I can preserve my limited energy.
M		I find that I spend a lot of my free time feeling bored.
A		When I try to do something fun or relaxing, I focus on how I'm feeling and not on what I'm doing.

A		I avoid participating in enjoyable activities with other people because I can tell they're having more fun than I am.
PS		Even a little obstacle can stop me from following through on an activity that might be enjoyable.
PS		I have pretty much stopped engaging in hobbies or other activities that stimulate me and help me feel good about myself.
Total: _____		Subtotals: A: _____ M: _____ PS: _____

The next step in this exercise is to add up the number of items you checked off for each type of response style. Indicate your score by circling the appropriate number in the following tables. Higher scores suggest greater susceptibility to depression traps and the overall depression compression experience.

Summary of Scores in the Three Types of Response Styles

A = Acceptance vs. Rejection of Unwanted Internal Experiences															
0	1	2	3	4	5	6	7	8	9	10	11	12	13	14	15
Fairly unlikely to reject unwanted internal experiences								Very likely to reject unwanted internal experiences							

M = Mindful Behavior vs. Living on Autopilot													
0	1	2	3	4	5	6	7	8	9	10	11	12	13	14
Fairly unlikely to operate on autopilot							Very likely to operate on autopilot						

PS = Problem Solving by Approaching Difficult Situations vs. Avoidance															
0	1	2	3	4	5	6	7	8	9	10	11	12	13	14	15
Fairly unlikely to avoid approaching problems								Very likely to avoid approaching problems							

Debriefing. Did any of these depressive behaviors ring a bell for you? Was there a big difference in your totals for your depressive behaviors in the four areas of health, relationships, work, and play? If this is the case, you might want to focus your efforts on the life area where you're exhibiting the most depressive behaviors. When you reach chapter 13, you may want to focus your life vision plan on this area as well.

What did you see when you totaled your response style scores? Was one response style decidedly more of a problem than the other two? This is not unusual, and again, it might provide you with some clues as to where to focus your efforts in this book. If you only have limited time to go through the ACT program, you can use the cheat sheet below to identify which chapters in part 2 are most likely to be useful for you based on your response style profile. However, if you have high scores for two or three response styles, the best bet is to work your way through the entire program, even if it takes a while to do so. In any event, we recommend that you complete all five chapters in part 1, as they lay the groundwork for the change-oriented work in part

2. You should also take the time to do the work in chapter 15, "Maintain Your Life Direction," as this will help you solidify your gains.

Response Style	Chapters to Target
Acceptance versus rejection of unwanted internal experiences	Chapters 7, 8, 9, 10, and 11
Mindful behavior versus living on autopilot	Chapters 6, 12, and 13
Problem solving by approaching difficult situations versus avoidance	Chapters 6 and 14

Try to view this initial exercise as an attempt to study where you are at this moment, rather than as an exercise in self-criticism. This isn't a test where you receive a passing or failing grade. It's just an opportunity for you to step back a bit and look at what's working and what isn't. Remember, you can only start from where you are, not from where you'd like to be! As with most life situations, if you decide to change your approach, you can immediately begin to change how things are going.

COPING STRATEGIES: PART OF THE SOLUTION OR PART OF THE PROBLEM?

Obviously, if the strategies you've been using to control your depression were successful, you wouldn't be reading this book, so we know that, on the whole, your efforts to manage your depression haven't been working very well. At the same time, it's important to size up the strategies you've been using. People use an amazing variety of strategies to manage depression. Some are positive coping behaviors, such as going to therapy, reading a self-help book, meditating, writing in a journal, exercising regularly, engaging in pleasant activities, or looking to friends for social support. Other coping strategies can actually increase your depression, such as drinking, taking drugs, overeating, isolating yourself, exercising less, staying in bed a lot, or trying to put on a happy face and pretend you aren't depressed.

Short-Term vs. Long-Term Results

Before we proceed with the next step of your self-inventory, we want you to learn the difference between short-term and long-term coping strategies. A lot of the depression behaviors listed in the previous exercise are short-term strategies designed to help you deal with your depression in the moment.

Depressed people often make decisions based on how they're feeling at the time, and these decisions are usually made so quickly that you don't even recognize what you're doing.

For example, if you decide to have a couple of drinks to help you feel better, you're using a short-term strategy to manage your depression; alcohol creates a high in the here and now. Notice that there's nothing inherently wrong with having a couple of drinks, and this is the tricky part about it. If you decide not to take a walk because you're too depressed and tired, you're engaging in a short-term strategy designed to help you function better; you're trying to preserve your scarce energy for "more important" things. Many of these decisions make a lot of sense when you make them, because most of us aren't used to second-guessing every single thing we do to relax or preserve our energy. This is part of the paradox of depression. It seems as though what you're doing would be beneficial, but it turns out that it isn't.

Long-term coping strategies often look quite different than short-term strategies. They're done to promote your health and well-being and are much less concerned with addressing how you feel right now. For example, instead of drinking to artificially change your mood, you might go out and walk briskly for thirty minutes, reminding yourself that shortly after the high you get from a couple of drinks, you'll feel low, as the alcohol depresses your nervous system. Exercise, on the other hand, is the real deal. It not only releases hormones associated with a positive mood, it also helps improve your cardiovascular health and elevates your metabolism, which could help with any weight problems. The problem is, exercise isn't a quick fix. It takes a while to do it, and it isn't always pleasant if you're out of shape.

The Paradox Involved in Short-Term Solutions

You have at your beck and call strategies you can use that will make you feel better right now. Some of them, such as alcohol, drugs, tobacco, food, and sex, create an artificial good feeling; others help you escape from situations that could make you feel bad, perhaps by staying at home, avoiding exercise, taking a long nap, avoiding confrontation, or missing work or school. You can do any of these behaviors at will, and most people do. The paradox, and the problem, is this: Most short-term strategies help you feel better right now, but in the long run, they create more depression. What a bummer! But it sure is tempting to use these strategies when you feel bad, isn't it? That's because you'll get some short-term relief. But in the long run, you'll pay for it, as Judy's story illustrates.

■ Judy's Story

Judy, a thirty-three-year-old mother of two children, ages nine and eleven, has been married for twelve years. Her husband is a construction worker who always drinks a few beers after work with his buddies before coming home. He often has a couple more beers at home. Judy's depression started two years ago after she discovered that her husband had an affair with a woman he met at the local watering hole. She chose to forgive her husband even though she felt terribly rejected by him. He still implies that her weight gain after the birth of their second child made her less appealing and led to the affair.

Judy believes that his drinking allows him to avoid interacting with her, but she hasn't said anything to him about it. She's afraid that confronting him might cause him to leave her or start another affair. Because of her limited job skills, she doesn't think she'd be able to make it on her own if he left her. She feels very isolated and alone, yet she can't generate the motivation to go visit friends. Her day is basically organized around her household duties, reading magazines, watching TV, and napping. She enjoys being with her children, but she's been spending less time with them.

JUDY'S SHORT-TERM VS. LONG-TERM RESULTS

In a minute, we'll ask you to analyze your depression behaviors and their short-term and long-term results. But first, let's take a look at what Judy came up with when she did this exercise.

Inventory of Short-Term vs. Long-Term Results

What I've Done to Control My Depression	Short-Term Results	Long-Term Results
I take a lot of naps during the day.	My mood gets a little better after I sleep. I don't have to listen to my children argue.	Later I feel guilty about not doing anything with my day. It increases my feeling that my life is stalled out.
I avoid large social gatherings because they sap my energy.	I feel relieved that I don't have to put on a happy face in front of others. My husband goes without me now and criticizes me for not liking to party. That makes me feel like I'm letting him down.	I haven't seen one of my close friends for over a year now and feel like I'm letting her down. I feel more and more guilty about this.

I try to talk to my husband about how depressed I feel.	He doesn't seem to listen and just starts lecturing me. I feel like he's criticizing me for being depressed. When he drinks, this gets so bad that I leave and go to my room.	I feel more and more isolated over time because my husband isn't helping me through this. These interactions are making my depression worse. I probably need to look for another person to talk to.
I take lots of walks with the dog.	This does give me peace of mind and helps my mood for a little while. I feel healthier after walking and don't see my problems in such a dark way.	The exercise has helped me feel more physically fit, so that's at least one problem I've actually been addressing.
I don't argue with my kids because it makes my depression worse.	I feel relieved that I don't have to battle with them and deal with their tantrums. I wait for my husband to get home so he can deal with them.	My kids are having more behavior problems at school, and I feel like I'm not helping them. This makes me feel like I'm failing as a mother.
I smoke cigarettes to calm down and de-stress.	I guess it helps me distract myself from things for a while. When I get stressed out, I can always step outside and relax with a smoke.	I feel like I'm addicted to cigarettes and am risking my health. When I try to cut back, I notice I get much more edgy.

Review. In Judy's answers, you can see the usual mixed bag of short-term and long-term strategies that depressed people typically use to try to control the way they feel. Notice that the strategies she assesses as least useful are basically avoidance behaviors (napping, smoking, and avoiding social situations and confrontations with her husband and children). What we know from clinical research is that this type of avoidance is a major cause of depression (Hayes et al. 1996).

Upon discussing her responses, it was clear that one of Judy's problems was that she was still using the negative strategies on a daily basis, even though she evaluated them as not being helpful. Why is that? At the time, these avoidance strategies were the easiest responses to engage in: Just lie down and take a nap; you'll feel better when you wake up. Just have a cigarette and focus on something else. Don't discipline your children, then they won't call you a bad mother and you won't feel bad. If the goal is to control your mood, these strategies might make a lot of sense. However, if the goal is to solve problems and live a vital life, these strategies will be totally ineffective.

EXERCISE: INVENTORY OF SHORT-TERM VS. LONG-TERM RESULTS

In this exercise, we want you to think back over the time since you first began to struggle with depression. In the left-hand column, describe the main strategies you've used to control your depression. Then consider the short-term and long-term results of each strategy and describe those in the next two columns. If you need more space, make a copy or print out another copy from the CD accompanying this book.

Inventory of Short-Term vs. Long-Term Results

What I've Done to Control My Depression	Short-Term Results	Long-Term Results

Debriefing. What did you discover in this exercise? If you're like most people, you will have compiled quite a long list of things you've tried. Were you able to identify some short-term coping strategies? When you step back and look at them objectively, how did these strategies end up working in the long run? Did you determine that any of your strategies have actually helped in the long run? If so, you'll want to use these strategies more often.

Depending upon your situation, you might have piled up a lot of short-term strategies that produce miserable long-term results. When your attempts to manage your depression don't work in the long run, you know it because you don't feel you are on top of your depression. Is your life working better than it did a month ago? A year ago? Is your life satisfaction improving or deteriorating? Are you living your life the way you want to live it? It's important that you honestly look at whether a particular coping behavior is working or whether it's hurting you. If it doesn't work, stop doing it. If it does work, do more of it!

HOW DEPRESSION PROTECTS YOU

Judy's example shows an important feature of depression behaviors: They're mainly short-term strategies that lead you to avoid or escape from emotionally charged situations that, for any number of reasons, you've decided are too hot to handle. The numbness and sense of detachment from life that characterize depression double as a protective shield. When you're depressed, your emotional world shrinks in scope, allowing you to avoid potentially painful life situations. This isn't something you're doing on purpose; it's the result of falling into a trap in which you trade dealing with your issues for keeping your mood in check. Unfortunately, this robs you of the will to address challenging situations, and those situations can and do worsen over time.

EXERCISE: DEPRESSION RISK INVENTORY

In this exercise, we ask to you step even further back, far enough away from your life situation to prevent you from being just your depression experiences. We're going to give you an opportunity to both observe and speculate on how your depression works for you. This requires you to look beyond your numbness and detachment and to size up your life situation in candid terms. Since you're on this mission alone, it's up to you to pull this off. The upside is that no one is likely to see what you come up with, so you have nothing to hide.

A wide variety of life situations can act as triggers for depression or, if allowed to fester, create chronic depression. These risk factors can operate in your relationships, your personal health habits, or your activities in both work and play. Read the list of depression risk situations below, and for any that might apply to you, rate the level of distress on a scale of 1 to 10, where 1 is minimal emotional distress and 10 is an extremely high level. In the right-hand column, indicate whether the risk factor is recent or more long-standing.

Depression Risk Inventory

Risk Situation	Emotional Distress (1=low; 10=high)	Longevity of Risk (recent or long-standing)
I'm in an unsatisfying intimate relationship.		
I don't have enough ways to spend my leisure time.		
I have problems with physical pain or poor health.		
I'm not really inspired by what I do for a living.		
I haven't allowed myself to grieve the loss of someone close to me.		
I don't feel good about how I'm taking care of my body.		
I have regrets about things I did earlier in my life.		
I don't have a spiritual practice.		
I believe that my friends have let me down or used me.		
I'm alienated from or have frequent conflicts with my parents or children.		
I'm struggling with memories of childhood abuse or trauma.		
I'm dependent on drugs or alcohol or use them excessively.		
I'm under a lot of pressure at home or at work.		
I live in poverty or reside in a dangerous setting.		
I'm involved in a physically or emotionally abusive relationship.		
Other (describe):		

Debriefing. What did you discover as you completed this risk assessment? Were you surprised to see that a number of these risk situations involve the absence of a positive habit or lifestyle? Did you mark a lot of areas or just one or two? How much emotional turmoil does each risk factor cause? Some of these problems might be chronic or long-standing issues and others may have surfaced only recently. Here are two basic rules of thumb for calculating your level of depression risk:

1. The more problems you have that create painful feelings for you, the greater your risk.

2. The longer these problems have festered in your life, the greater your risk.

EXERCISE: DEPRESSION AND AVOIDANCE INVENTORY

This part of the self-inventory helps you understand the impact depression is having on important issues or problems you may be facing. Since depression is fueled by avoidance of emotionally challenging situations, this exercise asks you to consider two different questions: "What unresolved issues might be feeding my depression?" and "How does my depression keep me from addressing and resolving these issues?" To make answering these questions manageable, we've divided them up into the same four life arenas we started this chapter with: health, relationships, work, and play. As always, don't use this as an opportunity to beat up on yourself. You've been doing the best you can, and this program will give you the new perspective and skills you need to make big changes in your life. Just stick with us and we'll get you to where you want to go!

Depression and Avoidance Inventory

My Health

Does a deficit in health-promoting behaviors feed my depression?

_____

_____

_____

_____

How does my depression keep me from addressing and resolving these issues?

_____

_____

_____

_____

My Relationships

What unresolved relationship issues might be feeding my depression?

_____

_____

_____

_____

How does my depression keep me from addressing and resolving these issues?

_____

_____

_____

_____

My Work

What unresolved work or school issues might be feeding my depression?

How does my depression keep me from addressing and resolving these issues?

My Play

What unresolved issues in my play life might be feeding my depression?

How does my depression keep me from addressing and resolving these issues?

Debriefing. Did you identify specific issues in any of these life arenas that aren't being addressed? In the past, have you noticed that you've used being depressed as a reason for not dealing with these issues? This is what we mean when we say that depression is protecting you from having to deal with some of the hard realities in your life. This exercise can be difficult when you're feeling depressed. Most people are so accustomed to seeing depression as the cause of their difficulties that it's hard see it differently.

JUDY'S RESULTS

When Judy did this exercise, she had some interesting observations on what was going on in her life and how her depression was fueling the fire.

Judy's Depression and Avoidance Inventory

My Health

Does a deficit in health-promoting behaviors feed my depression?

I've gained thirty-five pounds over the past five years, I smoke too much, and I don't feel very healthy. I'd like to trim down and quit smoking. I've even thought about joining the YMCA so I could exercise.

How does my depression keep me from addressing and resolving these issues?

I'm afraid to quit smoking or change my diet because smoking and snacking are how I stay calm. I think my depression level would skyrocket if I stopped. My mood is so down that I can't get myself to call the YMCA and join.

My Relationships

What unresolved relationship issues might be feeding my depression?

I'm sure that my husband and I have a growing problem in our marriage, but we never talk about it that way. We always just nit-pick each other and criticize what the other person does. Also, I don't have a clue what to do about my kids, who act up at home and don't mind their teachers at school. They're going to need some therapy or something.

How does my depression keep me from addressing and resolving these issues?

When I'm depressed, I feel unattractive and tend to avoid my husband. We don't talk much anymore, and most of what we say to each other is critical and negative. I feel that I'm responsible for my children's behavior problems, so they're better off if I stay out of the picture and let my husband deal with them.

My Work

What unresolved work issues might be feeding my depression?

I have a college degree but I've never pursued a career. I promised myself that I would get back to work once my children were in school, but I've never done it. I have a lot of anxiety about my ability to succeed out there.

How does my depression keep me from addressing and resolving these issues?

I have absolutely no motivation to look for work. I'm sure my depression would prevent me from getting a job or keeping one, so I don't even try.

My Play

What unresolved issues in my play life might be feeding my depression?

I don't really have a play life. I walk the dog and that's about it. I don't go to church anymore, and I can't think of the last time I did something that was actually fun. I'm sure this is setting me up for more mental problems.

How does my depression keep me from addressing and resolving these issues?

My depression feels so heavy that it seems like dealing with my play life is way down on the list of priorities. And if I can barely function at home and with my kids, what chance would I have at trying to do this?

■ *Judy's Journey Toward a Vital Life*

Judy struggled with her tendency to blame herself and avoid addressing her major life issues. The self-inventory exercises allowed a new idea to dawn on Judy: She was spending so much time and energy managing her feelings by avoiding things that her life was completely stalled out—and every problem she was avoiding was steadily getting worse. She felt trapped in her relationship because of her lack of job experience, and she was particularly afraid that her husband would walk out on her if she began to say what she wanted and needed from him.

She was even more afraid of the realization that her life was steadily going downhill. She didn't feel healthy, she felt trapped and humiliated in her situation, and she didn't feel like she was living in a way that reflected her values. She believed in being a good mother and an effective parent. She believed in having an intimate, loving relationship characterized by mutual respect. She believed in being a good friend, and she believed in promoting her health. To get her life back on track, she needed to turn around and face the music, for better or for worse. She had to act in the ACT sense of the word: accept, choose, and take action. She decided that if she and her husband couldn't develop the kind of relationship she wanted, she would move to end the marriage despite her anxieties about the future. She would deal with acquiring some job skills, and she would be a good mother to her children.

Judy realized that the mess she was in was caused by her reluctance to deal directly with her husband's affair and his lack of accountability about it. So one night when their children were staying at a friend's house, Judy brought up the affair and asked her husband to take responsibility for his behavior and apologize to her. She also informed him that his drinking wasn't going to work for her and that he needed to get help. He got up and left the table without saying a word, got into his truck, and drove off. Even as Judy wept, she felt released from her prison of numbness and isolation. She had learned what she needed to know to get on with her life: She could survive her most feared feelings if she was doing something she believed in. Her husband returned after a couple of hours and agreed to seek treatment for his alcoholism. He apologized for being unfaithful and finally admitted that it didn't have anything to do with the way Judy looked. He asked her to forgive him, and this time he meant it. Judy was on the journey toward a life worth living!

ARE DEPRESSION BEHAVIORS A CHOICE?

One thing we want to make abundantly clear is that we aren't blaming you for becoming depressed. We understand how difficult it is to remain focused on living in accordance with your values. It's easy to get sidetracked. That's why so many people experience symptoms of depression at some point in their lives. At the same time, when we abandon the idea that depression is a biological illness that's unrelated to the external world, we need to figure out what *does* contribute to the development of depression in the first place and what factors help perpetuate it. This should not be an exercise in self-blaming but rather an attempt to find out what the key depression factors are in your life.

It's likely that there's a relationship between your actions and the results you're getting in your life. In the ACT framework, we describe this as being "response-able," meaning that you are both responsible and capable of responding. Your action or lack of action does, in fact, put you in the exact life situation you are in at this very moment. But just as it's pointless to blame a bear for stepping on a bear trap, it's pointless to blame yourself for falling into the trap you're in. Even as you realize that you've unwittingly fallen into a trap, you can take responsibility for your situation. In subsequent chapters, we'll provide you with tools for extracting yourself from this trap, allowing you to continue your journey toward a rich and fulfilling life.

Secrets to ACT On

☞ Depression behaviors have the effect of making you avoid emotionally challenging situations or interactions. Think of your depression as a set of avoidance behaviors.

☞ Short-term strategies for coping with depression tend to be focused on controlling how you feel rather than solving problems. The long-term result is worse problems and more depression.

☞ Long-term coping strategies don't offer the quick fix you might want, but they provide stable, positive results.

☞ It's better to solve problems than avoid them, and better to face difficult emotions than run from them.

☞ Although depression offers a protective shield against having to deal with difficult life issues, not addressing these issues ultimately makes the depression worse.

The Coach Says

Depression is a parasite. It feeds on you by keeping you from addressing problematic situations in your life. If you learn to identify the depression trap and the behaviors that put you in it, you'll be in a position to change your actions and change your life. You have the ability and the strength to turn around and face the issues in your life. You can take actions that are consistent with your values and make dramatic changes for the better!

Sneak Preview

In the next chapter, we'll deconstruct the depression trap and show you the forces that keep you depressed. We'll look at how modern society feeds you certain rules about emotions and healthy living that set you up for depression. We'll also take an in-depth look at the first siren song: emotional avoidance.

CHAPTER 4

Recognize the Depression Trap

*We can't solve problems by using the same kind of thinking
we used when we created them.* —Albert Einstein

At the end of the previous chapter, we mentioned that you're in a trap. A well-conceived trap mimics the surrounding environment, provides an attractant as a lure, such as a piece of cheese or meat, and then *snap!* To understand the depression trap you're in, you must identify the factors that lure you into it. In this chapter, we'll help you understand how socialization, the basic training you receive from your social environment, makes you vulnerable to this process. When the ACT model was first developed, one of the main questions on the table was "How is it that bright, sensitive, caring people can find themselves in a situation where they experience symptoms of depression for months, if not years, and persist in using coping strategies that simply don't work?" This chapter describes the core process that functions as the bait that almost no one can resist. Armed with this information, you can recognize depression traps in your life and begin to respond in new ways.

UNDERSTANDING EMOTIONS AND HOW THEY WORK

Take a close look at this word: emotion. Notice anything unusual? Now, take a look at a slightly different version: e(motion). What do you see now? Do you see a word that describes movement? This is what the word "emotion" is meant to convey. It literally means "movement." Emotions are internal forces that propel us into action. To really get a handle on your depression, you first need to understand the role that emotions play in our lives and how we're taught to deal with our feelings. Inside the skin, our relationship with our emotions is an uneasy one. Many common emotional states, like rage, shame, anxiety, disgust, sadness, and so forth, are not fun. They are, however, absolutely vital to your overall health and well-being.

Emotions Are a Form of Intelligence

Long before children develop language and engage in higher-level thought processes, they have the ability to experience emotions and communicate these emotions. Emotion researchers have shown that preverbal infants can express primary emotional states in facial expressions (Ekman 1992). These primary emotions develop in early infancy regardless of race, culture, and ethnicity and exist before the infant is aware of the distinction between self and others. Sometimes infants will start crying just because a parent is crying. Before you even knew that you were you, you experienced and expressed emotions. This suggests that emotions are hardwired, meaning they are a core part of who you are. To be human is to have emotions. Why would we have evolved this way?

There is every reason to believe that emotions were the earliest form of understanding among prehumans. In comparison to the time humans and prehumans have been residing on the planet, language and higher-level thought appear relatively late in our history. This means that for eons, prehumans used emotions as a primary form of intelligence. Emotions were the organizing force among clans of prehumans. The primary emotion of sexual attraction was probably essential to procreation. The emotion of attachment was necessary to bring individuals into clans. If emotions were a harmful form of experience, they never would have survived the process of natural selection.

As human infants grow, they develop language and higher-level thought, and as they acquire these skills, they are trained to curb their emotions. Part of this is necessary for social order. You can't just go out and take any mate you're sexually attracted to. That would result in fierce and deadly fights between people attracted to the same potential mate. Learning to talk and to think at a higher level calms the fires of certain emotional experiences.

Another reason why we're taught to curb our feelings is because they produce strong reactions in other people. Ever hear a parent say to a child, "Stop crying or I'll give you something to cry about"? What the parent is really saying is "Your emotional expression is creating strong, unpleasant emotions in me. Stop expressing your emotion so I don't have to feel the emotions I'm having." In other words, our uneasy peace with emotions is due not only to the fact that emotions can be intensely unpleasant to experience, but also to the reality that our emotional expressions impact the emotions of the people around us. As we move into adulthood in a society that worships thinking and views emotions as the enemy within, we can find ourselves at odds with our internal signaling system.

We've already talked about this, but it bears repeating: Emotions are never accidental, they're never random, and they've evolved for several hundred thousand years because they're vital to our survival. Emotions are signals that something important is happening in your personal world. They motivate you to engage in various behaviors. When you numb yourself to this signaling system, you'll find yourself less able to adapt to life stresses. Whereas each primary negative emotion, such as anger, shame, disgust, fear, sadness, and abandonment, points to a specific event, depression is a general alarm that goes off when you feel trapped in a situation that is both humiliating and painful. In these situations, all of your primary negative emotions are in play: feeling angry, feeling ashamed of yourself, feeling disgusted with the situation, feeling afraid, feeling sad, feeling alone and abandoned. In your current life situation, do any of these emotions ring a bell for you? Our advice is don't kill the messenger; instead, read the message and spring into action.

THE CULTURE OF FEEL-GOODISM

In chapter 1, we mentioned that every year in the U.S. more than one in four people will develop a serious problem with their emotional health and well-being. Statistics like this are downright scary and indicate that there must be something fundamentally wrong with how we are being taught to be human. The ACT view is that current cultural conventions systematically dismiss the value of human emotions. In Western culture, we are socially conditioned to believe that unpleasant feelings, thoughts, memories, or sensations are a sign of bad health and, as such, are the principle cause of psychological distress and suffering. This derives from a culture where part of the definition of health is being free of distressing internal experiences. To achieve good health therefore requires us to eliminate any vestige of negativity in our inner world. We have to sweep the skeletons out of the closet; then, and only then, can we experience the good life. Out with the bad, and in with the good.

The ACT term for this is "the culture of feel-goodism." We are not taught to experience our emotions directly, for better or for worse. Rather we are taught to evaluate whether an experience is normal or abnormal: If an internal experience is deemed normal, then it's okay to have it. If it's deemed abnormal, then it's unhealthy for you and you need to get rid of it. The shift from directly experiencing emotions, whatever their nature, to evaluating their desirability and acceptability is a major problem because labeling is always *categorical*, meaning it involves thinking in either-or terms (for example, normal and desirable versus abnormal and undesirable). We're taught to evaluate things as good or bad and then use coping strategies to eliminate or control *bad* things—feelings, thoughts, images, and sensations labeled as abnormal. This social training leaves us highly vulnerable to depression, because the process of living, by necessity, involves unpleasant situations and distressing reactions. Indeed, these are the punctuation marks in life. Our experience of distress in response to painful life events isn't the problem; symptoms of distress are healthy responses to many stressful events in daily life. The problem lies in struggling to avoid unwanted painful events in life—events that are often unavoidable.

The Costs of Feel-Goodism

What are the costs of practicing feel-goodism in situations that just don't feel good? There's some interesting scientific evidence to answer this question. A worldwide study looking at the one-year risk of mental disorders in fourteen different countries showed that the United States has by far the highest risk of mental disorders in the world (Demyttenaere et al. 2004). In fact, it's 300 percent higher than in countries with the lowest risk, which brings us to a second finding to chew on: Countries heavily imbued in the Buddhist tradition (China and Japan) exhibited the lowest rates of mental disorders. As we'll discuss in detail later in this book, Buddhist philosophy is completely at odds with the culture of feel-goodism. Buddhists would argue that it is attachment to beliefs about the necessity of feeling good that creates suffering. Cultures that promote understanding and acceptance of life's ups and downs generally produce healthier people.

When considering whether negative feelings, memories, thoughts, or sensations are bad for you and mark you as unhealthy, look at it this way: Is it a sign of good health to grieve for two weeks for the death of a beloved spouse and cut it off there? Do you really admire a person who seems to endure the end of an intimate relationship without experiencing a long period of sadness? Is it possible to be fired from a job you like and need without feeling devastated? Should you be able to hear that you have cancer and not feel anxious and afraid? These questions point to the lure that lies at the heart of the depression trap. The bait is the unquestioned belief that to be normal and have a good life requires that you eliminate, conquer, and suppress unpleasant emotions, thoughts, memories, and sensations, no matter what life brings to you in the way of experiences.

The First Siren Song: Emotional Avoidance

In chapter 2, we mentioned that there are two siren songs that create and maintain depression: emotional avoidance and fusion. We'll deal with the problem of fusion in the next chapter. Here, we want to address the problem of emotional avoidance in light of the cultural training you've received. Basically, you've been trained to follow a cultural rule that encourages you to avoid your feelings, particularly your negative feelings. The problem is, when you don't allow your feelings in the room, you lose the ability to respond in an effective way. Experiencing your feelings directly would motivate you to act on the situation rather than become paralyzed.

THE DEPRESSION TRAP

This is the essence of the depression trap: You're doing all the right things in terms of your social training, and it isn't working. The more you work on feeling good, the less good feeling you get. What if our culture doesn't know squat about how to develop a vital, meaningful life? What if our culture is so sideways that it actually produces dysfunction on a massive scale?

Snap! *Trying to Control the Way You Feel Is the Problem*

In your self-inventory work in chapter 3, you probably discovered that, paradoxically, some of the very strategies you use to try to make your depression better actually make it worse. If so, you're coming face to face with the essential flaw of feel-goodism. If the internal experiences you're evaluating as bad, toxic, and unhealthy are actually signals that there's something in your life that needs to be fixed, you wouldn't want to control or eliminate these reactions; you would want to listen to them. But you can't listen to them or benefit from them if you're preoccupied with trying to suppress or eliminate them.

Snap! *Mental Events Are Uncontrollable*

There's an even bigger downside to the idea that if you could just control and eliminate emotional problems, you could have a satisfying life. As far as we know, it's impossible to prevent emotions, thoughts, memories, and sensations from occurring in the first place. They are part of your learning as a human being, and the nervous system doesn't work by subtraction. This means you can't unlearn thoughts, feelings, or memories once they're stored in your experience. They can show up at any time, in any situation, and you have no say as to when, where, and how they will make an appearance. This leaves you with one option for emotional control: avoid situations and circumstances that might trigger these reactions. If you pursue this strategy, your life space shrinks as the number of things you must avoid expands. And the irony is that the mental events you're trying to suppress are still there!

Snap! *Mental Events Become Bigger When You Try to Suppress Them*

There's one more quality of the depression trap you need to understand in order to extract yourself from it and avoid it in the future. This quality concerns what happens when you use suppression as an ongoing strategy. *Suppression*, one of the forms of avoidance, is the conscious attempt to squash a feeling, thought, memory, or sensation out of awareness. Here is a little exercise to show you why suppression doesn't work. Try this for a moment. Think of a campfire. Imagine the flames, smell the burning wood, feel the warmth of the air. Now stop. Stop having this image or memory, stop smelling the smoke, and stop the perception of warmth. Stop them completely. You are not to think of any of this from this moment on. What happens when you prohibit yourself from thinking about the campfire?

Now let's try something different. Think of something unkind that a teacher said or did to you. How old were you at the time? What were your teacher's exact words and tone of voice? Try to recall the room, your teacher's appearance, and all the other aspects of the experience in as much detail as possible. Now stop thinking about this unpleasant experience. Put all thoughts, memories, and feelings about it completely out of your mind.

How did you do? If you didn't do that well at getting rid of your reactions by trying to suppress them, you are by no means alone. Research shows us that conscious attempts to suppress or avoid thoughts, feelings, or memories will actually increase their intensity. This holds true not only for unpleasant thoughts or memories (Marcks and Woods 2005) but also for negative feelings (Campbell-Sills et al. 2006). So if you try to suppress an emotion, memory, or thought that you don't like, it will just come back to you in spades. It's another paradox: You can't control which feelings, thoughts, memories, or sensations show up in the first place, but you can make them much worse by trying to suppress them.

■ *Susan's Story*

Susan, a twenty-seven-year-old nurse, started experiencing symptoms of depression a year ago, when her marriage of seven years started to fall apart. Susan discovered that her husband, Bob, was involved with another woman. Even though she felt humiliated and rejected, she tried to keep the marriage together. However, Bob decided that he wanted a divorce so he could pursue his new relationship. Susan was devastated because she really loved her husband. She was shocked by his infidelity and horrified that he would want a divorce when she was willing to forgive him.

Susan stopped hanging out with friends that she and Bob had known because of the shame and pain it caused. It was also awkward because she wasn't sure if they were friends to her or to Bob. She started drinking at night to help calm her nerves. She and Bob had been active members of their church, but she stopped going for fear of meeting Bob and his new girlfriend there. Although she had enjoyed scrapbooking, she more or less stopped doing it after the divorce. She was an attractive woman, but she turned down every request for a date. She wanted nothing to do with intimacy or relationships because she didn't want to run the risk of getting hurt this way again.

EXERCISE: LEARNING TO SPOT THE DEPRESSION TRAP

It's difficult to recognize the inner workings of the depression trap, particularly when you're embroiled in your own struggle to control the way you feel. So, in this exercise, we'll ask you to look for suppression and avoidance strategies in the way Susan described how she was dealing with her failed marriage. Read each strategy and then circle the multiple choice item that defines the problem with Susan's strategy.

1. *I don't allow myself to think about my husband at all because when I do, I get more depressed. I start to cry and can't stop, and I feel like I'm losing it.*

    a.   Susan's depression will get better if she stops thinking about Bob.

    b.   Feeling sadness is unhealthy for Susan and means she's losing it.

    c.   Susan is having a lot of free-floating feelings because of trying to suppress her sadness about Bob.

2. *I don't see my old friends anymore. We had the same circle of friends, so they sometimes talk about him and his new girlfriend, which is painful for me.*

    a.   Susan is avoiding being with her friends to avoid feeling the pain and shame of the divorce.

    b.   Susan needs to stay away from her friends because it's unhealthy for her to be around them.

    c.   Susan needs to find new friends because her old friends are clearly more loyal to Bob than to her.

3. *I won't go on dates, even though I've met some interesting guys. I don't know if my heart can handle falling in love again.*

    a.   Susan's heart has been broken, and the best way to avoid its happening again is to avoid dating.

    b.   Susan is evaluating her sadness as so harmful to her that she must avoid situations that might produce more sadness.

    c.   Susan is just giving herself some downtime to recuperate from her loss.

4. *I try to feel positive about my life, but it doesn't seem to work. I know I should be moving on and starting to feel better now, but I feel horrible.*

    a.   Susan is trapped by programming that says she'll be healthy when she's no longer sad; she's getting even sadder because she's suppressing her grief.

    b.   Susan is trying to think positive thoughts about her life and needs to keep doing that to get healthy.

    c.   Susan is grieving for the loss of the relationship and shouldn't move on until her grief is gone.

5. *I try to do fun things, but it just backfires because I notice that I'm still sad and that depresses me.*

   a. Susan can't have fun if sadness and depression are present.

   b. Susan *should* get depressed when she does something fun and notices that it doesn't feel fun.

   c. Susan is trying to control her sad feelings by forcing herself to do fun things; when she notices it hasn't worked, she gets more depressed.

6. *I try to tell myself that I'm pretty and that I'm a good person, but the more I try to be positive, the worse my depression seems to get.*

   a. Susan is trying to suppress thoughts that she isn't pretty and isn't a good person and as a result is getting even more thoughts like this, leading to more depression.

   b. Susan is trying to be positive in her thinking, so it's unusual that she feels worse.

   c. Susan is putting on a happy face and trying to make the best of a bad situation.

7. *I try to be strong and forget about Bob, but I just can't seem to put it behind me.*

   a. Susan should be able to get over her feelings of loss, and there is something wrong with her if she can't.

   b. Susan is following a rule that strong people should simply suppress memories of a loved one who is gone, but instead is getting more and more memories of Bob.

   c. Susan understands that she will be healthier when she puts Bob out of her mind.

Key: 1: c, 2: a, 3: b, 4: a, 5: c, 6: a, 7: b

Debriefing. How did you do on this quiz? Do any of Susan's coping strategies seem familiar? Emotional avoidance and suppression usually show up in the form of behavioral avoidance. Notice that Susan is avoiding a lot of situations because they might trigger unpleasant feelings, thoughts, or memories related to her divorce. In fairness to Susan, the experience of living in depression is, as one client put it, "like a game of ping-pong, back and forth, back and forth, and it never ends." It's a game of trying to replace negative emotions, thoughts, and memories with positive emotions, thoughts, and memories, all in the pursuit of achieving health. Unfortunately, when you hit a positive emotion across the net, a negative one bounces back at you, and it never seems to end. The more of an effort you make to feel good, the less good you feel.

EXERCISE: AVOIDANCE AND SUPPRESSION

Now that you've had an opportunity to practice identifying avoidance and suppression strategies in Susan's life, we want you to apply what you learned to your life. To make this easier, we'll continue with the multiple-choice format, but this time the choices are going to be more generic. First, go back to the exercise "Inventory of Short-Term vs. Long-Term Results," in chapter 3, and identify the five coping strategies that you use most often in your daily life and that you rated as not working. Write them here and then circle any of the multiple-choice options that apply.

1. _____

   _____

   a. Avoiding situations that might trigger emotional pain

   b. Trying to suppress or avoid painful emotions, thoughts, or memories

   c. Distracting myself from or numbing myself to painful mental experiences

   d. Trying to force in positive feelings, thoughts, or memories

2. _____

   _____

   a. Avoiding situations that might trigger emotional pain

   b. Trying to suppress or avoid painful emotions, thoughts, or memories

   c. Distracting myself from or numbing myself to painful mental experiences

   d. Trying to force in positive feelings, thoughts, or memories

3. _____

   _____

   a. Avoiding situations that might trigger emotional pain

   b. Trying to suppress or avoid painful emotions, thoughts, or memories

   c. Distracting myself from or numbing myself to painful mental experiences

   d. Trying to force in positive feelings, thoughts, or memories

4. _____

   _____

   a. Avoiding situations that might trigger emotional pain

   b. Trying to suppress or avoid painful emotions, thoughts, or memories

   c. Distracting myself from or numbing myself to painful mental experiences

   d. Trying to force in positive feelings, thoughts, or memories

5. _____

_____

    a.   Avoiding situations that might trigger emotional pain

    b.   Trying to suppress or avoid painful emotions, thoughts, or memories

    c.   Distracting myself from or numbing myself to painful mental experiences

    d.   Trying to force in positive feelings, thoughts, or memories

Debriefing. As you went through this exercise, did you see any similar themes among your strategies? If you understand how the depression trap works, you can anticipate and look for the lures that draw you most often. When you see one, that's your cue to slow down and proceed with great awareness and intention. When you're tempted to avoid or suppress, you do have a choice: you can identify the avoidance or suppression move you're tempted to make and choose to do something different instead.

WHEN MANAGING YOUR MOOD IS THE GOAL, MANAGING YOUR LIFE IS IMPOSSIBLE

One pattern we frequently see in depressed people is that mood management becomes the reference point for most decisions about whether to engage in activities. If you look closely at Susan's statements, you can see that she's preoccupied with gauging the worth of activities based on their impact on her depression. She's following the cultural dictates of feel-goodism: Her definition of "getting over" her divorce is to no longer to be saddened by it or reminded of it, and to be free of the thoughts, feelings, and memories that went into both her marriage and the divorce. Ultimately, her social conditioning about what it means to be healthy, including the very concept of "getting over it," leads her to engage in a variety of behaviors that only serve to tighten the viselike grip of the depression trap.

Managing your life requires engaging in behaviors that are rewarding, behaviors that boost your confidence, and behaviors that address and solve personal problems. The dilemma is that when you're depressed, each of these behaviors could also trigger unpleasant emotions, thoughts, memories, or sensations. In order to control these unwanted internal events, depressed people usually try to avoid the situations that produce them. However, this ultimately restricts the scope and quality of a person's life. In fact, clinical research has shown that a variety of behaviors aimed at controlling emotions are actually causes of depression rather than solutions (Hayes et al. 1996). These emotional control behaviors take three common forms: decreasing positive activities, avoiding personal problems, and redefining what's normal.

Decreasing Positive Activities

Depressed people may drift into a pattern of decreasing the frequency of positive activities and other positive behaviors because they interfere with the focus on mood management. A person struggling with depression might say "My friend called and invited me to coffee, but I didn't want to burden her with my problems" or "I used to exercise two or three times a week, but I don't have the desire to do it anymore." Notice that in the first example, the implication is that the only reason for getting together with friends is to discuss personal problems, as opposed to just doing something fun. In the second example, the person is waiting to become motivated in order to do something. Unfortunately, being motivated is essentially the opposite of being depressed, so it's very unlikely that the person will ever start exercising again, even though it's known to improve mood. This pattern seems logical to the person, as his or her reasons for not doing positive activities appear to be valid. We'll discuss this problem and some solutions for it in much greater detail later in the book.

Avoiding Personal Problems

To address and solve personal problems, you must approach difficult situations. You can't solve a life problem unless you engage it, and this means figuring out what's going on, sorting out your options, and trying various solutions. When a person says "I'm too depressed to deal with my supervisor's constant badgering," his options appear to be limited to not going to work, or being passive and submissive in interactions with his supervisor. Here's another example: If someone endures an unsatisfying relationship and is unwilling to bring up her dissatisfaction directly, there's little likelihood that the relationship will change. Avoiding personal problems may result in a style of day-to-day living that doesn't reflect your values.

Redefining Normal Activities

As Susan's case demonstrates, one common emotional control strategy is to redefine normal activities in terms of the depression risk they pose and then avoid activities evaluated as presenting a risk. For example, dating a year or so after a divorce is a fairly normal thing to do at Susan's age. Dating doesn't require her to become more emotionally vulnerable than she is ready to handle. She could date just to have fun and to reenter the world of single people, where she might actually make some new friends. Activities like dating, spending time with friends, and going to movies create a balance in our daily living routines. When normal activities are redefined in terms of the depression risk they pose, a person's life gets more restricted—and, ultimately, more depressing.

■ *Susan's Journey Toward a Vital Life*

After analyzing her coping strategies, Susan realized that her emotional avoidance was generating and perpetuating the very feelings, thoughts, and memories she was trying to avoid. Once she accepted that grief is a healthy response to an unwanted divorce, she understood that her grief and sadness could help her heal if she didn't get in the way and try to suppress the process. She could go out with her friends and experience a sense of awkwardness. She could allow memories of Bob to come and go as such memories tend to do. She could give herself time to feel sad and cry about the loss of her relationship and the dreams she'd had for it. She could allow herself to experiment with new relationships while accepting the fear and anxiety that might come along for the ride. Susan realized she could do all of these things in the midst of feeling the way she felt, and that this was a life-affirming, emotionally healthy way to experience her pain. She began to engage the world again, and as she allowed herself to feel things directly, she noticed that her depression began to recede into the background of her life. Susan was on the path to living a vital life!

Secrets to ACT On

☞ Remember the rules of the depression trap and they will lose some of their power over your behavior:

> ☞ Unpleasant emotions, thoughts, and memories are bad for you and mean you're unhealthy.

> ☞ You'll be healthy when you no longer have painful experiences.

> ☞ You can control and eliminate bad experiences by replacing them with positive experiences.

> ☞ If you can't make this work, you're not trying hard enough.

> ☞ You must continue to try to replace the bad with the good, even if it means losing control of your life.

☞ Here's the secret your depression doesn't want you to hear: None of this is true!

The Coach Says

Your emotional pain is not the problem. In fact, your emotions are perfectly designed to help you live a valuable life. You can walk out of the depression trap if you choose to focus on engaging your life—solving personal problems, participating in valued activities, and protecting your health—with your feelings in tow. If Susan can do this, you can do it to!

Sneak Preview

In the next chapter, we'll take an in-depth look at the second siren song: fusion. You'll learn how language and thought, for all of their usefulness, can also trap you in following rules for living that simply don't work. We'll introduce you to two very important aspects of your mind—your wise mind and your reactive mind—and show you how reactive mind leads you into depression while wise mind leads you to a vital life.

CHAPTER 5

Understand Your Mind, Trust Your Experience

*What is troubling us is the tendency to believe that the mind
is like a little man within.* —Ludwig Wittgenstein

In earlier chapters, we suggested that depression is a sign that your life is out of balance in one or more areas of life. Ironically, remaining stuck in the depression trap may help you avoid potentially painful issues, but at the cost of building the kind of life you want to live. The process that has led you down this path is, in part, a result of your socialization. Following the rules you've learned about controlling negative feelings, thoughts, and memories can derail you. However, working outside the rules is easier said than done, because you have a mind that's always advising you about how to live your life. If you can't create some distance between you and your mental advisor, you're likely to keep following the same old rules. In this chapter, we'll look at some basic qualities of how the mind works and then help you put some checks and balances in place so you can use the advising mind when doing so is called for and use a wiser part of your mind to tune in to direct experience when this is the better option.

THE SECOND SIREN SONG: FUSION

In chapter 4, we examined the important role that emotional avoidance plays in developing and maintaining depression. We mentioned that one of the initial questions in developing ACT was how to explain the fact that bright, sensitive, caring people can persist in using coping strategies that simply don't work, often over the course of months or years, all the while losing any semblance of a vital life. This scenario implies that there must be some mechanism prohibiting the depressed person from understanding the direct results of these coping strategies. If a strategy is systematically making you feel worse, then the commonsense solution would be to stop using it and look for something else that might work better. But this usually doesn't happen in depression, and in a lot of other situations in which people are suffering.

One proposed explanation is that depressed people intentionally choose ineffective strategies because of low self-esteem and the resulting belief that they deserve to suffer, but that idea is preposterous. We have never met anyone who wanted to remain depressed. Most depressed people try everything they can think of to get on top of their situation, even if those efforts backfire over and over again.

Another possibility is that something is overriding the depressed person's ability to objectively assess the results of ineffective strategies. It isn't at all unusual for a depressed person to think something like "I know drinking is only going to make my depression worse" on the way home from work. Once at home, this same person may think "I feel angry, my life is going nowhere, and I can't stand this feeling of emptiness. The only way I'm going to feel better is to have a drink." Minutes after recognizing that drinking will only worsen the problem of depression, this person may get sucked in by other thoughts that propel him to drink to excess. These thoughts suggest that to feel healthy he must immediately eliminate "bad" feelings, such as anger and emptiness, and "bad" thoughts, like "My life isn't going anywhere." Unfortunately, the quick-fix solution of drinking too much will lead to more depression in the long run. This example highlights a dangerous mental process called *fusion*.

Think about fusion like this: If you have a thought or emotion, you can be the owner of it or you can be owned by it. When you're the owner, you could say something like "I'm having the thought that life is pointless" or "I'm aware of feeling sad right now." The thought or feeling would be "out there," separate from you in your mind's eye. Conversely, when you're owned by a thought or feeling, you might say "Life is pointless" or "I'm sad." In the example above, if the person takes it literally that life is pointless or thinks that the only emotion he or she will ever feel is sadness, then there would be a huge temptation to drink to escape that seeming reality.

When you own the thought, memory, or feeling, you are the master, and the thought, memory, or feeling is the slave. The tables are reversed when such private experiences own you: you identify with them and become trapped in a vicious cycle of trying to suppress, control, or avoid them. For example, it's very hard to accept an emotion like grief when you're owned by a thought that says "Unpleasant feelings like grief are unhealthy for you, and you shouldn't have them." In ACT terms, "fusion" means you're completely identified with whatever you're feeling, thinking, or remembering at the time. You're bonded with the mental event: If you think it, it's true. If you remember it, it isn't a memory; it's as though it's happening right now. If you fuse with an emotion like anger, you're likely to lash out without hesitation.

The tricky thing about fusion is that it is an essential feature of thinking and contributes mightily to our ability to operate in the world. For example, fusion allows us to hold hands and say "I love you" and consequently experience intimacy at the same level as if we'd just made love. Another example is a potter pulling up the clay for a large pot, who thinks "center" and experiences being one with the clay. It's fusion with untested, unquestioned, and inaccurate rules that causes us problems in life—not fusion per se. For example, when you fuse with a rule like "to be healthy you must get rid of your sadness," you will use the strategies demanded by the rule, such as trying to substitute positive thoughts for negative ones. If you add in a rule like "if this isn't working, it's because I'm weak," you have the perfect formula for continuing to use an ineffective coping strategy, like avoidance, over and over again even though it's actually increasing your depression.

Without fusion to unworkable rules, there would be no need for emotional avoidance because there wouldn't be any misguided rules that could own you. Primary emotions such as anger and sadness would support you in making needed course corrections. They would tell you that something in your life needs to change and motivate you to solve the problem. End of story—and end of depression.

As we'll explain, the conditions that allow fusion to occur are actually hidden in our language and thought processes. We'll try not to be too abstract about this, but you need to learn a bit of science geek information about how language and thought create the mind and, in turn, control our behavior. This is a little tricky because most of us aren't used to looking at our mind as a scientific oddity; rather, we're used to *being* our mind and following what it says. Let's start by looking at how Buddhism views the problem of having a mind.

The Uncarved Block

The Buddhist view of the human life cycle is very different from the Western perspective. In Buddhism, you are born with perfect consciousness, what Buddhists call the "uncarved block." This is raw consciousness, unadulterated by the mind's efforts to organize and label experience. As you mature, you lose perfect consciousness through the acquisition of mind, which is developed systematically through the process of learning language and higher-level thinking. As you develop these skills, your mind begins to play a more dominant role in daily experience. You internalize all sorts of cultural rules, norms, and expectations and learn to conform to them. This allows you to participate as a member of your culture, but it also begins to obscure the path to a blissful life because the knowing part of your mind starts to dominate the sensing part of your mind. Ideas and concepts that can be verbalized are reinforced, while such things as intuition and preconscious knowing are left out. At the same time, your mind begins to masquerade as an entity that's somehow bigger than you are. It begins to dominate how you shape and interpret reality.

The problem is, the creation of your mind is entirely dependent upon the people and cultural forces that have trained you to speak and think. The mind has no existence independent of this training. Buddhist practice is designed to free a person from the shackles of the illusion of mind as an independent entity. In essence, the goal of the life journey in Buddhism is to return to the perfect, simple awareness of the moment of birth. You're probably familiar with a Christian allegory that similarly emphasizes the destructive impact of verbally derived knowledge on one's ability to live in bliss—the tale of Adam and Eve being cast out of the Garden of Eden for eating the fruit of the Tree of Knowledge. What an interesting message—that the basis of all human suffering is the acquisition of the ability to know, compare, contrast, and evaluate!

How Your Mind Is Carved Up

One of the major recent developments in the cognitive sciences (the study of human intelligence) is *relational frame theory* (*RFT*; see Hayes, Barnes-Holmes, and Roche 2001). ACT is based in the premises of RFT, so we'll take a moment to describe some of the bigger ideas in more detail. RFT researchers systematically investigate how children learn language and internalize it (two inextricably intertwined processes, as indicated by the fact that thinking is sometimes referred to as "covert language"). Studying children as they develop the ability to think and speak allows researchers to uncover the ways that spoken and unspoken language govern behavior. As it turns out, Buddhist thought on this topic holds more than a grain of truth; acquisition of language is the main vehicle for understanding relationships and following social rules. It is the means by which we carve the world into categories, evaluate events and situations, and draw on the present to predict the future. Without language, we would be in the food chain, rather than at the top of it.

Rule-Governed Behavior

In RFT, the term *rule-governed behavior* is used to describe behavior that's under the direct control of the language system. Rule-governed behavior is a very powerful habit once it's formed. This means that once a rule is established in your language system, it will almost inevitably be followed even if the objective results are dismal. Sound familiar? One reason for this is that following mental rules is heavily rewarded by the culture, even when the rule doesn't actually work.

People learn rules about how to live life at the same time they learn to speak a language. They are promised rewards for following the rules, for example, "smile and the world will smile with you, cry and you cry alone." If the rule says "Negative emotions are bad for you and you need to get rid of them," following that rule will be more important than being aware of whether the rule actually works in real life. This is because the reward the rule promises (being healthy and happy) is so potent that you are just about powerless to stop your behavior.

One last point about rule-governed behavior: It's easy to program people with rules. Children absorb language like a sponge, and along with the way, they absorb the rules of the culture. It can take an adult many years to learn a foreign language and be fluent. It takes children only three to four years. This makes it easy to program children with all the rules necessary to maintain social order—and then some. By the time we become young adults, we are fully programmed to allow the "word machine" (another ACT term for the mind) to govern how we behave from moment to moment. If you take a minute to step back and look, you'll immediately notice that your mind is controlling your behavior all the time. You're receiving suggestions every few seconds about what you should attend to, where you need to be in half an hour, or what chore you need to get done. However, taking that step back and looking at your word machine whirring away in the background can be hard to do if you're not used to it. Don't worry; we'll help you learn how to become a world-class mind watcher in part 2 of this book.

Relational Frames

This is definitely science geek stuff, but we want to introduce you to the concept of *relational frames*. These are the basic building blocks of human language, and they appear in a developmental sequence as a child ages. A relational frame is nothing more than an association among two or more objects or concepts. Things you take for granted every day, like the ability to distinguish between nine in the morning and nine in the evening, require a complex set of language processes to occur. You have to understand that the number 9 on the clock corresponds to a particular time of day (later than 8 and earlier than 10). This means you understand that 8 is less than 9, and 9 is less than 10. You have a set of relations that help you know that even though both 9:00 a.m. and 9:00 p.m. use the same number, the second set of symbols, a.m. and p.m., provides you with another comparison that helps establish the time. Thus, you know that one of the 9s usually occurs in daylight and the other usually occurs when it is dark.

Young children don't know how to tell time because developing this skill requires acquiring all of the necessary elements of symbolic thought. When you see a parent showing a young child an object, giving it a name, and describing its age or any other property that links the object to something that the child already knows, the parent is programming a relational frame. Learning of this type is the cornerstone of human language—and of learning to think.

THE DEICTIC FRAME

To oversimplify, relational frame theory basically states that the complexity of language, and our thoughts and behaviors, is made possible by establishing relationships between things. Among the several types of relational frames, one in particular, the deictic frame, provides important insight into the mind and our relationship to it. The *deictic frame* allows an individual to distinguish between self and other. It establishes that I am different from you. Very young children can't engage in this type of relation, so they're unable to distinguish the emotions of others from their own emotions. Acquiring the deictic relational frame is thought to be the beginning of conscious self-awareness. Indeed, in Buddhism this is the first carving of the block. Until you know that you are you and that you are not the same as the person across from you, you cannot be fully aware, even though you are conscious. The deictic frame gives you a sense of self and enables you to be you. This process is so basic that it precedes the development of all other relational frames.

Deictic frames are also involved in distinguishing things from the perspective of the observer: here and there, now and then, and so on. Externally, this allows us to make such statements as "The photograph is there, in front of me" and "I was five in this picture; now I'm fifty." For the purposes of ACT, extending the deictic frame inward is very useful, because this creates a distinction between you and the products of your mental machinery. Once you've established the relation "me and my mind," you're able to say "I'm having the thought that I'm lonely" or "I'm having the feeling of being sad." At first, this distinction may seem surprising, maybe even mind-boggling, but just as you aren't the same person as someone sitting across from you, you aren't the same as your mind. It's more accurate to say that although you *have* a mind, you are not the same as your mind. Learning to undo fusion is, therefore, nothing more than strengthening your awareness of this relationship through practice, be it meditation, prayer, or mindfulness. Now there's a paradox, using the word "mindfulness" to describe a way of separating your self from your mind! Luckily, that one's just semantic. And as you'll soon see, having a mind isn't all bad; the key is to learn to access your wise mind.

CAUTION! WORD MACHINERY AT WORK

The ability to generate relations is what it takes to be a functional member of society. Once installed, language-based relations generate complex thoughts, images, emotions, memories, and sensations. They evolve into a tightly knit web of rules that we use to describe relationships among our experiences with objects, people, and events in the worlds of both public and private experience. You might imagine a patchwork quilt made up of words, pictures, emotions, and sensations. The quilt is as big as your life, and the pieces of fabric represent all of your experiences. You carry the quilt around with you 24/7 and thus become so accustomed to it that you often forget it's there. A key thing to understand about the assumptions that underlie language is that you can't observe them in process; you're only aware of the end product in the form of a whole thought, feeling, memory, or physical sensation. It's a system that largely functions beyond your awareness.

This should cause you a little anxiety, and we actually hope it does, because the same properties that make this system powerful in beneficial ways also can lead to destructive outcomes. For example, humans are the only species known to commit suicide. There's a limit to how much you can trust your mental machinery.

Programming Is Automatic and Resists Change

Do you think you're a racist? In response to this question, most people will state they believe in racial equality and stand against racism. Despite this, it's relatively easy to demonstrate that people have hidden programming that automatically labels some ethnic groups as good and some as bad. This is due to *implicit association*, a thinking process that's been extensively studied (Greenwald, McGhee, and Schwartz 1998). An implicit association is a built-in evaluation carried within the context of relational frames. As a result, you're preprogrammed to see an association between one event or object and a second event or object. When you see something that contradicts this bias, you have to work hard mentally to avoid acting in a way that is consistent with the bias. This often results in avoiding the memory or situation that triggered the bias. Later on, we'll introduce you to a type of implicit association that has been extensively studied in regard to depression: implicit self-esteem.

While there have been many interesting studies of implicit associations, the most famous is the Racial Implicit Association Test (RIAT). If you have Internet access, you can actually browse this name and find a website where you can take the test yourself. The basic way the RIAT works is as follows: You are presented with two faces, one Caucasian and one African-American. Positioned underneath the faces are one of two words: "good" or "bad." In the first trial, the word "good" is under the Caucasian person's picture and the word "bad" is under the African-American person's picture. In the second go-round, the locations of the words "good" and "bad" are reversed. Then you're given a list of words to place in the "good" or "bad" column. The words you have to sort are emotionally loaded words with good meanings (loving, kind, compassionate) or bad meanings (ruthless, dangerous, sneaky).

Here is what you're likely to find if you take the RIAT: It will be easier and faster to sort the good and bad words when the word "good" is under the Caucasian person's picture. When it's under the African-American person's picture, it will take you longer to sort the words and you'll make more sorting errors. This is an example of programming that's operating beneath your awareness. Interestingly, African-Americans usually have the same results as Caucasians, indicating that the programming of racial stereotypes is as basic as learning to speak English and think in English.

Programming Controls Behavior Outside of Awareness

Another interesting area of study in psychology is known as *priming*. Priming involves giving a person hidden verbal cues designed to influence the person's behavior in some type of simulated situation. When people are debriefed afterward, they usually aren't able to identify why they behaved in the way they did.

One of the more famous priming studies involved having college students memorize a list of words as part of a bogus study of memory (Bargh, Chen, and Burrows 1996). Two lists of words were used. One group of students was given a list that had words like peaceful, patient, cooperative, and unhurried scattered in it. The other group's list had occasional words like aggressive, impatient, intrusive, or racing. The real experiment involved assessing how the two groups of students would behave immediately after memorizing the words. After learning the lists, students in both groups were told to go to an office down the hall to get credit for participating. Unbeknownst to subjects, an actress played the role of a secretary who had come to see the assistant with the research credit slips. The job of the "secretary" was to go on and on about a personal problem and thus block students from getting their credit slips. To get the credit slip the student had to interrupt the secretary, and the time it took before the student did so was carefully measured.

Students who had memorized the list that included words related to aggression didn't wait long before interrupting the fake secretary, whereas students in the other group *never* interrupted the secretary. They would simply stand in the hallway and wait until the maximum time allowed for them to interrupt had expired! Interestingly, students in both groups weren't able to accurately explain why they chose to interrupt or passively sit by.

You are bombarded with cultural programming every day, and while there are no researchers manipulating the outcomes of your unique life experiment, you do take on rules that you aren't even aware of. Some come from our personal experience ("Don't cry; it just shows people that they got to you") and some come from our culture ("Go to college and you'll be happy and have a good life"). When these rules dominate, you may employ strategies that don't work over and over again without fully understanding the nature of the trap you're in. ACT strategies are very helpful in this regard. Many of them are designed to undercut the dominance of language by teaching you to recognize its limits. This will help increase your flexibility in working with the word machine.

EXERCISE: REVEALING THE BRITTLE SHELL

The operation of mind and language is so subtle and day-to-day in nature that we tend to take this system for granted. On the surface, it seems essential and correct to use it as our basis for day-to-day functioning. It helps us organize experience, plan, predict, and engage with the world. So what do Buddhists mean when they describe mind as an illusion? This exercise will help you understand this counterintuitive idea.

> *Get an egg out of your refrigerator, hold it in your open palm, and concentrate on it for a minute. What do you see? What do you feel? You see a white or brown shell, with a smooth, slightly sandy texture. Now notice how perfectly made the shell is in terms of its function. The entire structure is necessary for the shell to do its job. It is built exactly right and has been that way since the moment it came into existence as a tiny, tiny shell. Can you see the location where the shell started to become a shell? Is there an obvious starting point? What was the last part of the shell to grow? What is the living part of this egg? The shell? Or what is inside the shell?*

Debriefing. You may be feeling pretty good about the egg at this point. However, what if we asked you to let the egg fall from your hand onto the floor? Would you resist? Perhaps you would, as you know that would result in the end of the egg in its current form—and a mess on the floor! The shell, as perfect as it is for providing a lightweight protective covering for the potential life mass inside, is very brittle, and because of that, it is exactly the wrong kind of structure if the context changes. If you dropped the egg on your bed, it would probably make it, but not if you dropped it on the floor. Something that's a perfectly protective cover in one context can turn out to be exactly the wrong form of protection in a different context.

EXERCISE: CRACKING THE SHELL OF LANGUAGE

If the mind is like an egg, the shell is our language-based ability to think, feel, remember, and have physical sensations. It turns out that this shell grows and matures just like an eggshell, and it's also very brittle. How brittle is it? The following simple exercise has been used for decades (and in Hayes, Strosahl, and Wilson 1999, 154–6) to demonstrate the transparent nature of language and thought.

> First, think of the word "orange." Let all the sensations, memories, and images associated with that word come into your mind. Do you sense the tangy odor or the texture of the peel? Can you imagine the slightly bittersweet taste? Do you see color? Can you see the sections of the orange in your hand? Can you sense the gush of juice as you bite down on a section? Give yourself a minute or so to get a full picture of an orange in your mind's eye.
>
> Now find a clock with a second hand on it. For the next forty-five seconds, we want you to say the word "orange" over and over again as fast as you can. Just keep saying the word as fast as you can until the forty-five seconds are up. If you have trouble pronouncing it or lose your concentration on the task, just get back to it and keep repeating the word as best you can. Time to start. Go!

Debriefing. What happened to your relationship with the word "orange" as you did this exercise? Did you notice that the more you repeated the word, the more it started to sound like gibberish? Did you have more trouble pronouncing the word over time? What happened to the images and associations you had in the first part of the exercise? Did they disappear?

Let's consider the implications of the orange exercise for a moment longer. Initially, when we asked you to use the word "orange" as it's supposed to be used in your language system, the system functioned beautifully. It gave you not just the word "orange," but a variety of images and associations from your past history with orange. Then, when we asked you to use the word in a way that violates the rules of the system, it turned into an odd collection of sounds, mostly devoid of images and associations. You were simply uttering a sound that had no functional connection to your shell. This exercise actually works with most any word, phrase, emotion, or memory. Activities like this essentially crack the shell of language and reveal its contents, an aspect of the mind that exists beyond language. There is some formidable and essential wisdom in this part of your awareness, just as the essence of the egg is not the shell but what's inside the shell. The reason the egg is there isn't because of the shell. If there wasn't any life mass inside, there would be no need for the shell in the first place.

Learning to recognize that your shell is different from your essence is fundamental to living a vital life. You are the life mass, and although the shell protects you in some contexts, it's ineffective—or worse—in other situations. We'll help you learn when you can use your shell and when you need to shed it so you can access other important aspects of your mind. Don't worry about cracking the shell of language! It's very robust and will pull itself back together quickly.

REACTIVE MIND AND WISE MIND

We'll use the term "minding" frequently in this book. When we do, we're referring to the ongoing process of responding to and fusing with thoughts, feelings, memories, and sensations. When you're minding your mind, you're obeying its instructions, just as a child minds a parent. Only you can mind your mind, because no one else has access to your word machine. It's just you and your mind going at it. Your relationship with your mind is unique and determined by your learning history. In this way, no two minds are alike, even though we are trained from birth to comply with similar social rules, norms, and expectations. In part 2, we'll delve deeply into strategies to help you detect and prevent unproductive aspects of minding. For now, we want to create a basic distinction between two very different aspects of your mind: reactive mind and wise mind.

Like ACT, the Buddhist perspective views fusion with unwanted private events as a principle cause of human misery. Buddhists practice meditation to improve their ability to recognize mental events without becoming attached to them. As we've discussed, depression is fueled by fusion with rules about health and well-being that are inaccurate but compelling. Indeed, recent research suggests that depressed people who learn mindfulness-meditation strategies are less vulnerable to experiencing depression in the future (Segal, Williams, and Teasdale 2002; Williams et al. 2007). The ability to step away and use the deictic frame of "me and my mind" is a critical skill. If you can't step away, your unpleasant emotions, thoughts, memories, and sensations will seem toxic to you and you'll be unwilling to accept them. If you can't accept them, you have to try to suppress or avoid them.

Wise Mind	Reactive Mind
■ Intuition	■ Evaluation and categorization
■ Nonverbal knowing and inspiration	■ Reasoning, analysis, and logic
■ Free choice	■ Decision making
■ Values	■ Social norms and expectations
■ Present-moment awareness	■ Memory and future predictions
■ Simple awareness	■ Conceptualized view of the self and the world
■ Universal awareness and compassion	■ Stigmatizing forms of awareness (racism, prejudice)

Reactive Mind

Reactive mind lives in the shell of your language system. It is a built-in rule follower and advice giver, and it operates 24/7. It chatters at you, wants to discourse with you, and serves up an unending stream of woulds, shoulds, musts, and oughts, regardless of whether its advice is wanted or needed. Your reactive mind is full of judgments, evaluations, categories, and predictions. It strings together concepts that describe who you are in the here and now and how you got to be the way you are. It will tell you that you don't have enough of something, like love in your life, and too much of something else, like bad breath or fat. It tells you what will happen if you engage in some behavior ("If you leave your job, you'll never find another one") and what will happen if you don't ("If you don't quit, your boss will keep insulting you and you'll have no self-esteem"). This type of comparative, evaluative, and predictive activity is a breeding ground for depression. When you fuse with your reactive mind, you'll get caught in the trap of rule following and will be unable to adapt. In Buddhism, the reactive mind is viewed as a small and limited form of experience that must be held lightly in order for a different kind of mind to grow: wise mind.

Wise Mind: The Companion of Reactive Mind

It was Buddha who coined the term "wise mind." In this book, we'll teach you to use two forms of wise mind. One involves learning to focus your attention on the present moment of your life. In ancient Buddhism, this form of mind is called *poornata*, which means to be absolutely present and nonjudgmentally aware of everything around you. The second form of wise mind involves the ability to be *aware of your awareness*, to see that there is a you that is looking at the present moment. This state of being—a state of simple awareness—is called *shunyata* and is considered to be the path to enlightenment. These two forms of mind are developed through practice, not intellectual discussion. In part 2, we'll give you lots of ways to practice being in the present moment and contacting your simple awareness. Some scientific studies of brain function suggest that developing these two forms of wise mind result in permanent, positive improvements in brain functioning (Deshmukh 2006; Hankey 2006). When you learn to use your wise mind and free yourself of the monotonous chatter of your reactive mind, you'll be able to more easily see what's working in your life and what isn't.

Another way to think about wise mind is that it is observer of the antics of reactive mind. It's aware of what reactive mind is doing (thinking, feeling, remembering, sensing) but isn't caught up in what is transpiring inside the word machine. Think of your wise mind as the "me" in the deictic frame of "me and my mind." It is the place where you can be separate from the pull of reactive mind's evaluations, categories, prejudices, and instructions on how to behave.

Wise mind is the essence inside the shell; it is what remains after the reactive mind has expended its energy and flamed out. It is not defined by mental events like thoughts, feelings, memories, and sensations. Wise mind can see the shell of language and thought for what it really is, not what it says it is. After all, the shell has a specific purpose that is important and useful in the right situations. Because it is not in the world of evaluation, labeling, and comparison, wise mind is naturally compassionate and empathic and is focused on the here and now. It is fearless in standing in the presence of immediate experience and is keenly interested in the you that is doing the experiencing.

One of the cardinal signs that you are onto your wise mind is when you let go of troublesome private events—when you discover that in the tug-of-war between you and your reactive mind, the best move is to drop the rope. Your wise mind lets you see that it isn't necessary to struggle with things that can't be changed and that you can accept past events rather than continue to struggle with them. Once you understand that you construct your world, that it's basically an illusion of mind, then there is no real need to be afraid of or avoid anything in your life space.

Which Will You Trust, Reactive Mind or Wise Mind?

Now that you know the difference between your reactive mind and your wise mind, which do you want to rely on and for what purpose? In some circumstances, such as when you're planning a work task or crossing a busy intersection, the reactive mind is very useful. As we discussed earlier, reactive mind is able to plan, evaluate, and predict with considerable success in the external world. However, reactive mind isn't all that useful when it comes to matters between the ears. It tends to take the rules that work in the external world and to apply them mindlessly to your inner world. Since reactive mind labels, categorizes, and is a built-in rule follower, it insulates you from direct experience and the rich information available in the context of the present moment. Wise mind brings you in closer contact with your direct experience, because it isn't influenced by language and the rule-following built into it.

Here's a mental exercise to help you understand why reactive mind isn't always helpful: Imagine that you have $10,000 you want to invest and use for your retirement. You take the time to meet with an investment advisor, who presents you with all kinds of charts and graphs to show how much money he'll make for you if you invest with his company. You're impressed with his self-assurance and confidence. He seems to know exactly what he's doing, so you decide to invest your money with him.

After six months, he calls to tell you that your investment is doing extremely well and is currently worth $7,500. This means you've already lost $2,500. He says that if you just stay the course, you'll become very rich. He promises to update you in another six months with the good news. At the end of a year, he calls to enthusiastically inform you that his can't-miss investment model is just humming along, and your current worth is $5,000. This means you've lost half of your money. He explains that at this point, the main thing to do is stay with his investment program because it's going to be hot. After eighteen months he calls again, gushing that the investment model he developed has been written up in the money section of the newspaper. Other people are starting to get wind of his great ideas, and you're lucky that you got on the bandwagon with him early, as you'll benefit even more. He mentions that your current account value is $2,500, meaning you have now lost three-quarters of your money, and that you'll get rich and be able to retire early if you just stay with his approach.

In this scenario, when would you fire your advisor? Would you wait another six months and risk losing all of your money? For most people, the warning signals would start going off after six months, and certainly after a year. The investment advisor is like reactive mind, and his investment model is a set of rules he's blindly following. He provides mental chatter that says one thing is happening ("You're doing the right thing; you'll be rich"), while the results in the real world indicate something different ("You're losing your shirt"). Wise mind would allow you to cut your losses and pursue another strategy after the first or second indication that things aren't working out as you wish.

When Your Mind Is Incompetent, Hold It Softly

As the previous example illustrates, reactive mind can take you down the road to depression and will insist that you stay the course. However, that course is nothing more than the social programming your mind acquired when you learned to speak and develop your thinking skills.

Remember Susan, from chapter 4? After her divorce, this is exactly what she had to confront. Her reactive mind was telling her to avoid being with her friends because they weren't loyal to her and being with them would just worsen her depression. Her reactive mind was advising her to engage in a strategy designed to control her depression, but the strategy actually deepened her depression. Her reactive mind advised her that she needed to stop having negative emotions like sadness and grief about her divorce, but the more she followed this advice, the more depressed she got and the more dislodged her feelings of grief and sadness became. That didn't stop the mental chatter, of course. Her reactive mind kept telling her that other people could get rid of grief and sadness and get on with their lives. Why couldn't she? Susan's mental advisor simply couldn't admit that its strategies were never going to work, because it didn't have another plan of action to offer. Until Susan learned to listen to her direct experience using wise mind, she was powerless to resist the constant chatter of her reactive mind.

WORKABILITY: LEARNING TO USE WISE MIND

In addition to understanding the difference between reactive mind and wise mind, you need to have a way of penetrating the shell of reactive mind so you can access the wise mind's perspective on the results you're getting in your life. This requires you to adopt an odd but highly effective way of assessing (and negating) the influence of your mental advisor. In ACT, we call this alternative yardstick "workability." Workability is best thought of as living your life in a way that promotes an ongoing sense of direction, meaning, and vitality.

Workability Is About Results

Workability focuses on the direct results of strategies you're using in life. For example, Joyce described her life as having been workable when she took time to relax, play music, and be with her friends and family. The readings on her workability yardstick began to drop after several years of caring for her husband, whose health was declining rapidly. Her reactive mind told her she must stay the course and be there 24/7 for her husband. Even as she became increasingly exhausted, her reactive mind kept exhorting her to be a dutiful wife and evaluated any attempt to take time away from her husband as a violation of this duty.

When Joyce fused with this rule, she couldn't get in touch with the devastating results of pulling back from activities that brought her joy and peace. It was only when she let go of her rules and engaged her wise mind that she was able to see a clear path out of her growing depression. Being committed to her husband didn't require her to ignore her own health and well-being. She needed to engage in the rewarding aspects of her life just as energetically as she was taking care of her husband. Her wise mind had pulled the plug on her reactive mind!

Workability Is a Process, Not an Outcome

Since life is dynamic, workability in one's life moves up and down. This is a basic truth of living a vital life. Just as there will be good times, there are going to be bad times. In this way, living a vital life is a bit like learning to ride a bicycle. Riding a bike requires you to remain alert to the terrain and make continuous adjustments in how you distribute your weight and balance. As you pedal through your life, your wise mind helps you stay in direct contact with the terrain of your experience. And if you access your wise mind, it can help you make timely adjustments and keep your workability readings where you want them to be. When your workability is high, your sense of vitality in relationships, work, and play is strong. This doesn't mean you have peak life experiences every day, but it does mean that you know what's important to you and that you are moving toward it. Remember, a life worth living isn't defined by the absence of pain; rather, it's a path on which pain is accepted and experienced in a healthy way.

Workability Plays No Favorites

Another quality of workability is that it has no allegiance to any doctrine about how to live life. A life worth living comes in about as many flavors as there are people. And how you get there isn't about style points; it's about getting out of life what you want out of life. It isn't about what *should* work; it's about what *does* work. When you're zeroed in on using workability as your guide, you'll find yourself asking these kinds of questions:

- Is my drinking working for me?

- How has it been working for me to avoid dating?

- Is not talking to my husband about our marriage problems working for me?

- Is not looking for a more satisfying career working for me?

- What am I doing in my life right now that is working for me, and what's not working?

- How did my choices today work for me?

- Is waiting to be motivated before I take a walk working for me?

- Is not going to church working for me?

It takes courage to ask workability questions. Very often, the mere fact that you're asking means there's a difference between what your reactive mind is promising you and what you're getting in terms of results.

EXERCISE: THE WORKABILITY YARDSTICK

We recommend that you take a look at how your life measures up on the workability yardstick at least every three months. Make several copies of this blank worksheet so you'll always have a fresh copy. (Alternatively, you can print out fresh copies from the CD.) Use the workability scale below to rate your life on a scale of 1 to 10, where 1 means you feel that your life isn't working at all right now and 10 means your life couldn't be working any better. Circle the number that best describes where you are right now.

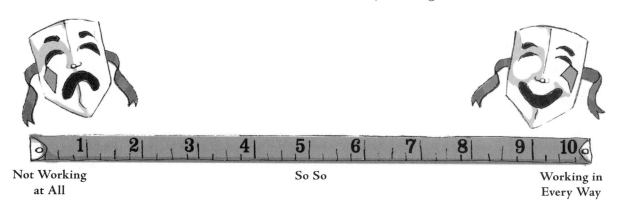

Not Working at All　　　　　　　　**So So**　　　　　　　　**Working in Every Way**

Now read through the two lists of words below and circle the words that best describe your life right now. Remember, the goal of all ACT self-inventory exercises isn't for you to beat yourself up; it's to honestly assess the situation you're in. The road to improving your life begins with figuring out what must be improved!

Low Workability	High Workability
■ Lethargic	■ Energetic
■ Lifeless	■ Vital
■ Apathetic	■ Purposeful
■ Withdrawn	■ Engaged
■ Bored	■ Interested
■ Inactive	■ Active
■ Isolated	■ Connected
■ Directionless	■ Directed
■ Meaningless	■ Meaningful

Debriefing. What types of words did you circle? Take a moment to look at each specific word you circled and ponder it for thirty seconds or so. Think about what went into picking that word. For words associated with low workability, what could you begin to change so that you'd be able to choose the corresponding word in the high workability column? If you circled a word in the high workability column, congratulate yourself for a job well done! How did you achieve that? How are you going to keep it going?

EXERCISE: WHEN LIFE WAS WORKING BETTER

This exercise will let you step back and look at how things were different when your life was working better. Can you think of a time when your life was working for you and you felt engaged and satisfied with your life? Keeping that time of your life in mind, answer the questions in the worksheet below. Try to use a few words from the high workability column in this exercise.

When Life Was Working Better

What was I doing to promote my personal health?

_____

_____

_____

What were my relationships and social connections like?

_____

_____

_____

What things engaged and motivated me in my work?

_____

_____

_____

What things engaged and motivated me in my play?

_____

_____

_____

Debriefing. What did you come up with in crafting your description of a more workable life? Chances are good that you said something about doing what's important to you, being satisfied with your relationships and social connections, enjoying yourself in various ways, and feeling a sense of life direction. In ACT, we see vitality as the main characteristic of a workable life. Vitality means having energy and feeling engaged and interested in the activities of your life. Living a vital life doesn't mean you have to be free of sadness or pain or be free of problems. It means approaching the pain and problems in life with the same energy and engagement that you approach the fun stuff.

EXERCISE: WORKABILITY ANALYSIS

This exercise will help you tune in to what your reactive mind is promising versus the results you're getting. It will help you assess how your wise mind and reactive mind participate in daily life situations that are causing you trouble. In the left-hand column, describe two troublesome situations that occurred fairly recently. In the next column, describe what your reactive mind told you to do. Next, describe what your wise mind said, and finally, in the right-hand column, describe what your eventual actions were and the results you got. This is a good format for practicing seeing things from the perspective of "me and my mind." However, it can be a bit difficult at first. If you have trouble with the exercise, read on; we've provided an example below.

Workability Analysis

Situation	What My Reactive Mind Said	What My Wise Mind Said	What Did I Do? Did It Work?

Debriefing. What did you find when you compared the responses of your reactive mind to those of your wise mind? Did you notice that your reactive mind just can't stop judging and carving up things into right and wrong or good and bad? This is a classic feature of the reactive mind, and it can be difficult to overcome. Chapter 9 provides a lot of help with this. How about your wise mind? Did you sense a quiet, calming response in the middle of your emotional upheaval that was encouraging you to let go, relax, and let things flow? That would be your wise mind showing up.

What about the results? When you fuse with your reactive mind and do what it says, what happens to your sense of vitality? Does your reactive mind advise you to take steps that actually work to solve the problem at hand? Once you're able to identify the types of situations where your reactive mind is leading you nowhere, you'll be in a good position to rein it in as need be. The more you practice this type of workability analysis, the better you'll get at turning away from your reactive mind when your wise mind knows better.

■ *Ted's Story*

Ted is a forty-five-year-old teacher who's struggled off and on with depression since adolescence. There are many triggers for depression in Ted's life. He responds to any type of criticism from colleagues—real or perceived—with intense down spells. He sometimes misses work to avoid being near people who have criticized him. He reacts similarly in conflicts or disagreements with his wife. Since he can't call in sick at home, he uses drinking as a way to avoid her.

When Ted began analyzing workability in his life, it provoked a lot of fear. He rated himself a 3 on the workability yardstick and circled the words "withdrawn," "isolated," "directionless," and "meaningless." As he put it, "I kinda know I'm doing things that aren't good for me, but I don't know what else to do. If I stop doing these things, will my depression just spiral out of control?" Here's what Ted came up with when he looked at the workability of his responses to two difficult situations.

TED'S WORKABILITY ANALYSIS

Situation	What My Reactive Mind Said	What My Wise Mind Said	What Did I Do? Did It Work?
I was criticized by the principal for not submitting test scores on time, even though I got the request for scores from him very late.	Stay home from work for a day and you'll feel better. You aren't smart enough to take him on; he'll make you feel like an idiot if you do.	I have a tight feeling in my chest, a lump in my throat, and lots of thoughts and emotions. I had the thought that maybe everything will turn out okay in the end, and I felt relaxed when I thought this.	I felt bad, like I was running away but not getting away, and embarrassed that I couldn't explain myself, so I called in sick again. I felt I was letting my students down.
I drank four beers after an argument with my wife.	If you drink, she can't get to you; you'll feel calm and she'll leave you alone.	I felt relaxed after drinking but woke up at 2:00 a.m. Unable to sleep, I felt a longing to be close to my wife. I love her and want her forgiveness.	My wife got on me about drinking. I felt like a coward, left home, and went to a bar to get away from her. I slept on the couch that night, and my wife wouldn't talk to me the next morning.

Review. Ted's workability analysis suggests that he's struggling to listen to his wise mind. Notice that his reactive mind is leading him to strategies that create additional problems, and that his wise mind isn't barking away at him as his reactive mind is. When we went over this exercise with Ted, we noticed the loving, compassionate comments about his wife that originated in his wise mind perspective. He loved her and wanted to be close to her. Following his reactive mind's advice was leading him away from what he truly wanted and valued. To have a satisfying intimate relationship, Ted has to show up for both the pleasant and the unpleasant moments in his marriage.

STARING INTO THE DARKNESS

For most of us, the darkness is the tendency to avoid difficult issues that surface when we strive for personal health, healthy relationships, and engagement in both work and play. These areas are critical for life satisfaction. The stakes are high, because you can't pretend that you're living a valued life. While painful, the first step is to admit that the strategies you've been using aren't working. Only then can you stop relying on them and start trying something new. As the old saying goes, "The journey of a thousand miles begins with the first step."

EXERCISE: IN A HOLE

This is a very well-known ACT exercise, adapted from the original book on ACT (Hayes, Strosahl, and Wilson 1999). We recommend listening to it now on the CD, because it will make the experience more powerful for you. Alternatively, you can read the instructions below and then take five to ten minutes to go through the visualization with your eyes closed. In either case, after you've done the visualization, answer the question following the text of the visualization.

> *You've been asked to walk the field of life blindfolded. Unbeknownst to you, this field is pockmarked with random holes of varying size and depth. To aid you in your journey, you're given a bag of tools. So, you begin walking the field of life, and sure enough, you eventually stumble into a very deep hole. The sides of this hole are so high that you can't climb out on your own. After mulling your situation over, you decide to open your tool bag to see if anything in there can help you extricate yourself. To your dismay, you discover that the only tool in the bag is a shovel. Determined to get out, you begin shoveling in all kinds of ways: You dig tunnels, you try to mound up some dirt, and you try cutting steps in the walls, but all of these strategies fail and the hole you're in just keeps getting larger and deeper. In frustration, you begin to analyze what you did to fall into the hole, and you get angry at yourself for being so stupid as to fall into a hole in the first place. You get*

even angrier when you think that other people walking the field of life are probably falling into very shallow holes and are able to get out with little effort.

Meanwhile you're still stuck in this very deep hole even though you don't really deserve this fate. So you go back to shoveling with even more determination, thinking that since you were given a shovel to dig your way out, the shovel must be the answer to your dilemma. You figure there must be experts out there who know how to use a shovel to get out of deep, steep-sided holes and that eventually one of them might come to the edge of your hole and give you the secret formula for success. Meanwhile, you just keep shoveling, and the hole you're in keeps getting deeper and deeper.

Now think about what you need to do as the first step in responding to this difficult situation. Write your answer on the lines below:

_____

_____

_____

Debriefing. In your answer, you may have focused on how to cleverly use the shovel in a different way. However, there isn't much use in using a tool that isn't working and probably won't work. It's easy to get so locked into a strategy like digging that you might not even notice if someone came along and dropped a ladder in the hole. Honestly, your reactive mind might even tell you to try digging with a ladder! However, no amount of digging will get you out of a hole. The answer is to put the shovel down. Digging's just making the problem worse.

Creative Hopelessness

Let's return to one of Ted's comments: "I kinda know I'm doing things that aren't good for me, but I don't know what else to do. If I stop doing these things, will my depression just spiral out of control?" Ted is fused with his reactive mind to the ground rules of feel-goodism. He fears what will happen if he disobeys his reactive mind. Although it's very unsettling, it's necessary to come to grips with this sense of apprehension. The following points may help you muster the courage needed to accept your dread and let go of the shovel:

- As long as you keep doing what you've been doing, you're probably going to keep getting the same results you've been getting.

- The time and energy you spend engaging in ineffective behaviors leaves less time and energy for you to try something different.

- While you don't know what your life will be like if you stop using unworkable strategies, you do know what your life is like now.

■ *Ted's Journey Toward a Vital Life*

By analyzing the workability of his situation, Ted realized he was following rules that were robbing him of his life. He valued his work as a teacher and took pride in his ability to be a role model and mentor for his students. He liked interacting with his fellow teachers too, and had learned a lot of good educational techniques over the years by watching how other teachers worked. He knew that work stress was bound to sometimes lead to sharp exchanges and that he needed to learn to deal with them. Ted was especially distressed about the direction his marriage was headed in. He came to see that intimacy involves fighting as well as loving, and because he didn't want the fighting part, he wasn't getting the loving part.

Ted made a commitment to go to work even when he was upset. He started speaking up when he felt unreasonable demands were being made of him, and to his surprise, his supervisor picked him to lead a committee charged with overhauling the curriculum for several core subjects. Ted made a commitment to cut back on his drinking and to eat dinner with his wife at least five nights a week. They had some less-than-pleasant interactions at first, because they had never really solved some of their basic differences about money, sex, and dealing with in-laws. But Ted persisted and the tone of their discussions gradually changed. Eventually, he asked his wife if she'd be willing to join him in some type of activity outside the home at least once a week. She eagerly accepted and they joined a bridge club. A few months later, Ted and his wife went on vacation together and had intimate relations for the first time in several months, and this seemed to rekindle some of their romance.

Ted still had his moments when he was overly sensitive to criticism, either at home or at school. But he didn't duck out of those situations, even though his reactive mind kept telling him to do so. Ted was on his journey to a life worth living!

To Dig or Not to Dig?

Ultimately, the question your life is asking you is this: Are you satisfied enough with your life to keep staying the course with your reactive mind, or are you willing to drop the shovel and try something new? If you drop the shovel, you must do so not knowing what will happen when you stop digging. All that you can know is that digging doesn't work, and that you won't find anything that works better if you continue digging. The choice is yours: To dig or not to dig.

If you're willing to try something new, we invite you to read on. If you're ambivalent about dropping the shovel, that's okay too. You might want to keep on as you have been and study how your strategies are working for you over a longer period. People differ in how they approach change, and some of us require more time and study before making a choice. There isn't a right or wrong way to do this, so take your time if you're not ready. This book will still be here when the time is right.

If you *are* ready to drop the shovel, continue with us on a journey designed to produce a life worth living. In part 2 of the book, we'll detail a nine-step plan designed to help you experience what life brings you—the good, the bad, and the ugly—while continuing to develop and pursue life directions based on personally meaningful values. Each of the chapters in part 2 introduces a different ACT strategy and offers exercises to help you apply the skill to your life. So go ahead: Drop the shovel and read on!

Secrets to ACT On

☞ Fusion, or being owned by thoughts, feelings, or memories, keeps people stuck in the depression trap.

☞ Fusion with cultural rules for how to deal with distressing thoughts, feelings, or memories leads to avoidance.

☞ The first step in extricating yourself from the depression trap is to stop following mental rules that don't work and that make your depression worse.

☞ Your reactive mind is a built-in rule follower; you must learn to separate yourself from it.

☞ Your wise mind doesn't follow rules; it looks at what works and what doesn't. To have a workable life, you have to learn to follow your wise mind.

The Coach Says

Use the knowledge of your wise mind to help you tune in to the results you're getting in your life. This isn't about what should work; it's about what does work. If what you're doing to manage your depression isn't working, you can stop doing it. You have the courage and commitment to stop using coping strategies that don't work. Put down the shovel and step away. Do it in the service of creating the life you want—and deserve!

Sneak Preview

In the next chapter, we'll introduce you to the fuel that drives a vital life: your values. We'll show you that depression is really the result of living in ways that aren't in accordance with your values. To turn the cycle of depression around, we'll help you identify your core values so that you can begin your journey toward a life worth living.

Step Out of Depression
and Into a Vital Life

In this part of the book, we'll introduce you to nine steps you can use to act on your depression. If avoidance, fusion, and lack of intentional living are the pathways into depression, the way out must be to approach emotionally challenging situations rather than avoid them, to detach from your word machine and all of its unworkable rules, and to identify your values and what you want to stand for. A life worth living involves making conscious, intentional choices in pursuit of those values and solving your problems by choosing actions based on your values. Once you learn to apply these strategies, your depression doesn't stand a chance. The amount of vitality in your life will expand your horizons and reverse depression compression.

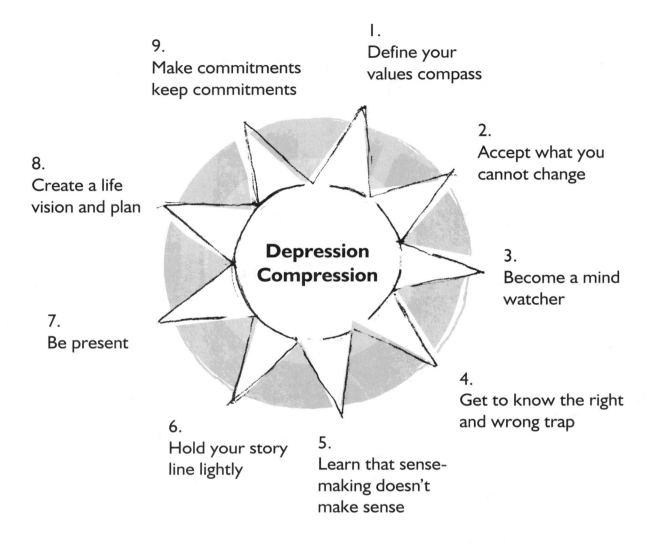

9.
Make commitments
keep commitments

1.
Define your
values compass

8.
Create a life
vision and plan

2.
Accept what you
cannot change

**Depression
Compression**

3.
Become a mind
watcher

7.
Be present

4.
Get to know the right
and wrong trap

6.
Hold your story
line lightly

5.
Learn that sense-
making doesn't
make sense

Here's a worksheet to help you keep track of your sense of confidence in taking each of the nine steps outlined in this part of the book. After reading each chapter in part 2, come back and rate your confidence in your grasp of the material presented in that chapter. As before, use a scale of 1 to 10, where 1 indicates that you need more help and 10 indicates that you've totally got it. You may already have practical experience with some of the strategies we offer. If so, don't be shy about devoting a lot of energy to using those, especially at first. It's best to work your way through the chapters sequentially, as some of the later chapters build on concepts and exercises in earlier chapters. However, it's fine to focus on the strategies that feel most natural to you. Other strategies may seem new and unusual; they might even fly in the face of what you thought was true. If this happens, try to maintain an open mind. You're likely to have an "aha!" moment later on, as all of this starts to come together.

PART 2 CONFIDENCE WORKSHEET

Need More Help			Not Confident			Confident			Got It!	
1	2	3	4	5	6	7	8	9	10

	Chapter	Confidence Level
6	Define Your Values Compass	
7	Accept What You Cannot Change	
8	Become a Mind Watcher	
9	Get to Know the Right-and-Wrong Trap	
10	Learn That Sense Making Doesn't Make Sense	
11	Hold Your Story Line Lightly	
12	Be Present	
13	Create a Life Vision and Plan	
14	Make and Keep Commitments	

Debriefing. If your confidence is 5 or less after reading any chapter, this may be a signal that you would benefit from rereading those parts of the chapter that were confusing for you. If you still have a low confidence rating after doing a second reading, consider asking a friend or other companion to read it and discuss it with you. This type of interactive dialogue and support can help keep you motivated.

CHAPTER 6

Step 1: Define Your Values Compass

If you don't figure out where you are going, you are bound to end up where you are headed. —Chinese proverb

So far, we've focused on how depression puts you in a trap. The trap involves lures that encourage you to avoid situations, events, and interactions that might make you feel bad. These lures are buried in your social training, so you probably aren't aware that they're influencing you. In addition, the symptoms of depression are sometimes so overwhelming and exhausting that you unintentionally fall into a pattern of avoidance, isolation, or withdrawal. You aren't doing any of this intentionally. You want to have your life work well, and you're trying as hard as you can to do that. However, your reactive mind lures you into using strategies that actually defeat your best interests. In our experience, very few depressed people actually understand how the depression trap works until it's explained to them. Understanding and observing how the trap works is an important and sometimes painful part of moving through depression and re-engaging in life.

Hopefully, you're beginning to get the gist of the ACT approach to depression. Life is relentless, and it doesn't take any prisoners. If you spend your time and energy on controlling how you feel, you forfeit control over your life direction. The strategies you've relied on to manage your mood are well intentioned, but they have the effect of removing you from a position of control over your life. This hidden part of the depression trap operates slowly and insidiously over time.

In this chapter, we'll introduce you to the first step in your campaign to dismantle the depression trap and reclaim your life: getting in contact with your values about living a vital life. When you plot a new course in life that's based in your values, you'll immediately notice that your sense of health and well-being is improving. You'll have the motivation to fight back and take actions that build a life worth living. In the end, your values are going to act as a compass heading for you in your journey toward a rich, meaningful, vital life. In this chapter, we'll help you investigate and clarify underlying values that can give you the inspiration and direction necessary to work through depressing situations in your life. Think of these values and the direction they will lead you in as your "true north."

ACT: A VALUES-BASED APPROACH

One of the unique features of ACT is that we don't like to dwell on the negatives in a person's life. Although part 1 of this book was devoted to exploring how your depression might be caused by avoidance of important personal problems, the solution is not to simply stop avoiding things. As we pointed out in chapter 5, it's hard to find a strategy that works if you're too busy using tactics that don't work. Dropping the proverbial shovel puts you in a position to look for other solutions. Now it's time to start looking at those solutions. In essence, the solution lies in a set of positive behaviors.

Each of the nine steps toward a vital life outlined in this part of the book is a positive behavior. Among them, defining your values might be the most positive of all. Once you're clear on your values, you'll be able to act on them. This means that no matter how long you've been depressed, there's a light at the end of the tunnel. Even if there's some personal pain present, values-based actions frequently produce feelings of health and well-being. In this way, valued actions are the antidote for depression compression. When you follow your values, your sense of vitality, purpose, and meaning won't be far behind.

ACCEPTING THE UNCERTAINTY THAT COMES WITH CHANGE

One of the first thoughts that may show up for you is "Why would I want to take this on?" That's a very good question—and an important one. After all, doesn't our culture suggest that we should let sleeping dogs lie? The reasons not to deal with this seem clear: You could be exposed directly to anxiety, fear, sadness, guilt, shame, anger, rejection, criticism, and disapproval from others. Things definitely could get worse before they get better. Being depressed is at least familiar. You know exactly what it feels like, and you may have modified your daily life to fit depression in as an ongoing reality. You don't know what will happen if you try something different. Things could get better or worse. But you *do* know what will happen if you stay where you are: You'll probably get the same results in your life you've been getting up to now.

In all honesty, you won't know how this turns out until you get there. Your reactive mind has absolutely no idea of what the future will look like, even though it might be predicting that you'll fail somehow, or that you'll be even more dissatisfied than you are now. So, for now, we want you to put your word machine on notice that you and your wise mind will be calling the shots from now on!

VALUES ARE THE FUEL

One reason you might want to take this on is the simple fact that humans want to have a say about how they live their lives. It is in choosing that we bring purpose and deeper meaning to our life experiences and directions. This option is there for you. It's a birthright of all human beings, but that doesn't mean it's delivered to you on a silver platter; you have to seize it. Only you can do this, and it won't be easy. You have to be willing to fail sometimes, to feel sadness and loss, to experience guilt and shame, to think distressing thoughts, and to remember unpleasant and frightening experiences from your past. The choice to deal with difficult aspects of your life might require you to face a variety of unpleasant and painful experiences—*and* it offers you the possibility of pursuing a healthy, vital life.

To make this move in your life, you first need to define a valued direction—a compass heading—and use it to guide you during your journey. Your values compass will provide the ongoing guidance needed to pursue a consistent direction and to deal with the inevitable barriers and potholes along the way. For our purposes, put aside any concept of values based on what our culture deems as appropriate. Your values are yours and yours alone. They are your personal beliefs about the way you want to live your life and what you want to stand for in your life. Here are some examples of values statements given to us by past clients:

- I want to be well educated and pass on my knowledge to other people.

- I want to be a loving, kind, responsible parent for my children.

- I want to be a spiritual being, and I will honor all forms of spirituality in others.

- I want to be a loving, compassionate, and supportive life partner.

- I want to continually challenge and improve myself as a person.

- I want to contribute to my community by performing acts of charity and volunteerism.

- I want to promote my physical and mental health over my life span.

- I want to be there for anyone I care about in his or her time of need.

When you get in touch with your values, they provide motivation for action even in the midst of depression experiences. They are a mental fuel that can propel you on the path toward a life full of meaning. In almost any life situation, there is no position to take that is more empowering than standing for your values.

The Danger of Running on Empty

If values are the fuel, living without them is akin to running on empty. Without them, you fall into patterns of daily living that don't reflect what matters to you and you find yourself without energy and enthusiasm. For example, let's say that one of your dearest values is to be in a caring, cooperative, and mutually supportive relationship. If you go through a period in which your primary relationship devolves into a cold war, you'll probably begin to feel a reduced sense of vitality because you're in a situation where you aren't living your values. All kinds of negative factors can push you in this direction and keep you there: You may feel overwhelmed. You may be afraid of the consequences of expressing your needs or standing up for your values. Your reactive mind will pump you full of messages that encourage you to reduce the amount of conflict in your life. As Amy's story demonstrates, when this system gets into high gear, it is extremely difficult to follow a valued course of action, or even to remember that you have a valued course of action.

■ Amy's Story

Amy, a forty-six-year-old divorced woman, lives with her cat, Emma. She struggled with depression during her twenty-one-year marriage to a charismatic man who had more than one affair. Amy had loved him, and the affairs hurt her deeply. More than once she had threatened to leave him, and his response had further destroyed her confidence. He'd say things like "Good riddance! You'll never find anyone desperate enough to want to be with you, and you'll end up alone. Go ahead if you think you're so hot—because you're not." Amy began to wonder if he might be right. For many years, she made deals with him that she would stay if he promised not to have any more affairs. And she made a deal with herself that she would stay until their sons left home. The final straw came after the boys had left, when she caught him sleeping with one of her friends.

Now, four years after the divorce, Amy goes to work, tends to Emma, and sees her sons when they find time to visit. She continues to work as an office manager at the same company she's been with for eighteen years. Years ago, she loved her work. It was challenging, and she felt creative and valued. But over the years a series of management changes put a real dent in her job satisfaction. Now, she works just to earn her paycheck and keep her health care and retirement benefits.

Amy doesn't have any close friends at work or in the community. Her husband remarried, and he and his new wife are involved with the group of friends that Amy had when she was married. She feels that her depression makes it hard for her to want to be social, so she hasn't made any new friends. She works long hours and doesn't feel she has the energy to do anything else. She's heard that exercise is supposed to help with depression and has started walking programs several times, but she doesn't keep them going. She's gained thirty pounds since the divorce and feels embarrassed by this. Concerning dating, she recently told her mother that she didn't think she could go through that again.

How Values Get Lost in the Shuffle of Living

From a valued-living perspective, Amy is definitely running on empty. Her life is just barely sputtering along because she's doing very little that embodies her personal values. Although one of her biggest complaints is that her life is dull, she goes from day to day just trying to get by.

In fairness to Amy, it's hard to live a values-based life in contemporary society. We're trained from birth to be obedient to the demands of our society, even though the interests of society don't necessarily coincide with those of the individual. The first step out of depression is to identify your values, connect with them, and embody them in your life. This doesn't guarantee you happiness or pleasure on a day-in, day-out basis, but we can guarantee you this: Breaking away from rules about how to live your life and embracing your personal values will provide you with the opportunity to experience greater well-being and satisfaction with your life. A life worth living can't be measured by the number of chances you *didn't* take, the distressing moments you avoided, or your allegiance to rules about feeling good. It's measured by the vitality that comes from living in accordance with your values and being willing to face both pleasurable and distressing experiences directly in the service of those values.

Values and Depression

When we start talking about values with depressed people, they often stare at us as if we just arrived from Planet Krypton. What could values possibly have to do with depression? Isn't the point of psychological interventions to help people gain control of depression so they can live the good life? This perspective clouds the very basic connection between how you live your life and how you feel about your life. When you feel as though your life isn't going very well, it's usually because your day-to-day life isn't giving you enough meaning.

When you begin to examine your values and how they are (or aren't) embodied in your daily activities, you may feel uncomfortable. This is because you're beginning to take note of what matters to you. Noticing a difference between what you do and what matters to you should and will cause concern. For example, if you value being a good friend but notice that you're frequently turning down invitations to be with your friends, you might feel bad about not living up to your values. This is actually a useful type of discomfort, as it can motivate you to have more awareness and intention, and make choices that are more true to your values. Be patient, go slow, and let the discomfort be there. You do have values, and they can be your guide. In the following set of exercises, we'll help you begin an ongoing process of revealing where true north lies in your life.

EXERCISE: STRANDED

This exercise will help get you in the mood to do some serious work on clarifying your values. Just relax and go along with this and see where it takes you. After you read the instructions, close your eyes to help you better imagine the suggested situation. If possible, use the recorded version on the CD; you won't have to work to remember the process, and it will make the experience more powerful for you. Allow yourself about ten minutes of uninterrupted solitude to do the visualization. The more you put into it, the more you'll get out of it. (This exercise and the next are based on Hayes, Strosahl, and Wilson 1999, 215–18.)

Imagine that you're on a trip to the South Pacific, and during a sightseeing trip in a small boat you rented, you experience engine trouble. As your boat starts to drift toward the breakers, you realize that you'll have to swim to a nearby island to avoid a catastrophe. You swim for your life, and you end up on the shore of a tiny, deserted island. You sleep in the sun, and when you are rested, you awaken and take stock of your surroundings. You look around and find some interesting things to eat and a protected place where you can rest. You realize that you have no way to communicate where you are, as everything was left in the rental boat. You hope that eventually you'll be found, but you don't know when that might happen.

Then your thoughts turn to your family and friends—the people back home. They will hear that you've disappeared without a trace and are presumed dead at sea. There will be tears. They will come together and speak of you and your life. They don't know that you're okay and that you'll be back with them soon. Eventually, they decide to remember you in a memorial service. They agree to write eulogies and come together to share them with each other to remember you. Eulogies usually speak to the more lasting traits a person is remembered for.

Imagine now that you can be there unobserved, like an invisible bird flying above them, and you listen to these heartfelt speeches of acknowledgment. What does your life partner say about you as a person? What would your best friend say? How do they describe you as a lover, a companion, and a playmate? If you have a child or children, what words do they use to describe your life and your advice about living life? How do they sum up your efforts to prepare them to go forward without you? What would your friends, your coworkers, and your neighbors say? What would people say about your spiritual life? What would you hear about your participation in the community in which you live? How do the mourners remember you in terms of your ability to have fun, relax, or engage in leisure activities?

After completing this visualization, fill out the worksheet below.

Stranded Exercise Worksheet

Based on how I'm living my life right now, what did I hear in the eulogy...

From my partner?

_____

_____

From my children?

_____

_____

From my closest friends?

_____

_____

From my coworkers?

_____

_____

From members of my community?

_____

_____

From people in my spiritual community?

_____

_____

If I could live my life any way I wanted to, what would I like to hear...

From my partner?

_____

_____

From my children?

_____

_____

From my closest friends?

_____

_____

From my coworkers?

_____

_____

From members of my community?

_____

_____

From people in my spiritual community?

_____

_____

Debriefing. Is there a difference between what you think you'd hear if the memorial service were held today and what you'd like to hear? Any differences give you important information. First, look at what you would hear based on how you're living now. You probably heard some things that warmed your heart, as you certainly do some things that reflect your values and some people will notice these things. At the same time, you may have noticed that in one or more areas of your current life, the news is not good. This is something to pay attention to, because it reflects the direction you're headed in. Second, comparing what you would currently hear with what you'd like to hear at your memorial service highlights values that you may have placed on the back burner. These may be important values that are being undermined by your avoidance of emotionally charged life problems.

Before reading further, make a list of the values or qualities that you wanted to hear but didn't. Just note them on a small card or piece of paper; you might even title it "True North." Place it in your wallet or someplace where you'll see it on a regular basis. This represents your initial heading as you begin to develop your values compass. The following exercise will help add a few more details to this important piece of paper.

EXERCISE: WRITE YOUR EPITAPH

An epitaph is what's written on a tombstone. Epitaphs are condensed statements about how a person is remembered by the living. For example, on the tombstone of one of our family members, the epitaph "Lover of life" is inscribed. This simple poetic phrase does justice to a man whose passion for learning and experience seemed to be without limit. What an incredible way to be remembered! Another family member's epitaph reads, "The smell of the rose remains in the hand who gives it." This loving remembrance celebrates the life of a woman who valued charity, equality, and the beauties of nature. This was a woman who never met a person she couldn't relate to.

In the space below, please write the epitaph you would like to see on your tombstone.

My Epitaph

_____

_____

_____

_____

Debriefing. How did you do with this exercise? Maybe you need to do some research or study to find the phrase that best describes how you want to be remembered. If you think about how you're living your life right now, is it in line with how you'd like to be commemorated on your tombstone? What areas of life are in sync and out of sync? Remember, this is your life and you can take charge and move in the direction of your personal values. This epitaph exercise underscores the very serious point that you only get to do your life once (unless you believe in reincarnation), and the clock is ticking.

EXERCISE: AIM FOR THE BULL'S-EYE

This exercise (based on one developed by Lundgren in 2006) will help you clarify your values in much more detail. You're probably familiar with a bull's-eye target, where the goal is to hit the bull's-eye in the center. The closer you are to the bull's-eye, the more points you get. Sometimes you might miss the target altogether, in which case you don't get any points.

This exercise asks you to identify your core values in four areas of life: health, relationships, work, and play. After clarifying your values in each area, we ask you to reflect on the previous week and evaluate the extent to which your activities of daily living have been consistent with your values. Don't worry if you find that some of your choices haven't been consistent with your values. When you're depressed, it's hard to stay in touch with values because the effort required to make it through each day is so great. It's as if you're in a fog. Making an effort to name your values will help clear this fog so that you have a better day-to-day focus and more opportunities to lessen the gap between what you care about and what you do.

Health Values

We encourage you to think about your values around promoting your health. Often, people think of health as a physical state, usually something like the absence of disease. In this view, you're healthy because you aren't actively ill. However, concepts like health have undergone a lot of rethinking over the last several decades. More-modern definitions look at health as a state that involves physical, emotional, and social roles, as indicated by the following definition: "A state characterized by anatomical, physiological, and psychological integrity; ability to perform personally valued family, work, and community roles; ability to deal with physical, biological, psychological, and social stress; a feeling of well-being; and freedom from the risk of disease and untimely death" (Last 1988, 57).

We like this definition because it acknowledges that health isn't simply a physical state; it's also a mental and social state. Only by protecting your physical, emotional, and social health can you be in a position to perform valued actions in the realm of family, work, play, and community. Conversely, even if you have a physical impairment like chronic pain or a chronic condition like diabetes, this doesn't automatically mean you're unhealthy. In fact, you can amplify your mental and social health by continuing to participate in valued activities in life. This can increase your overall sense of health even as you continue to suffer from a physical limitation.

Promoting health also means you have the self-care skills to address life stresses in a way that preserves your ability to move forward in a positive direction. Core self-care skills involve engaging in healthy behaviors in terms of diet, exercise, sleep habits, spiritual practice, self-growth, and hobbies. Health is also protected by avoiding or minimizing negative lifestyle habits, such as using tobacco, caffeine, alcohol, or drugs. In the following worksheet, describe where you'd like to be headed in terms of promoting your health.

Health Values

Diet: _____

_____

_____

Exercise: _____

_____

_____

Sleep habits: _____

_____

_____

Lifestyle habits (including ways to reduce stress): _____

_____

_____

Spirituality practices: _____

_____

_____

After writing out your health-related values, reflect on your actions over the past couple of weeks. To what extent were your day-to-day choices consistent with your values about health? Did your eating behaviors reflect a commitment to preserving and furthering your health? To what extent did you purposefully engage in exercise and relaxation activities? How much and how well did you sleep? Did you smoke or drink this week? If so, is this consistent with your values about promoting your health? Consider these and other types of behavior and then decide how consistent your choices were with your values about health. On the dartboard below, make an X to indicate how close or off the mark your activities were in relation to your values about health.

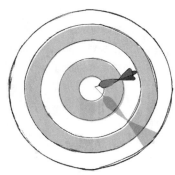

To help you focus in on opportunities for positive change in the area of personal health, write down a few examples of choices that show consistency with your values and a few that show inconsistency with your values.

Examples of actions that were more consistent with my values:

_____

_____

_____

_____

_____

_____

Examples of actions that were less consistent with my values:

_____

_____

_____

_____

_____

_____

Relationship Values

In regard to values about relationships, most people are probably much more alike than different. Most of us value honesty, trust, dependability, the ability to laugh and to forgive, the pursuit of win-win solutions, sensitivity, strength, and so on. Relationships are played out in many areas of life. For many people, the most important relationship is with a spouse or life partner. Other important relationships are with friends and family members, including family of origin, extended family, and children. Some values, like being honest and respectful of others, are usually relevant to all relationships, whereas other values may be more pertinent to a particular kind of relationship, such as being a parent versus being a friend. As you consider different kinds of relationships you have or wish to cultivate in your life, think about how you want to apply your values in each situation. In the worksheet below, describe where you'd like to be headed in your relationships. Describe the qualities that are most important to you in each type of relationship.

Relationship Values

Spouse or life partner: _____

_____

_____

Family: _____

_____

_____

Parenting: _____

_____

_____

Friendships: _____

_____

_____

Other: _____

_____

_____

After writing out your values about relationships, reflect on how you acted in regard to relationships over the last couple of weeks. To what extent were your day-to-day choices consistent with your values about relationships? To what extent did your actions support the development of relationships that reflect your values? Did your interpersonal behaviors reflect a commitment to preserving and furthering relationships with those you love as well as those you're less close to? Consider these and other types of behavior and then decide how consistent your choices were with your values about relationships. On the dartboard below, make an X to indicate how close or off the mark your activities were in relation to your bull's-eye values about relationships.

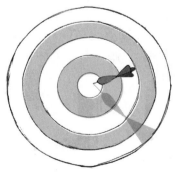

To help you focus in on opportunities for positive change in the area of relationships, write down a few examples of behavioral choices that show consistency with your values and a few that show inconsistency with your values.

Examples of actions that were more consistent with my values:

_____

_____

_____

_____

_____

Examples of actions that were less consistent with my values:

_____

_____

_____

_____

_____

Work Values

Now it's time to describe your values about work. Work activities include anything that makes you feel of use on a regular basis, whether that's a meaningful job, being a homemaker or caregiver, or donating your time to community or other volunteer activities. Examples of values in regard to work might include being reliable, maintaining focus, being persistent, cooperating with others, taking a team approach, being creative, and promoting more lightheartedness. In the following worksheet, describe where you'd like to be headed in terms of work.

Work Values

Work (includes homemaking, caregiving, and volunteering):

_____

_____

_____

   After writing out your values in regard to work, reflect on your actions over the past couple of weeks. To what extent were your day-to-day choices consistent with your values about work? If you value being cooperative or creative, to what extent did your daily activities reflect this desire? On the dartboard below, make an X to indicate how close or off the mark your activities were in relation to your bull's-eye values about work.

   To help you focus in on opportunities for positive change in the area of work, write down a few examples of behavioral choices that show consistency with your values and a few that show inconsistency with your values.

Examples of actions that were more consistent with my values about work:

_____

_____

_____

_____

Examples of actions that were less consistent with my values about work:

_____

_____

_____

_____

Play Values

Last but certainly not least, we want you to describe your values about play activities. For play, we find that images sometimes say more than words. One of us had a great-aunt who loved life fiercely. She had a loud, wild laugh, and she offered it freely. When other people didn't understand what struck her as funny, she laughed all the more and with great abandon. In depression, following your values about relaxation, leisure, and having fun is almost always an issue. A depressed mood tends to be serious in nature, so the idea of taking time to have some fun, relax, or engage in a leisure activity may be almost unthinkable. Countless times, we've asked depressed people the simple question "What do you do for fun?" Almost always, they say, "Nothing." If you can't relax, enjoy yourself, or dawdle away some leisure time, you'll have a very difficult time keeping your life in balance. In the worksheet below, describe where you'd like to be headed in terms of play, and make note of any relevant images as well.

Play Values

Having fun: _____

_____

_____

_____

Relaxing: _____

_____

_____

_____

Recreational pursuits: _____

_____

_____

_____

Creative activities: _____

_____

_____

_____

After writing out your values in regard to play, reflect on your actions over the past couple of weeks. To what extent were your day-to-day choices consistent with your values about play? If you did engage in playful activities, to what extent were your values about play demonstrated during those activities? On the dartboard below, make an X to indicate how close or off the mark your activities were in relation to your values about play.

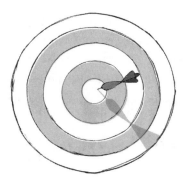

To help you focus in on opportunities for positive change in the area of play, write down a few examples of behavioral choices that show consistency with your values and a few that show inconsistency with your values.

Examples of actions that were more consistent with my values about play:

_____

_____

_____

Examples of actions that were less consistent with my values about play:

_____

_____

_____

Debriefing. In each of these life areas—health, relationships, work, and play—maybe you're mostly on target, maybe you're not. Whatever the results, view this exercise as an opportunity to clarify what your values are and where you're at in terms of following them. Most of us don't hit the bull's-eye every day, but over time and with additional practice, you can improve your aim!

■ *Amy's Journey Toward a Vital Life*

Amy was shaken when she examined her values using exercises similar to those in this chapter. In particular, she couldn't come up with an epitaph that felt satisfying because she didn't feel she was living a valued life. Instead, her epitaph read, "Hurt by her husband and never invested herself again." Her aim in terms of values about promoting health was quite a ways from the bull's-eye. Her biggest problems were a poor diet and very little exercise. She stated that she didn't feel physically or emotionally healthy much of the time. She was farthest off the mark in terms of relationships, placing her X off the target altogether. Her value was to have an intimate relationship based on trust, intimacy, and equality, yet she wouldn't consider dating or even agreeing to a male coworker's invitation to have coffee together. In regard to work, Amy wrote that her greatest work value was to be involved in a career that would use her natural strengths as a leader of coworkers but that she didn't even like the work she was doing. In regard to play, she placed her X in the outermost ring of the target. She described some attempts at engaging in creative hobbies (sewing and crochet) but said she didn't do them on a consistent basis.

Looking at her values was a serious wake-up call for Amy, and as a result she decided to enroll in night school so she could get an advanced degree in human resources. When the word got out to her supervisor that she was going to night school, he called her into his office and asked what her intentions were. She told him that she didn't like her job and wanted to work in human resources. Much to Amy's amazement, her supervisor offered to provide some financial support if she would agree to stay on, and said he could reassign her to the human resources department. Amy also developed a plan for eating better, which included not snacking at bedtime, and to further promote her health she started walking with a coworker at lunchtime. The weight she'd gained started to come off slowly but surely over several months.

Amy finally consented to have coffee with her coworker. She was petrified, because she believed that the only way she could avoid her fear of rejection was to stay away from any situation that might open the door to romantic feelings. Nevertheless, she made the choice to go into the situation with an open mind—and with her fear present. Her coworker became a close friend over time, and there was no romance involved. This challenged Amy's fear that men were basically out for sex and unreliable, and allowed her to choose to be available should the right man come along. Amy was on the pathway out of depression!

BE GENTLE WITH YOURSELF

If you've been struggling with depression, it's very tempting to take any information and turn it to negative purposes. After doing the work in this chapter, you may be tempted to beat yourself up because you aren't living out your values. Beware! Bashing yourself won't motivate you to change what isn't working. Try to look at your situation with compassion. You're doing the best you can. You aren't defective, broken, or a weakling. Life is tricky, and given our social conditioning, it's very easy to get stuck. Fortunately, once you learn the ACT approach you'll find it's just as easy to get unstuck. The main thing we want you to leave this chapter with is the sense that there's a bigger life out there. This is the life you'll be building as you progress through the ACT program.

Secrets to ACT On

☞ Your values can get lost in the fog of depression. The way out of depression is to find them and move your life in that direction.

☞ Your actions in life are what you'll be remembered for, not what is going on between your ears.

☞ Core values can provide a direction, like true north on a compass, to guide you through painful behavioral changes.

☞ While you may not always be consistent with your values, describing them and thinking about how you'd like your life to be will place you in a powerful position to push back the fog of depression.

The Coach Says

Living a valued life isn't easy, and sometimes it hurts to care. Can you do it anyway? Of course you can! The first step is to figure out where you want to be going in life. Then you can get out there and begin to live for what you care about. It may take time, patience, and persistence, but we know you can do it!

Sneak Preview

Someone once said, "You can't teach a pig to sing. It will only make the pig mad and frustrate you." In the next chapter, we'll help you learn what you can change and what you can't, and help you acquire the wisdom to know the difference between the two. We'll introduce you to an alternative to struggling and show how this stance will empower you to live a life worth living!

CHAPTER 7

Step 2: Accept What You Cannot Change

We cannot control the wind; we can only adjust the sails. —Kahlil Gibran

In the previous chapter, we asked you to look at your life and get in touch with what you want to stand for. We asked you to assess whether you're on a life course that's in keeping with your "true north." Sometimes this type of self-inventory reveals that you're quite far off course in one or more areas. Remember, this is not the time to start beating up on yourself! Instead, take a deep breath and call up some compassion for your very human predicament. In the remainder of this book, we'll teach you a variety of skills for making values-driven behavior a daily reality in your life. This is the antidote to depression compression.

In part 1 of the book, we explained how depression can be caused by emotional and behavioral avoidance—consciously or unconsciously acting in ways that insulate you from painful situations. Sometimes, avoidance functions to preserve your limited energy; other times, it's the result of dealing with the overwhelming feelings of isolation, worthlessness, hopelessness, and helplessness that characterize depression. However, the paradox of depression (and avoidance) is that strategies of avoidance and withdrawal actually strengthen depression.

A question that often comes up with the ACT approach to depression is "What causes people to avoid painful personal situations rather than simply deal with them?" One of the chief culprits is the human desire to control unwanted, emotionally distressing experiences. There are two basic forms of control that we're concerned with in ACT: active control and passive control. *Active control* involves attempting to suppress distressing feelings, thoughts, memories, or sensations from your awareness; for example, trying not to think about painful experiences from your childhood or trying to control your depression by attempting to think only positive thoughts. As discussed in part 1, this type of control strategy typically produces an upsurge in the very experience you're trying to suppress. Instead of getting fewer painful memories, you get more of them. And the more you try to think positive thoughts as a way out of depression, the more intrusive your negative thoughts often become. *Passive control* involves avoiding or withdrawing from potentially painful experiences. We refer to this form of control as passive because the strategy is based in nonparticipation. However, the hoped-for outcome is the same: to control your mood and reduce the weight of your depression symptoms.

ACCEPTANCE: THE ALTERNATIVE TO CONTROL AND AVOIDANCE

It's likely that you're already familiar with the concept of acceptance in the form of the Serenity Prayer so widely used in Alcoholics Anonymous and similar programs: "God grant me the serenity to accept the things I cannot change, the courage to change the things I can, and the wisdom to know the difference." The reason this simple prayer is so widely used and so effective is that it describes an important fork in the road we face over and over again in the process of pursuing a vital life.

From an ACT perspective, learning to discriminate between things that can and can't be changed is one of the keys to personal health. Whereas things that can be changed require one type of response, things that are beyond your control require an entirely different approach. In this chapter, we'll teach you how to make this very important distinction. When you learn what you have control over, you can direct your efforts toward exercising control where it's possible to effect change. And once you can identify what you can't control, you won't get sucked into the trap of expending your energy on strategies that lead to a dead end.

Learning to identify what can't be controlled allows you to practice an alternative strategy: acceptance. *Acceptance* is voluntary action involving a stance of nonjudgmental awareness and a welcoming orientation toward unwanted internal experiences. Rather than attempting to suppress or avoid a troublesome emotion, thought, memory, or sensation, you simply allow it to be there. In ACT we sometimes describe this stance as "making room" for something that's distressing you. By practicing acceptance when it's called for, you can free up incredible amounts of time and energy that can be redirected to aspects of your life that you can control. In a way, acceptance is the act of dropping the shovel. It is letting go of any urge to resist or avoid what is in front of you at this moment in time. Your immediate life dilemma won't suddenly disappear because you accept it, but acceptance does put you in a position to do something other than dig a deeper hole. It gives you a chance to check your values compass and make a new move toward your "true north." Practicing acceptance is extremely difficult when you're confronting personal pain, but the alternative is to struggle with things that can't be controlled. This struggle not only exhausts you emotionally but also worsens your personal pain and harms your overall health.

■ Bill's Story

Bill is a fifty-one-year-old man with chronic back pain and depression. He injured his back while lifting a pallet on the job about fifteen years ago. He returned to work after two months of leave but found that his back pain was too intense for him to continue his work. He quit his job and filed for permanent work disability, but his claim was denied after an independent medical examiner determined that there was no evidence of a permanent back injury. Nevertheless, Bill continued to experience pain on a daily basis. He was offered a vocational retraining option by the state but declined because he didn't feel he could work at any job with all the pain he had.

Bill consulted with several surgeons and underwent a spinal disk fusion that initially helped his pain but eventually left him with even worse pain. Bill feels that his doctors haven't taken very good care of him. He was prescribed narcotic pain medication about ten years ago. Now he's dependent upon it but still experiences a lot of pain. His current doctor has refused to increase his dosage, and Bill is furious that his doctor isn't helping with the pain. Bill describes his pain as a burning, stinging sensation, like someone is putting a needle in his back. His pain sensations radiate down his right leg, where he experiences numbness and tingling.

Bill's daily routine is to spend a lot of time at home lying on the sofa, as this gives him some relief. He doesn't really go out much anymore because upright activity tends to be associated with pain. He used to go to church with his wife a couple of times a week, but he stopped going after he had to leave a church luncheon because of a pain attack. There's a lot of tension in the household. Bill's wife complains that he doesn't help around the house and that he's short with her and their kids. They don't have much intimacy anymore, as intercourse is painful for him.

Bill believes his depression is caused by his chronic pain. The more he struggles to control his pain, the more angry and irritable he tends to get. He thinks about the day he hurt his back and whether he could have done something to prevent his injury. He doesn't see much hope that his life will turn around unless the pain is somehow eliminated. He's disappointed in himself for not being a good breadwinner, and he feels bad when he yells at his kids for no good reason. More than once, he's thought of killing himself because he feels his family would be better off without him.

EXERCISE: IDENTIFYING WHAT CAN'T BE CHANGED

Almost anyone hearing Bill's story would feel sorry for him. He experienced an injury, was weaseled out of his disability payments, and ended up basically homebound without much in the way of a life. He wakes up every morning with a little knot of anger in his stomach, disappointed and embittered at a world that seems to have given him a raw deal. Bill is a good person who loves his wife and children, and he was a good provider until he was injured. Then, *poof*! His life was vaporized by an act of fate, and depression became his daily companion.

Let's examine Bill's situation from the perspective of the Serenity Prayer. Does Bill know what he can and cannot control in his current situation? Is he practicing acceptance of those aspects that can't be controlled? Is he exerting control over the things that he actually can control? Take a few minutes to study the aspects of his situation listed below. For items that Bill can't change, circle A, for acceptance. For aspects he has control over, circle C.

Events or Situations in Bill's Life

A	C	1. Bill suffered an on-the-job injury.
A	C	2. Bill experiences back pain on a daily basis.
A	C	3. Bill was denied a disability pension.
A	C	4. Bill has thoughts that he has too much pain to work at any job.
A	C	5. Bill refuses to go through vocational retraining.
A	C	6. Bill underwent an unsuccessful back surgery that left him with more pain.
A	C	7. Bill spends a lot of time on his sofa to control the pain.
A	C	8. Bill doesn't go to church.
A	C	9. Bill doesn't exercise regularly because of the pain.
A	C	10. Bill takes larger and larger doses of narcotics to control his pain.
A	C	11. Bill experiences burning and stinging sensations in his back.
A	C	12. Bill experiences sensations of tingling and numbness in his leg.
A	C	13. Bill feels angry and irritable when in pain.
A	C	14. Bill remembers the injury.
A	C	15. Bill thinks about how he could have prevented the injury.
A	C	16. Bill yells at his children.
A	C	17. Bill is short with his wife.
A	C	18. Bill doesn't have intercourse with his wife because his back hurts.
A	C	19. Bill has thoughts that life has given him a raw deal.
A	C	20. Bill has thoughts that he would be better off dead.

Key: Acceptance: 1, 2, 3, 4, 6, 11, 12, 13, 14, 15, 19, 20; Control: 5, 7, 8, 9, 10, 16, 17, 18

Debriefing. Did your answers differ from those in the key? Bill has some control over quite a few things. He can influence the amount of time he spends on the sofa, his attendance at church, his participation in daily exercises, his use of narcotics, his behavior toward his wife and children, and his sexual relationship with his wife. And he could choose to challenge his assumptions about his pain and try vocational retraining.

Do these answers surprise you? Take a close look at the events and experiences that Bill has no immediate control over: not just physical sensations but also his spontaneous thoughts, feelings, and memories related to his pain and his personal history. Being in pain causes predictable private experiences, including negative emotions and thoughts. Unpleasant feelings, thoughts, and images show up in the moment for all of us in response to pain—and they show up more when we try to suppress or avoid them.

WHAT MUST BE ACCEPTED

Many difficult life situations, like Bill's experience of chronic pain, make the process of sorting out what one can and cannot change challenging: an unwanted divorce, a child with a serious illness, the death of a close friend, the diagnosis of a serious health problem, and so on. These types of painful circumstances may come into a person's life without warning. However, when you respond with avoidance and withdrawal in order to protect yourself from unwanted thoughts, emotions, or memories, you lose control over your behavior. By trying to wash your hands of responsibility for any aspect of the situation, you're likely to lose insight into which aspects of the situation you actually can exert some control over. In the meanwhile, you may be struggling to exert control over aspects of your human experience that can't be controlled, including the following:

■ Spontaneous feelings

■ Spontaneous thoughts

■ Spontaneous memories

■ Some physical sensations

■ An objective event, act of fate, or external stressor

■ Other people's behavior

■ Past events and personal history

These experiences occur within us in a very personal and immediate way. What could be closer than your own thoughts, feelings, memories, or sensations? What could be more in your face than rejection or criticism from someone you love deeply or the fading health of someone you care about? Like Bill, most people can't easily create space for the experience of physical or emotional pain and its unpleasant side effects. However, you can learn to create a little breathing room between you and these experiences, which will make acceptance easier.

Here's a key concept that will go a long way in helping you learn to accept difficult thoughts, emotions, and memories: Unwanted private events aren't toxic. They feel as if they're toxic and you may *think* they're unbearable, but they aren't. As a human being, you're perfectly built to experience whatever you experience in response to the situation you're in. These private experiences are normal, natural, and healthy, and they can't be prevented. They don't require alteration, and they don't need to be packaged to look good. While they don't feel good, you can feel them well! That's what acceptance means: feeling your uncontrollable and unwanted reactions for what they are, without evaluation and without struggle. If you just let your reactions be, they will function the way evolution has designed them to function. Have no doubt: Your own reactions aren't toxic to you, but avoiding your reactions through suppression and control can be very toxic indeed.

When we first suggested this possibility to Bill, he almost choked in disbelief. His first response was, "How could anyone expect me to do more when I'm in such horrible pain?" We asked Bill to take a deep breath and ask himself whether his pain literally prevented him from having a satisfying sex life with his wife, from exercising, from going to church, and from being kinder to his family. When Bill thought this through, he realized that his pain didn't actually preclude moving in these directions. When he considered the merits of continuing with his present approach versus creating values-based behaviors into his life, he decided to go for it, even though making some of these changes would be very challenging for him.

WHAT ACCEPTANCE IS—AND ISN'T

The word "acceptance" has a lot of different meanings, some of which we want to challenge. The type of acceptance we encourage you to practice is best thought of as a voluntary, intentional stance of nonjudgmental awareness of thoughts, feelings, memories, and sensations in the context of a triggering event. The key element of this definition is that acceptance is an action you take on purpose. It involves holding still in the face of what appears to be distressing private experiences. When you practice acceptance, you stay present with what is there instead of avoiding contact with it. Acceptance also involves withholding judgment and evaluation. It means that you're willing to be present with whatever is there. It isn't important to determine whether what you're experiencing is good or bad. It's just what you're experiencing, nothing more, nothing less. This kind of acceptance is often described as simple awareness.

It's important to understand that your level of acceptance can vary from moment to moment. Since acceptance is an action and not a result, it never remains at a constant level. Think of acceptance as a stance you try to adopt rather than a posture you maintain continuously. You might think of it as a difficult yoga pose. Most of us can learn to come close to that pose, but few of us could maintain it for an extended period of time.

Acceptance Is Not Resignation

Please don't mistake acceptance for resignation, or giving in to a life of misery. This would be akin to telling a person to just get used to being depressed for the rest of his or her life, something we would never condone. For example, we would never ask an abused woman to accept that she'll be beaten by her husband on a regular basis for the rest of her life. This is a situation in which she has some control over values-based behaviors. If she values positive intimacy, then she does have options. She can stay or leave or do something in between. What she has to accept is that if she does nothing, she'll probably continue to get the negative results in her relationship that she's been getting.

Acceptance Doesn't Mean You've Failed

Acceptance is not an admission of failure or defeat. When you give up the struggle with unwanted private events, you're simply giving up something that has never worked. This form of acceptance simply means that you recognize that this strategy isn't going to work. This is akin to dropping the shovel, and it's actually a prelude to success—to building a more flexible and effective response to the situation. Notice that this means acceptance and the workability yardstick are close companions. When the workability of your life is low, you not only have to accept that the reading is low, you also have to accept that what you've been doing isn't working—and then you have to be ready to accept what shows up between your ears when you stop engaging in unworkable responses.

Acceptance Doesn't Mean Tolerating Personal Pain

Another common misconception about acceptance is to confuse it with toleration. Think of the distinction between toleration and acceptance this way: Toleration is a form of acceptance "with strings attached." You're only willing to accept distress or suffering up to a certain level and no further. We all practice toleration when we go to the dentist: You tolerate the pain and discomfort of that big needle or the drilling because the consequences of avoiding the dentist will eventually be far worse than what you have to go through in the present. At the same time, you may have an evaluation of pain that says it isn't acceptable to have pain over a 7 on a scale of 1 to 10. So if the pain goes over that level, you'll alert the dentist or take action to control the pain, even if it includes leaving the scene! Or you may accept the pain in that moment but vow never to see that particular dentist again, which transforms it into a future avoidance move. So, toleration is a kind of acceptance, but it isn't the same as acceptance.

Acceptance Is a Posture

One question we're frequently asked is "How do I know if I'm accepting something or not?" There is no single correct answer to this question, but there are definitely places to look for clues about your stance. An important clue is how you talk to yourself when you're dealing with something that's causing personal pain. If you find you're using phrases along these lines, you probably aren't adopting a posture of acceptance:

- I just need to put this behind me.

- I want to get rid of these feelings, thoughts, or memories.

- I want to get on top of the way I feel.

- I need to leave the past in the past.

- I need to get a better handle on where these thoughts come from.

- I want to be able to control how I feel.

Notice how these statements suggest that the goal is to somehow get rid of or get the upper hand over painful private experiences. By now you're probably well aware that this is a losing battle, inviting you to either struggle with your pain or avoid situations that might produce pain. In contrast, talking to yourself along the following lines is a good indicator of acceptance:

- I'm willing to go through this.

- I know my reactions are a healthy part of me even though I don't like them.

- I can make room for the way I feel.

- I am willing to live with my past.

- I'll face this situation and do the best I can.

- I'm capable of feeling this way and doing what needs to be done anyway.

Our experience is that this type of self-talk fosters a state of acceptance, making you much more likely to act in accepting ways when you enter a troublesome situation or interaction. When you mentally rehearse these sorts of acceptance statements, they'll be at the ready to counteract your reactive mind and allow you to stay in a posture of acceptance.

EXCESSIVE SUFFERING

In ACT, we make an important distinction between suffering and excessive suffering. Together, suffering and excessive suffering make up your entire personal experience of a negative event, situation, or interaction in your life. Suffering is the original discomfort you feel in response to an actual event. Although it doesn't feel good, it's a natural and ultimately healthy experience if it isn't suppressed or avoided. Excessive suffering, on the other hand, is the pain you get when you struggle to control, eliminate, or avoid your original suffering.

In Bill's case, he's creating excessive suffering for himself by avoiding important aspects of his daily life in the name of managing his chronic physical pain. Consequently, he experiences the excessive suffering of a strained relationship with his wife and kids, as well as chronic anger, irritability, and negative thoughts. Whereas suffering is natural and often provides important signals that can help us make decisions that promote health and well-being, excessive suffering leaves us feeling traumatized and emotionally exhausted. If given the choice, most people would gladly return to their original suffering if they could somehow walk away from the excessive suffering they've become entangled in.

EXERCISE: SUFFERING AND EXCESSIVE SUFFERING

This exercise will help you assess how suffering and excessive suffering are playing out in your life. As you fill out the worksheet below, first take a few minutes to identify a difficult situation you've recently experienced. Try to be as specific as possible when you describe it. Next, describe the original suffering that's a natural consequence of this problem. Then describe how you might be generating excessive suffering in this situation. Describe the behaviors you're engaging in and the type of excessive suffering you experience, such as anger, resentment, guilt, shame, damaged relationships, and so on. Finally, consider the total amount of both types of suffering to equal 100 percent, then divide those percentage points between your original suffering and your excessive suffering; the total should add up to 100. This will allow you to see where most of your pain is coming from. You may wish to copy this worksheet or print out blank copies from the CD to analyze other issues.

Suffering and Excessive Suffering Analysis

Difficult situation		
		Score
Original suffering		
Excessive suffering		

Debriefing. This can be a difficult exercise, as it requires a great deal of honesty. What did you discover? Did the majority of your pain come in the form of suffering or excessive suffering? If you're like most depressed people, much of it can be chalked up to excessive suffering. Ask yourself which part of your suffering feels the most traumatic in terms of setting you back in life. In most cases, trying to suppress, control, or avoid the initial suffering or reminders of it is what leads to excessive suffering. If this is true for you, it's important to realize that you're not alone in subscribing to the culturally promoted belief that suffering means your life isn't going as it should. To help you see how this has played out in the lives of other depressed people, let's take a look at Bill's responses to this exercise.

BILL'S SUFFERING AND EXCESSIVE SUFFERING ANALYSIS

Difficult situation	I have chronic pain and can't do the things I used to do.	
		Score
Original suffering	I hurt almost all of the time, and I feel sad and frustrated by my inability to do the things I used to do.	20
Excessive suffering	I'm unwilling to accept all of the awful things this pain has done to me; instead I ruminate about how I've been mistreated by doctors and my employer in this whole nightmare. I've let my fears about my disability stand in the way of my return to work. And worst of all, I've allowed my pain to interfere with relating to my wife and kids the way I'd like to, and I'm afraid they don't love me anymore.	80

Review. Bill's response reveals that what turns an unfortunate but not uncommon life situation into something traumatic is the stance taken toward suffering. Again, it's the paradox of avoidance: The less accepting you are of your suffering, the more you try to suppress or control it; however, the more you try to suppress it, the more traumatic the resulting excessive suffering is. Consider this: If you could learn to stop creating excessive suffering for yourself but to do so you had to let the original suffering be there, would you be willing to make that trade? If this interests you, read on and we'll show you how to make this deal.

WILLINGNESS: AN ALTERNATIVE TO AVOIDANCE

In ACT, the concepts of willingness and acceptance are considered to be bedfellows. Think of willingness as choosing to enter a difficult situation with the intent of using a posture of acceptance rather than a posture of avoidance and suppression. Willingness allows you to expose yourself to what you are afraid of. Acceptance is what you do when you get there. Willingness is a voluntary, intentional action; it must be, because you're smart enough to know how to avoid situations you'd rather not experience. Usually, low levels of willingness tend to correspond with high levels of excessive suffering.

EXERCISE: WILLINGNESS AND ACCEPTANCE PLAN

This exercise will help you develop a willingness plan that you can implement in your daily life. It builds upon the results of the previous exercise. The goal is to begin to shift points from the excessive suffering category to the original suffering category by practicing a stance of willingness and acceptance in situations you've identified as producing a sense of excessive suffering.

First, copy your descriptions of your original suffering and excessive suffering from the previous exercise onto the form below and record your percentage for each type of suffering under Day 1. Then, at the bottom of the worksheet, describe specific behaviors you'll engage in that demonstrate a posture of willingness (this usually means choosing to enter the situation) and acceptance (simply allowing what shows up in your awareness to be there). It's helpful to include a description of what you can and cannot control in this situation so that you're clear on what you must be willing to accept.

After you've implemented the plan for a week, come back to this exercise and record your new percentages for your original suffering versus excessive suffering. Hopefully you'll see progress. If not, it may help to talk this over with a friend. Sometimes you just need more practice; or it may be that you need to revise your plan.

Willingness and Acceptance Plan

		Score	
		Day 1	Day 7
Original suffering			
Excessive suffering			
Willingness and acceptance plan			

Debriefing. What results did you see after your first week of practice? Did some of your percentage points shift out of excessive suffering? If not, don't be afraid to experiment with different strategies. Bill's completed worksheet appears below, so you can see how this process played out for someone else.

BILL'S WILLINGNESS AND ACCEPTANCE PLAN

		Score	
		Day 1	Day 7
Original suffering	*I hurt almost all of the time, and I feel sad and frustrated by my inability to do the things I used to do.*	*20*	*35*
Excessive suffering	*I'm unwilling to accept all of the awful things this pain has done to me; instead I ruminate about how I've been mistreated by doctors and my employer in this whole nightmare. I've let my fears about my disability stand in the way of my return to work. And worst of all, I've allowed my pain to interfere with relating to my wife and kids the way I'd like to, and I'm afraid they don't love me anymore.*	*80*	*65*
Willingness and acceptance plan	*I'll attend a class for people with chronic pain that my doctor recommended. At the first meeting, I'll read my values statements to the entire class.*		

Review. Bill had serious doubts as to whether a class could make a difference for him, but he decided to give it a try. Though it would be difficult, he decided to try to shift his excessive suffering numbers by stating his values to the class at the first meeting. Not only would this reaffirm his values, it might also create a greater sense of committing to them, as is often the case when we disclose our goals publicly. He received a great deal of positive support from others in the class, and they were very interested in his experiment with his willingness and acceptance plan. This reminded Bill of how he'd once been a leader and creative thinker at his job.

EXERCISE: WILLINGNESS, DEPRESSION, AND VITALITY DIARY

When you begin studying your willingness level, you will notice that it vacillates minute by minute. However, the realities of contemporary living make it very difficult to stay focused on such intricacies in the moment, even though doing so is an important element of vital living. Because of this, you'll need to practice some type of observation of your willingness levels on a daily basis. The daily diary form that follows can help you in this regard. You may wish to make copies of this blank form so you can continue to keep the diary over time. (Alternatively, you can print out fresh copies from the CD.)

Complete the form near the end of each day, when you can reflect on the entire day to come up with your responses. You'll assess your willingness in the column labeled "W," your depression in the column labeled "D," and your vitality in the column labeled "V." Assess each using a 1 to 10 scale in which 1 means none and 10 means extremely high. First rate your willingness to experience unwanted and possibly distressing experiences over the course of the entire day. In the notes column, describe any factors that may have contributed to higher or lower levels of willingness. Next, rate your depression level and, again, describe any factors that pushed your depression level up or down. The third rating is the most important. Assign whatever number best reflects the extent to which you felt your activities were purposeful and meaningful during the day and, in the notes column, describe anything that contributed to a higher or lower sense of vitality. Make particular note of any spontaneous, natural moments when your willingness or vitality levels were high. At those times, what were you doing that elevated your willingness or vitality?

My Willingness, Depression, and Vitality Diary

Day	W	Notes	D	Notes	V	Notes
1						
2						
3						
4						
5						
6						
7						

W = Willingness (1–10); D = Depression (1–10); V = Vitality (1–10)

Debriefing. What did you see in terms of the relationship among your daily willingness level, depression level, and sense of vitality? Did you notice that your willingness and vitality ratings fluctuated from day to day? That's normal when you first start practicing willingness. What occurrences seemed to spark higher levels of willingness and vitality? What factors decreased your willingness level? When you notice factors that drive your willingness down, you might consider putting together a new willingness and acceptance plan to use when those factors are at play.

To give you a sense of how this daily practice played out for someone else, let's take a look at Bill's responses. This will show you how much information can be gleaned from doing this exercise in earnest for just one week.

BILL'S WILLINGNESS, DEPRESSION, AND VITALITY DIARY

Day	W	Notes	D	Notes	V	Notes
1	1	Many doubts, pain was real bad, was down on myself	10	On the couch most of day	3	Reviewed my values, read from a book of poems and the Bible
2	3	Thought about what I could do even with pain	7	Outside for a while in a.m. and p.m., helped to be in sunshine	4	Read more poems, wrote one, offered to garden with wife
3	4	Wrote more on values	7	Decided I would go to pain class	4	Told wife and kids about class
4	5	Shared values about family with kids and wife	6	Class supportive of me, told me they'd be there	5	Told wife about class and asked her to help me keep moving
5	4	More pain, angry at life and doctors for screwing me up	8	Mostly watched TV all day, bored and feeling life is going nowhere	3	Trying not to think about pain, trying to be positive
6	8	Decided to plan day with walking, activity, and getting out	2	Outside a.m. and p.m., called a friend	7	I can choose where I want to go in life; I'm not a prisoner
7	9	Called someone from class for coffee, invited wife to a movie	2	Outside a.m. and p.m., less pain meds needed, felt I belonged	8	Long embrace with wife, had the thought that I can do this

Review. As you can see from Bill's diary, his ratings of willingness, depression, and life vitality tend to dance together in certain patterns. As his willingness goes up, his depression tends to go down and his sense of vitality tends to go up. Although the overall trend is for the better, Bill's diary does show a day where his willingness level goes down and his depression goes up. This is common, and occasional setbacks are inevitable. To Bill's credit, he doesn't stop trying, and he uses his experience to figure out effective strategies to restore his willingness.

■ *Bill's Journey Toward a Vital Life*

When he implemented his willingness and acceptance plan, Bill noticed that he enjoyed social connections with his classmates and that his pain levels seemed to decrease when he was focused on the class. He was surprised to find that he could go to a movie and sit through the whole thing without a pain episode of huge proportions afterward, as had always happened to him in the early years of his chronic pain problem. He realized that he had previously gone to movies alone and wondered if the difference this time was because he went with his wife and he was willing to have pain in order to do something positive for their relationship. Bill began to plan daily activities that would engage his attention in areas of his life he wanted to build, including spending more quality time with his children. He found that he could go to the park with them if he did it at the start of the day. He could then rest strategically to restore his physical strength.

He began stretching regularly a couple of times each day to help manage his pain, even while accepting the fact that he would probably experience pain for the rest of his life. He still struggled occasionally with anger about his fate, particularly on days when his pain flared up. However, he stuck with his planned activities even when he was in pain. His relationship with his wife improved to the point where she told him he was like a new person. Bill was on the pathway out of depression!

Secrets to ACT On

☞ One of the more difficult aspects of living a values-driven life is learning what can and cannot be changed.

☞ Things that can't be changed must be accepted.

☞ For the most part, you can't directly control internal events, like spontaneous feelings, thoughts, images, and physical sensations; you also can't control your personal history or the actions and attitudes of other people.

☞ The thing you have the most control over is choosing to act in ways that promote your values in any life situation.

☞ Being willing to suffer in the service of your values, rather than avoiding suffering, can prevent excessive suffering.

☞ When you understand the relationship between willingness, depression, and vitality, you can consciously increase your daily levels of willingness and thus increase your sense of vitality.

☞ When you focus on practicing willingness and acceptance in the pursuit of vital living, your depression doesn't stand a chance!

The Coach Says

Take a stand—a stand that says who you are and who you want to become. Hold strong to that stand, breathe in and out, and get ready to adjust your sails. You are on a powerful journey, and the wind knows where to take you if you will just let it!

Sneak Preview

In the next chapter, we'll show you how your mind tricks you into losing the posture of acceptance and willingness. We'll revisit the issue of reactive mind and wise mind and compare how each would have you address your most troublesome life situations. You'll learn strategies to detect the mental trickery of your reactive mind so you can bring your wise mind into conscious, powerful play!

CHAPTER 8

Step 3: Become a Mind Watcher

If you gaze for long into the abyss, the abyss also gazes into you. —Frederick Nietzsche

In the previous chapter, we introduced an alternative to avoidance, which can lead to depression. This alternative is to accept rather than struggle with things that cannot be changed. We discussed what types of things you can change and what types you can't. Basically, you have the most control over how you *behave*, or take action; you can "vote with your feet," as the saying goes. You have less control over the spontaneous thoughts, feelings, memories, and physical sensations you experience in difficult situations. And you have almost no control over the opinions, beliefs, or actions of others, even though you may care deeply about them. When you can't control something, it's best to accept it for what it is: something that may be painful to experience but is also part of a healthy, vital life.

RULE FOLLOWING: THE ARCHENEMY OF ACCEPTANCE

Although the idea of adopting a willing, accepting stance sounds simple in theory, it's difficult in reality. You might enter a situation with the intention of using acceptance only to discover that you've been pulled back into trying to suppress or eliminate unwanted internal experiences. Although your mind is very useful in helping you address challenges and problems in the external world, it can be the cause of enormous struggle and suffering when applied to events inside the skin. In fact, your mind may be your worst enemy when it comes to addressing personal problems and dealing with personal pain.

For example, you might have a dream of going back to college or vocational school to get enough education or training to pursue a different career because you don't really like your current job. The last time you tried to go to school while working, you had trouble keeping up with your studies. Putting yourself back in that situation means you must risk failing again. If you're depressed, it's likely that your reactive mind will give you the suggestion that to avoid the pain of struggling academically, you might be better off not going to school or pursuing a less meaningful goal. If you follow your reactive mind's advice, you'll end up living in a way that isn't consistent with your values. Yes, you avoid the possibility of failure, but in doing so you also relinquish control over a valued life direction.

There are specific properties of minding that tend to make you mindless in such situations. You'll tend to automatically protect yourself by withdrawing from any painful event. This is not to suggest that you aren't thinking during such times, but rather that your thinking is dominated by an attachment to provocative and rigid rules about (often exaggerated) dangers posed by distressing thoughts, feelings, memories, and other unwanted internal experiences. When you can't separate yourself from your reactive mind and its rules, it's hard to respond in a flexible way. Instead, like the person stuck in a hole, you pick up the same old shovel and start digging again. The ACT term for this mental trap is "rule following." When you're caught up in rule following, you use strategies that *should* work rather than strategies that *do* work.

In this chapter and the three that follow, we'll teach you to recognize the various ways that your mind draws you back into rule following. Our goal is to help you fight the tendency to get drawn into your mind so you can stay in the present, use behaviors that work, and improve the quality of your life.

YOUR MIND IS PHISHING YOU!

Unless you've been living in a cave for the past decade, you probably use the Internet on a regular basis. The information age spawned by the Internet has had a huge, mostly positive impact on our ability to acquire information, transmit knowledge, and create a true world community. However, there's also a dark side to this powerful tool. Identity theft has become a major threat to personal security, and one of the primary tactics employed to this end is the practice of phishing. When you are being phished, you receive an e-mail that presents you with either highly exciting personal news ("You've just won an all-expenses-paid trip for two to a tropical paradise!") or highly distressing personal news ("We have reason to believe that your credit card has been used by someone else"). Along with this news is a request that you provide personal information. The main tactic in phishing is to create a powerful emotional state that makes you give away personal information without thinking first. This is a textbook example of a mindless action. You are certainly engaging in complex action when you provide the information requested, but you're doing so automatically, without an appropriate level of awareness.

Like the Internet, your mind is a hugely positive addition to your bag of tools as a human being. Its job is to provide you with a constant stream of intelligence that's potentially useful for your survival and promoting your best interests. Although it hasn't been scientifically established how many thoughts, feelings, memories, and sensations a person experiences in a typical day, the number is clearly astronomical. In the background of your awareness, you automatically and continuously sort through this vast array of information and decide what's important and useful, and what isn't. If you had to consciously evaluate every iota of intelligence in your mind, you would literally be paralyzed with information overload. So your job as the recipient of your mind's activity is to look for the most useful intelligence and pass on the rest.

A lot of what your mind gives you is instantly useful for your survival, like when it tells you to wait for a car to pass before crossing the street. If you ignore that kind of intelligence, you're going to live a very short life. This is the tricky thing about having a mind. In many real-life situations, it is important to listen to it and follow its advice, sometimes without taking the time to analyze what it's doing. But minds aren't right about everything—and worse, minds are along for the ride even when they aren't all that helpful, such as in emotionally charged situations. Those are times when your mind can phish you. It can get you to attach to a thought, feeling, memory, or sensation and ratchet up the negative intensity. It can get you to respond automatically in ways that aren't good for you.

An excellent example of how you can get phished deeper into depression is when you get hooked into ruminating about why you're depressed and why you can't end your depression. This is a common problem for depressed people. In terms of phishing, rumination occurs when you bite on three provocative lures: First, your mind tells you that because you're depressed, you aren't like everyone else. Second, your mind says you should prove you're normal by consciously changing from a depressed state to a positive state—and that you have the capacity to do this. When you're unable to control your mood directly via willpower, your mind phishes you with the third lure: the thought that there must be something terribly wrong with you and that you need to analyze where all of this personal weakness comes from.

Phishing for Fusion

When you're being phished by your mind, you're being invited to respond as if what your mind is telling you is the absolute truth, with a capital T. Like a phisher on the Internet, your mind is pulling you in based upon the emotional pull of the intelligence you're being given. To refresh your memory, this is fusion. When you're fused, you've lost the distinction between you and your mind. You quite literally become your thoughts, feelings, memories, images, and physical sensations. There is no *you* left to sort through the products generated by your mind and to determine what, if any of it, is of use in deciding a course of action in the here and now. When you lose this witnessing stance, it's almost impossible to practice acceptance. Instead, you usually do what your mind is telling you to do, even if it's something that hasn't worked before, no matter how many times you've tried it. Since fusing with your word machine means you're buying rather than owning your thoughts, it will be very difficult to practice willingness and acceptance in an emotionally charged situation.

Signs You're Being Phished

Interestingly, a practical strategy for avoiding being phished on the Internet is also helpful when your mind is phishing. Here's how it works: First, step back, observe what's happening, and avoid the tendency to jump in impulsively. Then examine the message you've received for signs that it might be bogus. So, assuming that you've taken a step back, here are some surefire warning signs that your mind is phishing you with bogus intelligence:

- Your mind is giving you a negative message about who you are as a person: "I'm a loser," "I'm fat and ugly," "I'm unlovable," "I'm defective in some basic way."

- Your mind tells you what you can and can't afford to think, feel, remember, or sense: "I can't be angry at my spouse if I want us to remain close," "I can't allow myself to think about my childhood if I want to be happy," "I shouldn't think about addressing my own needs at home because that would be selfish."

- Your mind predicts what will happen if you take a step to approach and solve a personal problem: "My kids will hate me if I punish them," "I'll get demoted or fired if I bring this concern to my supervisor," "I'll come out on the bottom end of this argument with my friend just like the last time I tried."

- Your mind tries to compare how you're doing in life right now with how you should be doing: "With all the good things I've got in my life, I should be happier than I am," "I've wasted a lot of my life struggling with my feelings and still don't feel good," "I'm going nowhere with my career and have wasted my potential."

- Your mind compares how you're doing in life to how other people are doing in their lives: "Other people don't seem to be depressed all the time, so why am I?" "Everyone else seems to have a direction in their life, so why don't I?" "Relationships seem to be easier for other people than they are for me."

- Your mind focuses on mistakes you've made in the past as proof that you'll never have a meaningful life: "I can't ever forgive myself for giving my two children up to my ex-husband," "I stayed too long with my abusive husband and have been permanently damaged as far as ever finding a new life partner," "I can never forgive myself for being an alcoholic for ten years."

■ Your mind insists that other people can tell how badly you're doing and that you shouldn't use them for support: "If I go to the party, other people will be able to tell I'm depressed," "I shouldn't go visit my friends and burden them with my problems," "It's humiliating to go to church and have everyone see how unhappy I am."

Each of these phishing lures has a set of qualities you should learn to recognize. First, the intelligence your mind gives you tends to be in black-and-white terms, negative, and extreme in tone. Second, these messages encourage you to avoid real-life situations. Third, and most important, this intelligence comes in the form of "I" statements, creating the impression that this is you speaking about you. However, this is actually your mind speaking to you and trying to disguise it so that it looks as if you're speaking to yourself. Your mind presents you with intelligence, and you can either act upon it or ignore it. Unfortunately, when you're being phished this distinction can become very unclear and will often disappear altogether. It will be helpful if you identify some of your mind's favorite phishing lures; this will make it easier for you to see them even in murky situations.

EXERCISE: PHISHING LURES

Take some time to think about past and present situations in which your mind may have hooked you with the phishing lures just described. Write down the particular form this "intelligence" takes as closely as you can. Leave the nickname column blank for now; we'll return to it later in the chapter.

My Phishing Lures

Intelligence about my negative personal qualities and shortcomings:	Nickname:
Intelligence about what I can or can't afford to think, feel, remember, or sense:	Nickname:
Intelligence about future negative results if I try to address a personal problem:	Nickname:
Intelligence comparing how I'm doing in life to how I should be doing:	Nickname:
Intelligence about how I'm doing in life compared to how other people are doing:	Nickname:

Intelligence focusing on personal mistakes I've made and how they'll keep me from having a meaningful life: _____ _____ _____	Nickname:
Intelligence suggesting that other people can tell how badly I'm doing: _____ _____ _____	Nickname:
Intelligence suggesting that I shouldn't burden others with my problems: _____ _____ _____	Nickname:

Debriefing. What did you discover as you worked through this exercise? Did certain themes reappear in various categories? Did you sometimes argue with yourself that certain lures might represent the truth? This is what lures do; they get you to swallow them and then struggle with them once you've been hooked. The more you struggle, the deeper in the hook is set.

■ *Helen's Story*

Helen is a twenty-seven-year-old African-American woman. Her mother died when she was thirteen, and she spent the remainder of her adolescence living with her father, who worked as a car salesman and had a problem with drinking. After his second wife died, he became more irritable and tended to isolate himself at home. When Helen began to gain weight at age sixteen, her father ridiculed her, often in front of family and friends. He would tell her to get out and exercise like everyone else and stop eating everything in sight. Even when Helen dieted and lost some weight, he would still say things that had a critical edge: for example, that she was "built solid" and "looked stocky." Helen started to experience symptoms of depression at that time and her struggles continue today.

Because her high-school grades weren't high, Helen decided she wasn't smart enough to go on to college. She had a couple of intimate relationships in her early twenties and was rejected both times. One of her partners was quite verbally abusive and made negative remarks about her physical appearance on more than one occasion. She stopped dating four years ago. She works as a bank teller and likes the job but is also concerned that there aren't very many prospects for job growth. When Helen completed the ACT phishing lure self-inventory, she made some interesting discoveries about how her mind was phishing her.

HELEN'S PHISHING LURES WORKSHEET

Intelligence about my negative personal qualities and shortcomings:

The hardest one for me to handle is that I'm fat and not worth much. I also get hooked on the idea that I'm not very smart. I have to battle these messages all the time.

Intelligence about what I can or can't afford to think, feel, remember, or sense:

I really get shaken up when something triggers memories of my childhood, especially all the things my father said and when my mother died. I try really hard to stay positive and not let myself go back there. When I fall into this pity pot, I can still see my dad looking at me in disgust. I even hear his voice saying that I'm fat.

Intelligence about future negative results if I try to address a personal problem:

Secretly, the thing I want most in life is to have a husband who loves me for who I am. When I think about dating someone, I get hooked on the idea that I'll be too fat for him and I'll be rejected again or, even worse, that he'll like me the way I am and then he'll die and leave me alone. These thoughts seem completely true and scare me to death.

Intelligence comparing how I'm doing in life to how I should be doing:

I get hooked on the idea that I should be married by now. What is so bad about me that I can't find a partner? I just can't seem to feel any happiness, and then I blame myself for that too. Who would even consider getting involved with me if I'm always sad?

Intelligence about how I'm doing in life compared to how other people are doing:

I really struggle with the fact that most of my coworkers are married and have children. I envy them. They seem to be so happy and content with their lives. I get hooked on my sense of being different in bad ways—never really able to have a good life—that I just drew bad cards and it doesn't matter how I play them.

Intelligence focusing on personal mistakes I've made and how they'll keep me from having a meaningful life:

What I get hooked on is blaming myself for getting fat and that I've never taken care of this weight problem. I think I did it because I was so sad about my mother dying. My other big mistake is that I didn't care enough about my grades in high school. I get hooked on images that I'm at a dead end in my job and that I'll never get a better job. Probably the worst hook for me is that losing my mother was somehow my fault.

Intelligence suggesting that other people can tell how badly I'm doing:

I really get hooked on the idea that people can tell I'm not happy. A couple of times I've cried at work and had to go to the bathroom to get myself together. I'm sure all the other tellers noticed. They probably talk about me when I'm not around. When I go to a wedding, I always think that if I ever married, people would pity me because I don't have a mother and I have a bad relationship with my father.

Intelligence suggesting that I shouldn't burden others with my problems:

I don't get lured very much here. I don't really have anyone to talk to. Even if I did, I don't know how they could help. What lures me more is the feeling of aloneness that I have.

Review. Helen's responses are pretty typical of a person who's being phished by the mind on multiple levels. She's dealing with intelligence that not only is she unattractive as a person, she's also at a dead end at work and hopelessly alone. Her lures present her with gloomy predictions about her future, and as she attaches to them, she begins to experience a wide range of negative feelings, sensations, and memories.

How Fusion Begets Fusion

One of the more vicious aspects of phishing is that once you begin to fuse with your mind, the process of fusion seems to pick up speed and energy, not unlike the cascading chain reactions that fuel an atomic explosion. As more and more fusion takes place, the heat, light, and explosive intensity of the reaction increases. Applied to the process of mental fusion, this leads to something called a *ratcheting effect*. Once you get the process of fusion started, it picks up momentum and is increasingly difficult to reverse. In fact, the more you fuse with your mind, the more your mind wants to fuse with you.

Mind as a Child Throwing a Tantrum

Imagine that you're at a department store with a small boy. Initially, he's behaving, so you only monitor his whereabouts, but eventually he sees a toy that he really, really wants. When he asks you to buy it, you say no. He starts to throw a temper tantrum, complete with crying, screaming, jumping up and down, and throwing things. So you switch out of monitoring mode and move into control mode. You order him to stop the tantrum, only to see him kick into higher gear. You move closer and, using your most stern voice, order him to stop. This is met with even greater resistance. He screams and runs at you and then away from you. In an effort to restrain him, you pick him up, and you feel yourself turn red as he thrashes his arms and legs, screams, cries, and tries to get free. In the fray, you've stopped doing what you came to the store to do: shop.

At times, your mind can be like a child throwing a tantrum. First it gives you provocative content to get you to pay attention to it. As is true for the parent who argues, threatens, persuades, or attempts to comfort a child throwing a tantrum, simply paying attention to your mind's behavior can reward and strengthen the very things you'd like to control or stop. When your mind detects that you're fusing with a piece of distressing intelligence, it will give you more of that kind of tantrum, perhaps other intelligence related to the same types of issues. This is why you bounce from one negative thought, feeling, memory, or sensation to another when you're in a downward depressive spiral.

So, what's the antidote for this negative cycle? When you confront a child's temper tantrum, it's best not to engage the child in a test of wills, as described above. Rather, you quickly remove the child from the store and place him in the car, where his undesirable behavior isn't rewarded. As you stand outside the car, you can observe him calmly through the car window. This time-out context allows time for the child to calm himself. As the adult in a time-out context, you're still very aware of the child, but you don't encourage unworkable behavior by engaging in a struggle.

The same principles apply to fusing with mental tantrums. When this process gets over-the-top, you can put your mind in a time-out. As the human in the situation, you'll be aware that your mind is still blabbering at you a mile a minute (just as a child in a time-out may get a little louder for a few minutes). And while noticing this, you can engage in actions that work for you in the situation that has set your mind off.

As an example, suppose you're in a disagreement with a spouse or partner over the lack of intimacy you're experiencing in the relationship. Your mind might quickly tell you that, given all your personal defects, you're lucky to have any relationship at all. Then your mind threatens you with the idea that your spouse or partner will leave you if you don't quit making these unreasonable demands. Then your mind yells that if your spouse or partner leaves, you'll never have another relationship because you're ugly and unlovable. In the midst of this tantrum, you refocus on your values about intimacy and continue to assert what you want. In this example, your job as the human is to avoid reinforcing your mind's tantrum and to leave it in time-out while it settles. The next few exercises will teach you some practical strategies to help you establish a time-out with your mind when it's throwing a tantrum.

EXERCISE: RAILROAD CROSSING

You've probably had the experience of stopping at a railroad crossing to wait for a train to pass. Next time this happens, notice what you do. Most people fix their attention on a single car, follow it a little ways across their field of vision, then drop their gaze and shift their attention back to a newly arriving car. What prompts you to give your attention to a particular car? It could be the shape or color of the car, or perhaps something printed on the side of the car draws your eye. Maybe it's simply that the car looks different from those around it. When watching a train, most people just watch the cars pass by without getting locked in on a particular car to the point of running beside the train to follow it!

In the exercise that follows, we want you to think of your thoughts, feelings, memories, and physical sensations as railroad cars in a train moving across your mental field of vision. Your job is to let each railroad car pass in front of you without fusing with the thought, feeling, memory, or sensation the railroad car carries. This exercise will help you practice the skill of just noticing the contents of your mind—being aware of mental events without becoming fused with them. Go to a quiet place and read the following instructions. Then take a few deep breaths and allow yourself to go into the suggested experience. Or, even better, play the version of the exercise on the CD.

> *Imagine that your car is first in line at a railroad crossing and a long train is traveling very slowly in front of you. It's dusk and you're on your way home. You are in no hurry. Since you're right in front of the train, it's really the only thing you can see. Now, imagine that the boxcars of this train are unique. They have large whiteboards on their sides, and they invite you to write a message on their sides. Your messages can be thoughts, feelings, memories, or sensations that you experience as you watch. They can be images that your mind offers up. When you notice any type of mental event, take it and place it on the boxcar in front of you. Let each mental event go with the boxcar as it moves on down the track. Notice the next mental experience your mind offers, and place it on the whiteboard on the next boxcar. If you notice that you're no longer watching the cars and putting mental events on the whiteboards, simply notice that you left the exercise and bring yourself back to the railroad crossing. Continue for at least five minutes, bringing your attention back to the railroad crossing as needed.*

Debriefing. What did you notice when you tried this exercise? Most people have trouble staying with the task of simply observing mental events. Did you have a thought like "I'm not doing this task right" or "I'm trying to put mental events on the cars, but they won't go on"? The trick is to take *those* thoughts and put them on boxcars too, allowing them to be there and pass by just like your other experiences. Were there certain thoughts, feelings, memories, or sensations that totally drew you out of the posture of just noticing? That's what happens when your mind phishes you. When you fuse with a private event, such as a thought, memory, or feeling, you lose the observer perspective and will be prone to acting automatically, and often in ways that defeat your best interests.

EXERCISE: DOWN THE TRACK

This exercise builds on the previous one and is a little more challenging. Go back to your responses for the exercise "My Phishing Lures," earlier in this chapter, and give each of your lures a nickname. In ACT, we encourage you to give feared and unwanted private experiences a nickname. This creates a little mental separation between you and the complex of thoughts, feelings, memories, and sensations you might be tempted to fuse with. Nicknames are often exaggerated terms that can actually be quite humorous. When you notice that an unpleasant experience has shown up, you can welcome it by greeting it with its nickname. For example, a nickname for the thought "I'm never going to measure up to others because my mother beat me and my dad was an alcoholic" might be Born Loser. Be creative as you assign your nicknames and try to have some fun with it. Lightheartedness and humor are excellent remedies when you're being phished.

Once you've assigned nicknames to each of your personal phishing lures, write each nickname on the front of a separate 3 by 5 index card, leaving the other side blank for now. Now, as in the preceding exercise, go to a quiet place and read the following instructions. Then take a few deep breaths and allow yourself to go into the suggested experience. Or, even better, play the version of the exercise on the CD.

You are taking your time and simply watching the same slowly moving train. Now reach down and pick up a nickname. Let yourself generate the thought, feeling, memory, sensation, or image that goes with that nickname. Now place it on the boxcar in your mind. Look at it on the side of the boxcar and simply allow the boxcar to move on in its own time. The train may stop briefly and then resume a more regular pace. Respect the pace of the train and just notice it as it is; don't try to control it. Then pick up the next lure and do the same thing. If you start to experience a negative emotion or thought in response to one of your lures, simply put that thought or emotion on the next boxcar. Continue in this fashion until you've placed all of your lures on the train. If you notice you're getting phished by some other content provided by your mind, simply put it on the train as well. Just watch the train, stay in your car, and remember that your destination in life is different than the train's destination.

Debriefing. Did you notice any difference in the degree of difficulty between these two exercises? Was it harder to put certain lures on the boxcars? In this exercise, your mind might phish you more powerfully, causing you to lose sight of the task more readily. Did you get lost in your own mental activity? Were you sometimes tempted to just give up? Most people report getting drawn out of this exercise over and over again, so if that happened to you don't beat yourself up about it. Just let it serve to underscore the importance of a daily practice of exercises designed to develop the skill of just noticing—or mindfulness. These types of mental exercises will help you strengthen the ability to make the distinction between you and your mind. This allows you to voluntarily withdraw from a fused state when you recognize that your mind is phishing you. By the way, you'll use the index cards with the nicknames for your phishing lures in the next chapter, so store them somewhere you can easily find them again.

EXERCISE: THANK YOUR MIND

Since you can't keep your mind from thinking, feeling, remembering, and sensing, learning how to distance yourself from your mind when it's provoking you is important. Our experience is that expressing gratitude to your mind—out loud—for the intelligence it is giving you is one sure way to create and hold a space between you and your mind. This allows you to respond voluntarily to your word machine rather than fall for phishing lures and fuse with your mind. This strategy also requires you to do something else that's very important: give a name to the type of mental experience you're having.

Here's how it works: When you notice an unpleasant mental event unfolding, simply say "Thank you, mind, for giving me the [thought, feeling, memory, sensation] called [describe the cue for the lure]." Try to get in the habit of doing this any time your mind is phishing you. In Helen's case, she thanked her mind in the following ways:

- *Thank you, mind, for giving me the thought called fat, ugly girl (or FUG).*

- *Thank you, mind, for giving me the thought called you're messed up (or MUP).*

- *Thank you, mind, for giving me the memory called my dad thinks I'm disgusting (or DD, "disgusted dad").*

- *Thank you, mind, for giving me the feelings called sad and scared (or SAS).*

- *Thank you, mind, for giving me the sensation called chest pain (or Ticker).*

- *Thank you, mind, for giving me the feeling called loneliness (or OTL, "Only the Lonely").*

Review. By describing the lures your mind phishes you with and creating nicknames for them, you're building skills for sorting through the intelligence your mind offers and deciding whether it's useful or not. Another benefit of this approach is that it establishes that you don't just mindlessly follow your word machine. This is a crucial step toward maintaining a posture of willingness and acceptance in highly charged situations.

EXERCISE: THERE AND THEN, IF AND WHEN

This exercise allows you to look at the lures that your mind phishes you with and practice expressing your gratitude to your mind for being a mind. In general, minds don't experience the here and now very well, so in the here and now, you're likely to hear your mind chattering at you about your "there and then" (your past) and your "if and when" (your future). This will tend to draw you out of the present moment and make your responses to current situations less effective.

One of the greatest challenges in learning to be mindful is in knowing how to defuse from provocative mental content. Practicing the following exercise will help you see when you're being lured into the there and then or the if and when. This will help you respond to situations in the here and now with greater flexibility. It will also make it easier for you to see what you're doing that is and isn't working. In this exercise, focus on lures involving negative past experience and lures that predict a negative future. Feel free to record more than one lure for each category.

There and Then, If and When Worksheet

Thank you, mind, for lures about the there and then, including…

The thought called

_____

The feeling called

_____

The memory called

_____

The physical sensation called

_____

Thank you, mind, for lures about the if and when, including…

The thought called

_____

The feeling called

_____

The memory called

_____

The physical sensation called

_____

Debriefing. What happened when you began to thank your mind for specific problematic thoughts, feelings, memories, and physical sensations? Did you have a different kind of experience when you faced your mind, thanked it for doing its job, yet remained in the position of the mind watcher? Previously, your typical stance with respect to this material may have been to fuse with it or try to ignore, avoid, or suppress it. The welcoming posture of thanking your mind (while turning down its invitation to fuse with it) is a very important characteristic of an acceptance-oriented response style.

EXERCISE: TAKE YOUR MIND FOR A WALK

It's important to practice new ways of relating to your mind and its never-ending efforts to provide you with bogus intelligence. Different people find different techniques more helpful or relevant, so we offer you a variety to choose from. This exercise (based on Hayes, Strosahl, and Wilson 1999, 161–62) helps you learn how to make choices even as your mind blabbers at you. It's easier to learn to do this when the emotional stakes aren't high, so in this exercise you'll work with a partner and do a role-playing exercise in which each of you takes a turn at being the human while the other plays the role of the mind. This exercise is really fun to do with a close friend, your spouse or partner, or someone else who knows your hot buttons. If you do this with someone who doesn't know you as well, take your written phishing lures and show them to the other person. This will take some guts on your part, but it will make the exercise much more effective.

In this exercise, your goal is to take a walk, with you the human deciding how to walk and where to go. You can walk fast, slow, or on your hands and knees if you like. You can go forward, sideways, or backwards. You can change direction at any time and without any reason. The goal is for the human, not the mind, to choose each aspect of this walk.

You and your partner are to walk for about twenty minutes. For the first ten minutes, one of you is to be the human and the other is the mind. The mind must walk behind the human no matter where the human goes. The mind's task is to try to engage the human by offering up the most effective lures (without being too hurtful, of course). This could involve questioning every choice the human makes, or making fun of or criticizing how the human is walking—whatever it takes to get the human to argue or otherwise engage with the mind and stop walking. Any time the human responds in any way to the mind, the second this is recognized the human is to say, "Never mind my mind!" The human's task is to take a walk in which the human is choosing everything about the walk—while being exposed to the mind's constant harassment. After ten minutes, reverse roles and do the same thing again.

Debriefing. When you've finished this exercise, it's useful to sit down and share your experiences of what each of you went through as the human and what it felt like to be in the role of the mind. You may notice that you and your partner experienced some of the same difficulties in being the human. You may have stalled out momentarily when the mind hit one of your hot buttons. If so, just notice what that hot button was based in. Later on you might write a thank-you note to your own mind for giving you that lure. It's a good idea to practice this exercise on a regular basis. It's really a type of walking meditation in which your partner is teaching you to recognize the activities of the master phisherman!

Secrets to ACT On

☞ All minds are alike in the ways they phish the human who owns them.

☞ When you, the human, are phished by your mind, you lose your sense of being in the present, and with it some of your flexibility in responding to challenging situations.

☞ By engaging in exercises designed to help you notice your private mental events (thoughts, feelings, memories, sensations, images, and so on), you can become more skillful at detecting and detaching from bogus intelligence.

☞ Creating nicknames for common lures will help you learn to identify them and detach from them more quickly.

☞ Exercises such as saying thank you to your mind aloud can be particularly useful in responding to the mind's phishing lures, as they create lightness as well as space.

☞ Using physical exercises like taking your mind for a walk can help you develop a better appreciation of how you are not the same as your mind.

The Coach Says

The best defense against being phished is a good offense. Develop your acceptance skills by practicing them! Set up a schedule for practicing the railroad cars exercise, write a thank-you letter to your mind and read it daily for a few weeks, and recruit a partner to help you take your mind for a walk and make it a weekly date for the next month.

Sneak Preview

The next chapter will help you learn how to utilize your wise mind as an antidote for your reactive mind. We'll teach you how your reactive mind tricks you into acting on evaluations and following rigid rules about living. While some of these rules seem logical, compelling, and even "healthy," they don't map onto the real world well. We'll also introduce you to the four poison pills of depression and give you some antidotes for their toxic effects.

CHAPTER 9

Step 4: Get to Know the Right-and-Wrong Trap

Expecting life to treat you well because you are a good person is like expecting an angry bull not to charge because you are a vegetarian. —Shari R. Barr

In the previous chapter, we explained why fusion is the archenemy of acceptance and willingness. When you're fused with your reactive mind's thoughts, feelings, memories, and sensations, it's difficult, if not impossible, to see these experiences for what they are (just mental events) instead of what they advertise themselves to be (*really important stuff* that you must act on immediately). We explained how your mind lures you into these entanglements and how to identify the signs that your mind is phishing you. In this chapter, we'll teach you some additional skills for responding to being phished by your reactive mind.

THE PULL OF REACTIVE MIND

One of the major difficulties you'll face when trying to stay in an accepting posture is that your reactive mind will try to get you to fuse with unworkable rules for living. As you acquired language and thought, you also learned to categorize, analyze, evaluate, and predict. This has its good points, among them that it's the basic advantage that keeps us near the top of the food chain. At the same time, when these mental functions are focused on achieving a misguided result, it can have a devastating impact on life satisfaction. The reactive mind is hyperactive, always wanting to chatter, discourse, evaluate, and label. It becomes so overly involved in your basic experience that it begins to distort your perceptions. This dangerous feature of human thought has been recognized for centuries in most of the world's religions, perhaps nowhere more so than in Buddhism. As mentioned in chapter 5, one aim of Buddhism is to neutralize the raging, out-of-control effects of reactive mind using the balancing functions of the wise mind.

The wise mind looks upon emotionally charged situations in a more detached way than the reactive mind, yet it is not withdrawn. It is present and silent at the same time. It is the source of great intuition and other forms of preverbal understanding without being intrusive. Most of all, wise mind is full of compassion, both for yourself and for the people you're involved with, now and in the past. Both reactive mind and wise mind are valuable in daily living. Each serves important but different functions, and they must be in balance for your life to feel harmonious.

Why is the distinction between reactive mind and wise mind so important for overcoming depression and developing a life worth living? Research into thinking styles and depression has consistently shown that depressed people tend to think in highly charged, negative, and self-critical ways (Alloy et al. 2006). Depressed thinking is characterized by a rigid, black-and-white, moralistic, and catastrophic tone. Indeed, many approaches to the treatment of depression focus on correcting this tendency toward exaggerated self-criticism. In short, one major cause of depression is a serious imbalance between your reactive mind and your wise mind. Typically, when you feel the most depressed you'll also notice that your reactive mind is going a mile a minute and you're just along for the ride. Because your reactive mind is so noisy, the silent understanding of your wise mind can't be heard above the din.

HAVING THOUGHTS, HOLDING THOUGHTS, AND BUYING THOUGHTS

In the ACT approach, we take a slightly different angle on what to do about depressive thinking. ACT doesn't focus on making sure all of your thoughts are logical and rational, because the reactive mind is prone to being illogical and irrational at times. We know that a large percentage of negative thoughts, feelings, and memories are self-focused, meaning that they refer to you ("I'm ugly," "I feel awful," "I can't stop thinking about my dead mother," and so on). In fact, it appears that the human word machine tends to be biased toward producing negative, provocative information. Why is this so? In all likelihood, human intelligence evolved to help detect, predict, and prevent threats to our physical survival. Your body is built to respond to these warning signs with the fight, flight, or freeze response. This was appropriate in the prehistoric world, where humans faced many physical threats to survival, but by comparison the contemporary world is a pretty safe place. Sure, we have crime, drunken drivers, and other threats to deal with, but this is nothing compared with the daily life of early humans.

The irony is that as we've become safer, more comfortable, and more long-lived, we've fallen into a different kind of trap: having too much time to think about things. In the absence of genuine physical threats to survival, the bored reactive mind turns its attention to warning you of every conceivable kind of internal danger; for example, "You aren't attractive or smart enough" or "Past events prove you're a loser, so you're likely to fail at this." As the often quoted Zen saying goes, "The mind is a rambunctious thinker." Like your liver, lungs, and heart, the organ on top of your shoulders operates 24/7, which is why you can wake up from a frightening dream with your heart racing or even with tears in your eyes.

You can't turn off your reactive mind because you actually need it to survive the physical world; plus, it's hardwired into you. You can't—and shouldn't—try to stop it from producing negative thoughts, feelings, memories, and sensations. The key to a life worth living is to avoid the temptation to identify and struggle with your reactive mind, and instead simply see thoughts as thoughts, feelings as feelings, memories as memories, and so on. This means you must learn to *hold* your thoughts lightly rather than buying them hook, line, and sinker. Holding a thought means that you recognize the presence of your reactive mind and take an observer stance toward it.

Let's look at this in terms of a situation in which a mother is trying to address her teenage son's slipping grades and escalating drug use. A parent in that situation is bound to be bombarded with thoughts about what to do, emotional reactions triggered by the teenager's angry statements, physical sensations of arousal triggered by heated interactions, and even memories of similar experiences the parent endured as a teen. Buried in this array of private reactions are some provocative thoughts about the role of anger and what constitutes a healthy result in this troublesome situation. One thought might suggest that a "healthy" outcome is making sure the teenager is no longer angry at his mother after the consequences and remedies for his misbehavior are put in place. If the mother buys this rule, she no longer sees this as a set of thoughts but rather as truth with a capital T. This is likely to shift her aim from setting limits and enforcing consequences to trying to eliminate her teenager's anger.

If, instead, the mother held these provocative thoughts as thoughts, she might look at it this way: "One thing I'm aware of is this thought that says a healthy ending to this conflict is when my son is no longer angry at me. Another thought I'm aware of is that it's very important to make him understand that there are limits to misbehavior, and my value is to enforce the consequences for violating those limits, even if he's angry at me for doing so." In this scenario, she's aware of the competing nature of different thoughts rather than becoming fused with any particular thought. When you can hold a thought, feeling, memory, or sensation rather than buy it, you can choose to act in a way that's consistent with your values.

Holding thoughts is easier said than done because your reactive mind is always chattering at you, and some private events are harder to leave alone than others—especially negative, emotionally laden internal events. These are precisely the types of mental events that depressed people are likely to struggle with. As previously noted, the reactive mind isn't self-policing. It doesn't disqualify itself from situations it knows nothing about. It will have an evaluation, opinion, or prediction about everything.

Another problematic aspect of the reactive mind is the immediate nature of the minding process. Your mind doesn't notify you in advance that it's about to give you a provocative thought, image, or memory. You have just a split second to notice what's going on and decide whether you need to pay attention to the incoming message. You won't have time to figure this out each time you have a thought, so you need to learn general rules for identifying suspicious incoming messages.

Rules About Living

We tend to organize the world in terms of evaluations and predictions about how things should be. These assumptions are buried so deeply in our day-to-day language that we usually don't even recognize them for what they are: evaluations that reactive mind has secretly injected so as to make them masquerade as reality. For example, let's say you assume your boss is out to get you at work, even though you haven't actually talked with your boss about her attitude toward you. Operating on your assumption, you'll act in a self-protective way at work so your boss can't find fault with what you do on the job. Alternatively, you may begin to look for a new job on the side or look to transfer to another department. All of these behaviors are driven by your initial assumption. Notice one more important feature of a hidden evaluation: It can be totally made up. If you buy the evaluation as reality, it will guide your behavior even if it's entirely fictitious or entirely wrong. One of the reactive mind's most effective phishing lures is to present you with carefully disguised evaluations about life and its complexities such that you behave in ways that are inconsistent with your best interests. As you read on, we'll help you better understand how your reactive mind phishes you with unworkable assumptions—and what you can do about it.

One way to access some of your basic assumptions is to look at the sayings about life that you carry around. As an example, one saying a lot of people adhere to is "No pain, no gain." Taken literally, this seems to suggest that you have to be in pain to experience some type of benefit. Does it mean you should slam a door on your hand every day to make sure you have enough pain to gain benefit? Of course not; these are really figurative instructions that communicate a general rule about life. In this case, the rule states that you achieve personal growth by going through painful life situations and that such pain is unavoidable. This prepares you for painful situations and allows you to both endure them better and see the potential for personal learning in them. You may have found yourself using this saying at some point in your life when you were in a lot of emotional pain.

EXERCISE: FAVORITE LIFE SAYINGS

This exercise involves three tasks. In the left-hand column of the worksheet, write down five of your favorite sayings about life, either popular clichés or sayings that aren't well-known but are important to you. Next, identify the area of living that the rule applies to: how to treat other people, how to deal with personal pain or problems, how you should be treated by others, and so on. Write that in the middle column. In the right-hand column, write out the figurative instruction carried in the saying, as we did on the previous page with "No pain, no gain. If you have difficulty with this exercise, take a look at the example from Jose, which follows the worksheet.

My Favorite Life Sayings

Saying About Life	Area of Living It Relates To	What It Tells Me to Do

Debriefing. Now go back and look at each saying using a different lens. Do you remember when you first heard this saying? Was it something your mother or father told you, or someone else in your family? Was it a teacher you looked up to in school or a friend you hung out with? How many times have you used this saying to guide you through difficult or complicated situations? If you've used a particular saying a lot in your life, why do you think that is? When you last were in a situation where you used the saying, did it help you deal with the situation effectively, or did it get in the way? Sometimes assumptions in the form of sayings can be very useful; at other times, they can set you up for frustration and failure. As with other mental products, the key is to remember that a saying hails from your reactive mind. Don't buy it or act on its advice without first looking at whether it's appropriate in the current situation.

■ *Jose's Story*

Jose, a thirty-six-year-old married man with three children, used to work as a firefighter. His problems with depression began after he suffered a serious knee injury playing basketball at the fire station. After surgery, he was told that he could never play sports again. Since the accident, he has lived with knee pain on a daily basis. Because of his injury, he can't work as a firefighter and receives a modest disability payment that barely covers his family's basic costs of living. He used to be very involved in sports and loved all sorts of outdoor activities, but now he's unable to run or jump and is all but confined to walking with a severe limp. His prospects for long-term improvement are modest at best.

Jose has become increasingly depressed, angry, and withdrawn over time. He gets angry at his wife and kids over little things and then continues to fume for hours. He believes he's failing in his role as a father and a husband. Lately, he's been drinking more than usual and has been driving under the influence. When Jose took a look at his favorite life sayings, he came up with some revealing answers.

JOSE'S FAVORITE LIFE SAYINGS

Saying About Life	Area of Living It Relates To	What It Tells Me to Do
If you can't do something well, don't do it at all.	Undertaking any kind of task	Nothing short of perfection is acceptable, and you should never settle for less.
The mark of a man is his family.	My public and private image	Nothing is as important as being a good father and husband.
The apple doesn't fall far from the tree.	Providing a role model for my children	My children will be a lot like me, so I need to be a good role model for them. If they mess up, it's on my shoulders.
Where there's a will, there's a way.	Overcoming obstacles	If you believe in yourself, you can overcome anything in life.
He who hesitates is lost.	Making important decisions	You can't second-guess yourself. You have to act decisively, and if you don't you'll never succeed.

Review. You can see from Jose's life sayings that some of his hidden life rules could affect him in ways that would cause him to stumble in certain circumstances. Not being willing to do anything less than perfectly in the arena of being a father means he'll have a hard time accepting the fact that he can no longer play sports with his children. Believing totally in the power of will is going to be dangerous when it comes to his physical recovery. He may push himself so hard that he incurs another, more serious injury; or when his willpower fails to win the day, he might stop trying altogether and conclude that he's a failure. His implicit worldview is that only the strong succeed and to be less than strong is a form of failure.

IMPLICIT WORLDVIEW

Another way your reactive mind secretly injects evaluations that can stall you out comes in the form of your implicit worldview. Like the implicit associations discussed in chapter 5, your implicit worldview is hidden from sight. It operates behind the scenes such that you see the world from that point of view. It's like a pair of tinted sunglasses you've forgotten you're wearing. The tint becomes so familiar to your eyes that you no longer realize certain shades and colors are highlighted, and others are suppressed.

Because your implicit worldview is a product of your reactive mind, it's organized along the lines of evaluations, categories, and predictions. Children receive a lot of training that creates an implicit worldview because this is the source of a person's morals. An implicit worldview is necessary for you to operate as a member of your culture. The problem is, the reactive mind goes far beyond what's necessary and begins to use this worldview to construct a grand picture of how life and even the universe are organized. This picture is influenced by a lot of cultural messages, such as the sayings you identified in the previous exercise. This grand yet hidden picture sets the stage for what you expect life to give you, and these expectations are often the source of great suffering. As one depressed person put it, "I have these ideas about how the chips are supposed to be distributed by the big poker dealer in the sky, and I'm getting screwed!"

In Jose's case, much of his difficulty in adjusting to his misfortune was his implicit worldview that life is organized to reward people who are strong and willing to play by the rules. He felt he had followed the rules, and this made the loss of his physical prowess seem unfair, as if he had been cheated by life. As we shall see next, your implicit worldview can be the source of some of the most poisonous forms of evaluation you may fall prey to.

EXERCISE: RULES ABOUT LIFE

In this exercise, we'll present you with a number of statements about life that we've heard over the years from depressed people. Since no statement like this is ever completely true or completely false, complete this exercise based on how you think about these things the majority of the time. Read each statement closely, and then, based on your beliefs, mark whether you tend to agree or disagree with the statement.

Statement About Life	Tend to Agree	Tend to Disagree
If you do all the right things in life, good things will surely come your way.		
When something bad happens to a person, the person probably did something to deserve it.		
If someone wrongs you in some way, the person will eventually pay for it.		
If you're always kind to other people, they will be less likely to take advantage of you.		
If you suffer some uncontrollable trauma, like being abused as a child or being physically deformed, life should make up for it later by giving you some breaks.		
There are good and bad people out there, and it's easy to see the difference.		
If you don't have something positive to share with others, it's best to keep things to yourself.		
If you don't put your best effort into something, you shouldn't expect much in return.		
What goes around comes around. Bad things will inevitably happen to bad people.		
You should be able to overcome any obstacle in life if you try hard enough.		
When you violate a trust or fail to live up to what's expected of you, you should expect to suffer.		
People who take advantage of others deserve any bad things they get.		
If you're generous and charitable to others, they will like you and treat you fairly.		
Everything you face in life is given to you for a reason, even if you can't see it.		

Debriefing. Did some of these statements remind you of things you have said to yourself? Did you notice that some of these statements pulled more emotional responses than others? When you notice that pull, you might be tapping into a part of your implicit worldview. How many of these statements did you find that you mostly agree with? Generally, if you marked a lot of these statements as agreeing with your beliefs about living, you might be more susceptible to being phished by your reactive mind in an emotionally challenging situation. Think about situations you've been in lately where your beliefs about living were activated. Were you able to respond in an effective way, or did you feel your hands were tied? Usually, the more provocative the situation, the more likely it is your worldview will be activated. It is very important to learn what the signals are that this often hidden system is in the "on" position.

FOUR POISON PILLS: HOW YOUR EVALUATIONS MAKE YOU SUFFER

While there are countless ways your reactive mind can make you suffer, four areas seem to be particularly dangerous for depressed people. We refer to these as the four poison pills. All of them involve evaluations: right versus wrong, good versus bad, fair versus unfair, and assessments of responsibility and blame. In a sense, all are variations on the theme of right and wrong. Whenever you sense the presence of any of these forms of reactive mind, you need to move into a posture of holding your thoughts rather than buying them. Let's take a look at each poison pill, and then we'll explore some strategies to help you detect and deflect toxic evaluations.

Right and Wrong

The belief that something isn't right implies that an injustice is being committed and someone is the victim of that injustice. There are some obvious examples of injustice, such as being physically or sexually abused. However, what's right or wrong is far less obvious in many situations. A prime example of this is expectations about how other people should treat you. You have your own unique set of rules about what must happen for a relationship to be right, and the other person has his or her own unique set of rules too. Evaluating that an offense has occurred when your rules are violated implies that your rules are the right ones. Beware: This is your reactive mind phishing you with the thought that it knows how all human relations must be conducted, that it knows what the other person's intentions are, and that you are entitled to be judge, jury, and executioner.

When you swallow the poison pill of right and wrong, you're far more likely to act on your anger and desire for vengeance. Although you probably value being loving and respectful of others, your evaluation of right and wrong might lead you to say or do things that are mean and hurtful. The other side of this coin is that you'll begin to see yourself as a victim. When you look at yourself in this way, you're likely to withdraw, act in a passive way, and see the other person as having evil intentions. Be very careful when you see thoughts like "This isn't right" or "I shouldn't have to go through something like this."

Good and Bad

Good and bad describe the qualities of an object or event in terms of how desirable it is. If you say you're a "good person," this means you evaluate *all* of your personal qualities as desirable. When you have an evaluation such as "He's a bad person," you're essentially saying that *all* of his qualities are very undesirable. This very basic form of evaluation is hidden in our everyday language, and one of the trickiest ways your reactive mind delivers this poison pill is through negatively charged words: loser, defective, boring, untrustworthy, liar, hopeless, empty, unlovable, ugly, and so on. These kinds of words constantly flow through our daily conversations and thinking. The emotional pull of good and bad is strong, and we don't want to associate with bad stuff (unlovable, loser, ugly) because it's unhealthy to do so (another good-bad evaluation). We only want to associate with the good stuff (lovable, winner, attractive). The problem is, most human events don't fit easily into one category. They are neither all good nor all bad. Rather, they often are a combination of good and bad.

Fair and Unfair

The evaluation of fair versus unfair has a special twist to it. Fair implies that you deserve a certain outcome. When something is evaluated as unfair, it means you've been arbitrarily punished or deprived of something you deserve. This particular type of evaluation can be a real impediment in situations that require you to act in a purposeful way. Taking the stance of being unfairly treated usually results in a person standing still and throwing a temper tantrum at life. Unfortunately, other people involved in the situation see it differently. People who struggle with long-term depression often buy the evaluation that life hasn't been fair to them. The problem is, just because you followed a certain set of rules about how to get a good life doesn't mean you'll have mostly positive feelings and experiences. Life doesn't work that way. Life is not fair, nor is it unfair. What's more, life doesn't care whether you think it's fair or not. The time and energy you spend under the influence of this poison pill would be better spent pursuing a valued life.

Responsibility and Blame

The fourth category of particularly toxic evaluations involves trying to determine who or what is responsible for an unwanted outcome. The assignment of responsibility feels extremely important when negative life outcomes are present. To illustrate the dangerous side effects of this poison pill, let's consider a depressed woman who thinks, "If I hadn't been so domineering, my husband wouldn't have gotten involved with that woman." In essence, she's making herself responsible for her husband's actions—and the other woman's actions. In reality, this doesn't seem too likely, does it? This type of evaluation is toxic because it clouds the issue of who is responsible for what and overlooks the fact that there are some things that can't be controlled. Depressed thinking is often organized around the idea that the person is somehow responsible (and to blame for) events not entirely within his or her control: the unexpected death of a loved one, a divorce, a child's drug problems, and so on. While you are "response-able" (meaning you have the ability to respond), you aren't necessarily to blame (in control of the outcome).

EXERCISE: POISON PILLS

In this exercise, you'll identify some of your hot-button situations and look at how these may be fueled by buying evaluations that lead you into an unworkable stance. In the left-hand column, describe one of your hot-button situations—a situation, event, or type of interaction that really sets you off emotionally. Take a moment to think about which of the poison pills might be at play in your response to this situation: right versus wrong, good versus bad, fair versus unfair, or responsibility and blame. Then, write the poison pills that apply in the middle column, each in a separate row. In the right-hand column, describe the private experiences (thoughts, feelings, memories, and so on) that show up as a result of buying each evaluation you listed in the middle column. Once you've completed this analysis for the first hot-button situation, do the same for a few more. You may wish to do the exercise on a copy of this blank form, or you can print out fresh copies from the CD. If you have trouble doing this exercise, take a look at the example from Gloria later in the chapter.

 Poison Pills Worksheet

Hot-Button Situation	Poison Pills	Private Experiences (thoughts, feelings, memories, sensations, etc.)

Debriefing. What did you discover when you examined life situations that act as hot buttons for you? Did you notice that your hot-button situations involved violations of certain assumptions about how life is organized? Is there any particular poison pill that shows up repeatedly? When you look at the situations that push your buttons, do they share common features? For example, are they mostly intimacy conflicts, mostly interactions with peers at work, and so on? What types of private experiences come along for the ride in these situations? Do you notice having a lot of provocative thoughts or intense emotions? Are you barraged with memories of earlier situations in life that seem similar?

Remember, this isn't an exercise in self-criticism or self-blame. *Everyone* has hot buttons, because everyone has a reactive mind. The purpose is to allow you to take a look at the topography of these situations from an observer perspective. If you develop the ability to detect poisonous evaluations, you can learn to hold them lightly, thereby creating some needed space between you and your word machine.

■ *Gloria's Story*

Gloria, a fifty-six-year-old married woman with four adult children, has had several episodes of depression since her teenage years. She was sexually abused by her older brother for more than two years, starting when she was seven. When she finally told her mother about it, her mother didn't believe her. Instead, she asked Gloria's brother whether he did it, and when he lied she believed him. Gloria has never forgiven her mother for this and they never talk about it.

Gloria places tremendous importance on loyalty and trust in her relationships. She's been married to her second husband, the father of her two younger children, for fifteen years and has struggled with depression throughout the marriage. There have been problems throughout the marriage with blended-family issues. In Gloria's view, he has never been as close to her two older children as to his own children, even though he promised her he would be a good father to all of the children. Gloria feels betrayed by her husband in this regard and doesn't feel she can trust him when he makes promises to her about other things that matter to her. Their intimacy has suffered because of these trust issues. She doesn't socialize much and feels uncomfortable in social situations. She isn't sure whether people like her or not, and she feels anxious when she's around strangers.

GLORIA'S POISON PILLS WORKSHEET

Hot-Button Situation	Poison Pills	Private Experiences
My husband seems to be paying more attention to our kids than my kids.	Right vs. Wrong	This is a violation of what he promised me when we got married. I'm angry and withdraw from him. I won't tell him why I'm angry. I feel he's betrayed me again. If he loved me, he would follow through on his promise. He's a liar.
	Fair vs. Unfair	What did my kids do to deserve this? I need to protect them from his neglect because it will hurt them as adults. What did I do to deserve this? I treat him well and what I get in return is that he ignores my feelings.
	Responsibility and Blame	I should have known better than to trust him. Now my kids are going to be in another messy situation; they're going to be hurt again and it's my fault.
Having dinner with my own family, including my brother, last weekend	Good vs. Bad	I can't believe what a piece of crap he is; he just keeps conning my mom. I can't get myself to be jovial and converse; I just keep staring at him. He and I both know the truth about how awful he is.
	Fair vs. Unfair	My mom is just in love with him, and she doesn't have the time of day for me. I'm the one who was abused, and she doesn't care about making up for it. I feel sad and alone.
My husband comes on to me in our bedroom.	Good vs. Bad	I've tried to be good to him, but all he wants me for is sex; he doesn't really care about me. I don't respond to him, and he walks away. I think, "Good riddance."
	Fair vs. Unfair	I shouldn't have to deal with his advances since he has never paid attention to what I want and need.

Review. Clearly, Gloria is heavily fused with her reactive, evaluative mind and is buying a lot of her negative, provocative thoughts. Some of her evaluations originate in her implicit worldview and, as such, probably obscure her ability to accurately assess her present situation. (For example, "I treat him well and what I get in return is that he ignores my feelings" is a violation of the view, "When you're kind and giving to others, they'll treat you the same way in return.") It is as if she has a set of glasses on her nose called "Can I trust you? Are you going to understand and believe me?" Her reactive mind is so busy recasting interactions in terms of this issue that it would be very difficult for her to approach her husband, mother, or brother with any type of compassion or understanding.

When we asked Gloria whether it would be possible for her to hold these thoughts lightly, she became distressed and asked, "Are trying to tell me I wasn't sexually abused? Are you saying that any person who went through what I did wouldn't be looking for someone they could trust?" These are actually two *very* different questions, which we will now turn our attention to.

DESCRIPTION VS. EVALUATION

What is so tricky about the reactive mind is that it will weave together descriptions of events or situations and evaluations of the same events or situations. A description is an objective, factual statement about the qualities of some thing or situation based on information received by your primary senses (sight, sound, smell, taste, and feel). If you look at a vase full of flowers, you can describe what the vase looks like (its shape, texture, color, height, and so on) and what the flowers look like (size, shape, and color of the flowers; whether the stems are smooth or thorny; and so on). If we ask ten people to write a description of that vase full of flowers, we would probably see a lot of consistency in the primary attributes. The aspects of situations, objects, or events that are perceptible to the senses are primary properties. They are an integral part of the event, object, or situation being described.

Evaluations contain qualities that the individual injects into a description. An evaluation takes a clear crystal vase with yellow long-stemmed roses and transforms it into an elegant vase of beautiful yellow flowers that have been expertly arranged. If we ask the same ten people to write their impressions of this vase full of flowers, their responses would vary much more widely. Some might even report that they find it to be objectionable; perhaps they don't like hybrid flowers, or perhaps they view cut flowers as frivolous. When we unleash the evaluative, reactive mind on even a simple object, the results become far more subjective.

Now we can return to Gloria's two questions. Yes, it is true that she was sexually abused, and she could concretely describe each episode of abuse in terms of primary attributes: the setting, the events that transpired, and so on. However, we run into a problem with her second question, which implied that a person subjected to this type of event must evaluate it in terms of trust and must focus on trust issues from that point on. Granted, this type of childhood experience is not to be taken lightly. However, evaluations such as "This means I can't trust anyone" and "No one ever believes me or understands me" need not be inevitably linked to the primary properties of the event. They are added in by Gloria; these are evaluations she developed at the time and that she continues to apply to most situations in her life, no matter how unrelated.

Here's the rub: It's impossible not to have evaluations of objects, events, interactions, and so forth; that's what the reactive mind does for a living. The problem is, we often begin to fuse with our evaluations as if they were actually descriptions. Once an evaluation is taken as a description, you can no longer discriminate between what naturally exists in the situation and what you're injecting into it. It is woven together so tightly that it's nearly impossible to separate description from evaluation. And when the evaluations involve right versus wrong, good versus bad, fair versus unfair, or assignment of responsibility and blame, you're dealing with poison pills that can have extremely damaging side effects, as they've had for Gloria. At some point, she is actually generating mistrust in her relationships because her evaluations are so tightly interwoven with her descriptions.

EXERCISE: OBSERVE YOUR EVALUATIONS

This exercise will help you practice making the distinction between describing things and evaluating things. In this exercise you'll study an object, a person, and an event. For each, we ask that you observe your reactive mind as it gets busy phishing, simply notice that it's doing that, and then say (aloud), "Thank you, mind, for giving me the evaluation that _____." While this is similar to the exercise "Thank Your Mind," in chapter 8, it has a twist in that you insert the word "evaluation" when you thank your mind. This exercise also gives you an opportunity to see similarities and differences among your reactive mind's responses to objects, people, and events. You can use blank paper to do this exercise.

1. Select an object that you want to focus your concentration on for few minutes: a teacup, a piece of furniture, a picture, a flower arrangement, whatever. Look around you and choose something specific, then zero in your concentration on this object for a few minutes, focusing only on describing, not evaluating, the object. On a blank sheet of paper, write out your description of the object. Next, write down any evaluations that may have crept in. Finally, thank your mind for each of these evaluations.

2. Next, do the same for a person. In this case, the evaluations that creep in may involve the person's state of mind, what you think the person thinks of you, or what you think is good or bad about that person. After you've written your description and then written about the evaluations that crept in, thank your mind for each of those evaluations.

3. Finally, do the same for a difficult event in your life. It could be from your childhood, teenage, or adult years. Choose something that's been a problem for you in terms of the emotional reactions it triggers. Focus your mind's eye on this event for several minutes until you're sure you have the image in

full detail, then write your description of the actual event. Finally, note any evaluations that crept in. These may include how it affects you now, how it has changed your life, or evaluations of right and wrong or good and bad, such as "disgusting" or "traumatic." Once again, thank your mind for these evaluations.

Debriefing. What did you notice as you proceeded through this exercise? Often, the reactive mind tends to insert more evaluations as the emotional stakes become higher. Looking at a cup is a very different experience from thinking about a painful personal memory. You might have noticed that you remembered your painful life event *primarily* in terms of evaluations. For some people, the evaluations are so built-in that it's actually hard to get back to the original event and describe it in factual, objective terms.

NOTICE YOUR EVALUATIONS AND CHOOSE WHAT YOU CARE ABOUT

We aren't proposing that evaluation in and of itself is a dangerous activity (though we often suspect that it is). The danger lies in forgetting that there is an "I"—a self who is receiving these evaluations from the mind. When you fuse with evaluations as though they were reality, this puts you in a rigid position, with less flexibility to respond to events as they actually are rather than as you evaluate them to be. When you're able to separate your self from your evaluations, you'll have a powerful response available: caring. We normally think of caring as an action directed toward another person, such as caring about your parents or your children. However, caring can also be viewed as investing yourself in something or someone—including yourself. In caring, your values are in play and you try to align your actions with your values. Caring is a powerful and vital stance in any setting.

Caring also applies to private events, such as negative thoughts, painful feelings, distressing memories, or alarming physical sensations. You can choose to care about these events—to invest yourself in them—in which case you are likely to struggle with them and suffer. Another strategy is to let those events be there while you choose what you want to care about in the situation at hand. Here's an example: Let's say your mind gives you an evaluation like "If you go to dinner with your friends, they'll notice that you're depressed and they'll think you're a weakling." You could choose to care about this thought—so much so that you don't go. You can also choose to make room for that thought and act in a way that's consistent with your values about friendship. You could say to yourself, "I know this thought may plague me tonight, and I could spend the night caring about whether that thought is there. What I really care about, though, is being with my friends, so I'll go to dinner anyway." This form of caring means you'll be taking the negative evaluation "your friends will think you're a weakling" along with you to dinner. You need not invest yourself in this thought or try to control whether it shows up while you're at dinner. And ultimately, it comes down to acceptance anyway; what your friends really think of you is something you can't control. What matters most is choosing to act in a way that shows what you really care about in terms of your values.

EXERCISE: WHAT DO YOU CARE ABOUT?

To complete this exercise, you need to get out the 3 by 5 index cards you created in chapter 8, with the nicknames of your phishing lures. This exercise is a little tricky, but we think you'll get the gist of it as you read on. Here's how it goes:

1. Take one index card and consider the phishing lure represented by that nickname. Then, take your time and imagine a meaningful life situation that could trigger that phishing lure.

2. Read the card again and imagine that your mind is giving this private message to you in that life situation.

3. Turn the index card over and write down what you want to care about in the imagined situation. In other words, if you were to choose to act in accordance with your personal values, what would you do, even while being in the presence of the negative thought, feeling, memory, or sensation represented by that phishing lure? Don't argue or struggle with the content of the lure, and don't try to squash it or imagine it isn't there.

4. Go through this process with each of your phishing lures.

Debriefing. When you've completed this exercise for all of your lures, look through your index cards, front and back, and for each, ask yourself this question: "Is there any reason I can't have the distressing thoughts, feelings, memories, or sensations that make up this lure and at the same time engage in the action described on the back side?" When you're buying your thoughts, it may seem that the lure on the front side of the card prohibits you from engaging in the valued action listed on the flip side, but is that really so?

This is the hook that evaluations set into you. If you evaluate the lure as true, then you're likely to believe you shouldn't or can't engage in the valued action. You may even withdraw from the situation altogether. Although it may feel as though you're protecting yourself from emotional injury, it is actually the avoidance of action that's inflicting emotional damage. Why? Because when you undermine valued actions, you're undermining what you believe in.

■ *Gloria's Journey Toward a Vital Life*

For Gloria, fusion with her reactive mind's rules about protecting herself and being on the lookout for betrayal was actually creating the very relationship results that she feared the most. Unable to see situations or interactions for what they actually were, she always assumed her interwoven evaluations of betrayal, rejection, and deception were true. As she learned to take a step back and separate herself from her evaluations, she understood that she played a role in these situations and had a choice to make. What did she want to care about? Proving that her negative predictions about people being untrustworthy and deceptive were true? Or moving toward her values about intimacy and personal relationships in her life?

When she worked on her values, Gloria was very clear about what she wanted in the realm of relationships. She wanted to have an intimate and mutually respectful relationship with her life partner, and she wanted to have a loving, safe, and respectful family setting. Yet all the while, she had chosen to care about having her negative predictions prove true. Finally seeing the disconnection between her values and how she'd chosen to act was an "aha" moment for Gloria. She realized she wanted to start interacting with her husband and children with a posture of acceptance. They were who they were.

Rather than continue to buy the evaluation that her husband was playing favorites, Gloria decided to approach her husband directly and ask him about the issue. He responded with surprise, saying that he loved all of his children and considered her children to be his children. She then asked him if he'd be willing to legally adopt them, and he said yes. He said that the toughest part of being a father to Gloria's children was his sense that nothing he did was good enough for her, and that she tended to get overprotective and aggressive when he tried to parent her children.

Gloria became defensive when she heard this and had an evaluation that she couldn't get close to her husband because he would turn out to be a fake, use her for sex, and then reject her. Instead of buying this evaluation, she simply let it be there as a thought. She also noticed feeling afraid at the same time and simply let that feeling be there too. Along with the fear came an image of being held down by her brother while he molested her. Gloria allowed herself to hold that memory, even though it was really tough. After a while, she noticed that this image of her past was entirely irrelevant to the current interaction.

Gloria and her husband went to dinner that night and later slept in the same bed together for the first time in months. Gloria didn't want to rush into physical intimacy, and her husband seemed okay with that. He just held her through the night, and she felt close to him for the first time in years. Gloria was on the path toward a vital, purposeful life!

THE ULTIMATE RIGHT-AND-WRONG TRAP: SUICIDE AND SELF-DESTRUCTIVE ACTIONS

We have yet to address a very sensitive issue that is often associated with depression: dealing with the risk of suicide and other self-destructive actions, such as cutting, overdosing repeatedly, or abusing alcohol or drugs. Stories about suicide in depressed people usually focus on the tragic nature of the situation but do little to educate us about the real causes of self-destructive actions. As far as we know, humans are the only species in which individuals deliberately terminate their own existence. How is it that a person can become so fed up with daily existence that nonexistence seems like a more attractive option?

In our view, suicidal thoughts and behavior are less a symptom of depression than a response to depression. There are probably two primary factors that fuel the thought that death is preferable to living. They're related to avoidance and fusion, those siren songs that can lead you into depression, and just as in Greek mythology, they can also lure you to your destruction. The first primary cause is the presence of intense emotional pain that is evaluated as intolerable, unending, and inescapable. This type of pain usually falls into the excessive suffering category and is probably due to not taking a stance of willingness and acceptance with respect to a situation that's producing intensely unpleasant feelings. As attempts to suppress, control, or avoid negative feelings feed into the downward spiral of depression, the person begins to feel out of control emotionally. Suicide may be seen as the only way out, but in the end, it's clearly the ultimate form of avoidance.

A second cause is when the person gets fused with poison pill evaluations about hot-button situations, particularly fair-unfair evaluations. Evaluations that seem to trigger suicidal actions often involve a profound feeling of being cheated in life or being wronged by another person who deserves to be punished for those transgressions. Perhaps the ultimate siren song is fusion with a vision of being dead as a peaceful state, free from all suffering. The truth of the matter is, we simply don't know what being dead feels like. The idea that being dead is peaceful is another example of the reactive mind giving us advice on something it knows absolutely nothing about.

If you've contemplated suicide, or even tried to do it, we want you to look at the process that brought you to that point and ask yourself, "If I took a posture of willingness and acceptance into the situation that has triggered my suicidal feelings, what would happen to my sense of suffering? Would I still experience excessive suffering if I were willing to stand still and accept my original suffering? Am I inserting toxic evaluations into the situation that make it impossible for me to separate the original facts from my evaluations of those facts? Am I fusing with an image of death as a peaceful state, even though I have no practical experience with what it's like to be dead?" We can guarantee you this: If you spend the time required to seriously contemplate these questions, you're very likely to see that there's another way out of this bind. There's an old saying that makes this point better than we can: Suicide is a permanent solution to a temporary problem.

Secrets to ACT On

☞ The root of excessive suffering, including depression, is often attachment to evaluations about self and others in the past, present, and future.

☞ Your reactive mind's implicit worldview clouds your ability to see the world as it actually is; instead you see the world in terms of arbitrary rules and expectations.

☞ Your reactive mind weaves evaluations into the fabric of everything you experience—things, people, and events—making those evaluations seem like indisputable truths.

☞ You can choose what you want to care about: your evaluations or your valued actions.

☞ You can welcome your evaluations, see them for what they are, and act in ways that build a life worth living!

The Coach Says

The mind is *not* a terrible thing to waste when it comes to its evaluations of you and others. The mind's evaluations are often inaccurate and self-defeating. Once you understand how to short-circuit your reactive mind, you'll be able to focus on what you really care about in life: living out your values in a way that gives you vitality, purpose, and meaning.

Sneak Preview

In the next chapter, we'll introduce you to another dangerous form of evaluation: the reasons you give for your behavior. We'll show you how reason giving creates the very life results you want to avoid. We'll also help you understand the importance of being very skeptical about the accuracy of the reasons you use to explain your actions, both to yourself and to others.

CHAPTER 10

Step 5: Learn That Sense Making Doesn't Make Sense

Like a thief, reason sneaked in and sat amongst the lovers eager to give them advice.
They were unwilling to listen, so reason kissed their feet and went on its way.
—Rumi

In the previous chapter, we showed you the problems associated with the reactive mind's ability to inject hidden evaluations of events, situations, and interactions, making them seem like indisputable truths about how life works. These rules set you up for suffering when situations, interactions, or life events don't turn out as you had hoped. We described four poison pills that constitute the most dangerous forms of hidden evaluations: right versus wrong, good versus bad, fair versus unfair, and assigning responsibility and blame. When you buy your evaluations, you may act in ways that increase your depression and diminish your sense of vitality. The antidote to these poison pills and other hidden evaluations is to let your wise mind be your guide. When you notice you're being sucked into depression compression, you can create space for your wise mind to express itself by simply observing your evaluations and assumptions for what they are—mental events, not reality.

In this chapter, we'll explore how to recognize and overcome another potentially dangerous feature of reactive mind. This involves learning to have a healthy mistrust of explanations you have about why you behave the way you do. On the simplest level, we develop explanations for specific things we do or don't do on a daily basis: "why I didn't go to church last week," "why I yelled at my kids today," "why I'm not going to work today," and so on. This ongoing process of self-evaluation is of tremendous importance in determining the quality of your life, in both positive and negative ways. Without the ability to explain events, situations, and interactions, we would be hard pressed to function at all. This is an essential mental tool that helps us solve all kinds of problems of living. However, when this powerful analytic process is turned inward, it can pose a real danger.

For most depressed people, even simple explanations of behavior can take a negative twist: "I didn't go to church because there's nothing in my life worth praying for," "I yelled at my kids because I'm a bad parent," "I didn't go to work because I'd just screw up again if I did." This can dramatically affect your self-confidence and willingness to engage in vitality-producing behaviors, particularly in negatively charged situations. The problem is, the processes of reasoning and explanation occur in your reactive mind, and you, the human, interact with the reasons it generates on a daily basis. This means you have to learn when it is useful to create reasons and explanations and when it is not.

In this chapter, we'll help you see that your reactive mind's explanations for certain kinds of events, situations, or interactions not only are inaccurate but also can actually lead you down the wrong path in your quest for a vital life. Looking directly at how your mind explains things about you and your world is about as up close and personal as you can get with your reactive mind. Your reactive mind is going to be plenty upset as you read on, because explaining events is a huge part of its job description and it's very attached to this role. Consequently, you can expect to hear a lot of chatter and back talk as we systematically dismantle the illusions it creates to explain why you behave the way you do. This back talk may take the form of inviting you to not believe anything we're presenting to you. You may have thoughts that your situation is different and that you do know why you do what you do. You may experience anger at us for having the audacity to suggest that your life narrative is fraught with memory errors, selective filtering of events, and questionable assumptions about cause and effect. Like Gloria, you might even have the thought that we're denying you had specific life events that were hard on you. If you notice any of this going on, thank your mind for giving you these evaluations of what you're reading and continue on as best you can. Remember, our goal is to help you live life with greater freedom from the depression-promoting maneuvers of your word machine.

SENSE MAKING

Sense making involves explaining why you do what you do, why others do what they do, and why life events unfold as they do. On a daily basis, sense making takes the form of explaining your immediate actions and interpreting the actions of others. In ACT, we call this ongoing daily process of analysis "reason giving." Because reasons originate within your language system, and because of the way language and the reactive mind work together to link things in conceptually similar groups, reasons start to take on themes that can span weeks, months, or years. Think of this as your ongoing life narrative, which is basically your explanation of who you are and how you got to be that way. In ACT, we call this your "story line." This form of reason giving is so powerful that we've devoted the next chapter entirely to this topic. In this chapter, we want to focus on the basic process of reason giving as you try to understand why you do what you do and why others do what they do. It turns out that the inner world of depressed people is filled with this type of sense-making activity. For example, when you try to analyze why you're depressed and why you can't seem to enjoy life like other people do, you're trying to make sense of your situation.

The problem is that, for certain types of life problems, sense making creates the impression that there's one specific answer ("I'm depressed because my job sucks"), when in reality there might be many other explanations that are just as plausible ("I'm depressed because I've stopped exercising," "I'm living on junk food," "I'm not dealing with my problems with my daughter," and so on). In most life situations that involve personal pain, sense making is dangerous because it can lead you down the wrong alley. Certain types of reasons you may come up with, such as citing past events to explain your depression ("I'm depressed because my father constantly criticized me"), leave you with no way out. Since you can't undo your personal history, this type of explanation leaves you with very few avenues for overcoming your depression.

REASON GIVING

As mentioned, reason giving involves trying to establish a cause-and-effect relationship between two potentially linked factors. For example, suppose a man promised his wife that he'd pick her up after work and drive her home. For some reason, he forgets that he made this agreement and doesn't show up. She's pretty peeved about this and asks him why he didn't show up. She's asking him to generate a specific kind of cause-and-effect relationship: what happened that caused him to not show up. You are trained from an early age to produce a socially acceptable response ("I didn't show up because I left my calendar at home and didn't remember I was supposed to pick you up") and to avoid using reasons that are violations of social norms ("I forgot" or "I thought about coming to pick you up, but I decided not to").

Think of reason giving as a vehicle for both explaining and justifying your actions (and those of others) to yourself and to others. Reason giving always originates in your reactive mind. However, as we say in ACT, "Just because you think it doesn't mean it's real." Although your reactive mind is able to generate explanations for events and interactions in your life, that doesn't mean your explanations are necessarily accurate! To understand why this is the case, let's take a look at how reasons emerge from the reactive mind, how they function in the social world, and why there is every reason to be suspicious of the reasons your mind gives you.

The Illusion of Cause and Effect

Defining cause-and-effect relations is a basic property of human thinking—one that gives us a tremendous advantage as a species. For example, imagine that it's a bright and sunny summer day outside and you spend several hours sitting in the sun. You get badly sunburned and immediately learn that being in the sun causes you to get burned, which is very painful. To prevent this cause-and-effect relationship from playing out again, you develop a cause-and-effect rule that tells you to cover up or use sunblock the next time you'll be in the sun for a long time. If you don't follow this rule, you'll get sunburned again. This is an example of developing a *track*, a mental rule that maps correctly onto a physical relationship between you and the external world. Tracks are very helpful in organizing your behavior in the physical world.

There are also times when what appears to be an obvious cause-and-effect relationship is, in fact, an illusion. One good example is sunrise and sunset. To the mind, it looks as if sunrise is caused by the sun's moving up and emerging above the eastern horizon and as if sunset is caused by the sun's descending below the western horizon. For centuries, people assumed this to be true and believed that the sun (as well as the moon and stars) orbited around the earth. This is, of course, an illusion. In reality, the apparent motion of celestial objects is caused by the earth's rotating on its axis. And on a cosmic scale, the entire solar system is moving through space at an unimaginable speed. However, we directly perceive none of this, because our frame of reference is limited.

There are many illusory relationships in the world between the ears—a world full of symbolic activity that's constantly ebbing and flowing. As the human brain has evolved, it has expanded its ability to expand tracks to areas of living where tracking doesn't work very well. For example, if you go to a party and become extremely anxious to the point of choosing to leave early, you might develop a track along these lines: "The party caused me to be anxious; therefore, to prevent being anxious again, I need to avoid going to all parties." Superficially, it resembles the cause and effect involved in being in the sun and getting a sunburn. However, while we can confidently say that ultraviolet rays from the sun hitting unprotected skin is what causes sunburn, we can't as confidently presume that being at the party is what caused the anxiety.

There could be a multitude of other causal factors at work to produce the anxiety. Some could be fairly straightforward, such as lack of sleep, too much coffee, or seeing an accident on your way to the party. Others might be more complex. Maybe you were afraid you might run into your ex, or maybe this was the first office party you attended at a new job and you were desperate to make a good impression. Though a list of possible factors could become quite lengthy, notice that the track (going to a party leads to anxiety) implies that there's one main causal agent. This presents a very serious problem: When the reactive mind is bent on finding a simple reason for a complicated situation, the odds of that explanation being accurate or exhaustive are pretty slim.

Reasons Maintain Social Control

In ACT, we believe that reason giving is a basic social skill that's necessary for social order. Being able to justify your behavior is a fundamental part of your role as a social animal. For example, if one kid hits another kid in a kindergarten class, the teacher will ask, "Why did you hit Johnny?" If the kid can give a socially approved reason for why he did what he did, such as "I hit Johnny because he took my crayons," he will get a much better response from the teacher than if he said something like "I hit Johnny because he's short and I like hitting him in the face." This social training in reason giving begins early and continues throughout life. Suppose you miss a day of work and your boss asks you why you didn't come in. You aren't likely to say "Because I didn't feel like it," even if that's the truth. You know you need to say something like "I was ill" or "My child was very sick with a temperature of 102 degrees."

Reasons Are Easily Programmed

As you've learned, the reactive mind is capable of generating reasons for almost anything it comes across. As one ridiculous example, the sentence "The brown grocery bag caused me to drive off the road" could function as a reason why a person ran into a tree. The minute you read that explanation, your reactive mind begins to generate various ways that a brown grocery bag could cause a person to drive off the road. Maybe your windows were down, the bag caught the air, and it landed on the dashboard, blocking your view. Notice that as you read that explanation, your reactive mind created an image of the scenario that might actually seem credible. If we asked you to come up with three more scenarios explaining how a brown bag could cause a person to drive off the road, you could do that.

Your reactive mind is programmed to respond to all cause-and-effect relations as if they were plausible. This is because the external world is full of cause-and-effect relations, and to operate in that environment, you need to have a mind that is constantly attending to those relationships. There are often good ways to test cause-and-effect reasoning in the physical world. If you don't believe that sunblock prevents sunburn, go outside without any sun block on and test the idea. However, there's no good way to test this same kind of thinking when it's applied to the world between your ears.

Let's go back to the example of the kid who hit Johnny. His explanation basically boils down to "Johnny took my crayons, and this caused me to hit him on the head." When you really look at this, you can see that this is an absurd explanation. "Johnny took my crayons" didn't actually, physically *cause* him to raise his hand and hit him, right? There might have been any number of other forces at work. He may have been tired and irritable. He might have been hungry. He might have just shared a toy with another kid, who refused to give it back. Dozens of things could have contributed to this simple act. But the kid has learned, at some level, that a socially approved answer works best. As children, we quickly learn that giving an accurate account of our behavior isn't nearly as important as coming up with a socially approved reason. The fact that your mind has been socially programmed to provide less-than-accurate reasons to others raises the very real possibility that it's doing the same thing to you, in the world between your ears.

The Myth of Emotions as Reasons

Now let's complicate the situation. If you're that kid in trouble, to really get the teacher off your back you have to add a mental state that acts as the middle man between Johnny taking your crayons and you hitting Johnny. This mental state is anger. Once the teacher understands that you were angry about having your crayons taken, it doesn't make hitting a permissible response, but it does provide your teacher with an explanation for why you did what you did. But check this out: Did anger really make the kid hit Johnny over the head, or does it boil down to a choice? Describing an event (like having your crayons stolen) or a state of mind (anger) is not the same as explaining what caused the behavior (hitting Johnny). Although he may have experienced anger when Johnny took his crayons, there isn't a cause-and-effect relationship between those events and choosing to hit Johnny. A variety of responses were possible in that situation.

EXERCISE: LOOK AT YOUR REASONS

As the example above suggests, cause-and-effect explanations are often used to justify doing things that aren't socially acceptable. Since depression often involves withdrawing from or avoiding socially expected actions, it's likely that you've frequently found yourself in a position where you needed to justify why you did or didn't do something that was expected of you. As you read through the following statements that depressed people often use to explain their behavior, consider whether you've ever used any similar statements to explain your actions (or lack of action):

- I was too tired to go walking.

- I didn't go to work because I was so depressed.

- I can't deal with my kids because I'm too depressed.

- I have no motivation at all, so I just sit around.

- I would eat better if my mood weren't so bad all the time.

- I can't stop smoking because my mood just goes in the toilet.

- I don't date because I'm still trying to get over my divorce.

- I drink alcohol because I'm depressed.

- I won't argue with my partner because I just get more depressed.

- I didn't get together with my friends because I felt so lousy.

- I didn't go to church because people there don't understand what it's like to be depressed.

Review. Do any of these statements ring a bell for you? If you're like most depressed people, you probably recognized several statements similar to those you've used to explain your depressed behavior. Don't beat yourself up about this! Just notice that there's a common way that we are trained to explain our actions. Let's deconstruct what's carried in these sentences: First, there's a negative behavior, such as avoiding friends, not dating, drinking too much, or overeating, that has to be explained. Next, you must provide a reason for the behavior. This reason is portrayed as the cause for why you did or didn't do something; in this case, the reason is your depression. What these sorts of statements say is that your depression literally causes your behavior and actions.

THE CART AND THE HORSE

If you flip the reason-giving sequence we just reviewed on its head, you run into a very basic problem that plagues most depressed people when they attempt to do something about their situation. In the early years of ACT, we were struck by the tendency of depressed people to explain nearly everything going on in their lives in terms of depression. It was as if a little man or woman named Depression were stationed at the master control panel of the person's life and was pushing all the wrong buttons. As we continued to investigate the process of reason giving and how it fuels depression, we began to wonder whether depression was causing the action (or lack of action)—or whether the action (or lack of it) was causing depression.

Remember Jose, the disabled firefighter from the previous chapter? When he completed this exercise, he discovered a rather complex way that he used reason giving to explain his quandary: "I've stopped playing with my kids because my knee injury prevents me from running with them like I used to. Since I can't play with them the way I did before, they would just be disappointed in me if I tried to play. Then I'd feel like even a bigger failure." In essence, Jose's reason suggests that his choice not to play with his kids is literally caused by the thought that he would be a failure if they were disappointed in his physical abilities.

If you look at Jose's situation, you can see the trap of reason giving in stark relief. Jose is waiting for something miraculous to happen to his knee so that he can return to being the person he once was. He cites the injury as the cause of his depression and in turn blames his depression for his angry, sullen, and withdrawn behavior at home. His withdrawal from family life is based on a reason that says he'll just be a disappointment to his wife and children since he isn't the same as he was before. However, his lack of participation means that he's falling down on the job of being a husband and father, even though this is the very arena that's most important to him. Jose is trapped in a complex sequence of reason giving that tricks him into not acting in accordance with his values.

Most of us are familiar with the old saying, "Don't put the cart before the horse." This reminds us that workable strategies rely on being clear about cause and effect. If you try to use a cart to pull a horse, you won't get very far. When it comes to explaining depressed behavior, this is not a trivial issue. If you view your depression as the cause of action or inaction, then the path to recovery would look like this: First you must eliminate your depression; then, and only then, can you act effectively. If, on the other hand, action or lack of it produces depression, then the path out of depression would look like this: First you engage in effective action; then you see a reduction in depression.

It turns out that most people believe depression causes ineffective action, so the elimination of depression seems to be the obvious solution. To help dispel this widely believed myth, let's turn to what three decades of psychological research on depression has taught us. As it turns out, the scientific understanding of depression is exactly the opposite of this commonly held belief about depression. In fact, it is an ever-expanding pattern of behavioral avoidance that causes depression. Another way of saying this is that depression is the result, not the cause, of acting or living in ways that don't reflect your values. This suggests a totally different way to move through depression: approaching difficult situations and engaging in meaningful activities that support your values, even in the midst of depression.

Unfortunately, people who follow the culturally supported view of how depression develops will actually experience an increase, not a decrease, in depression. In ACT, we call this the "unworkable change agenda." If you wait for your depression to lift and make that a condition for being able to behave in more effective ways, you'll continue to avoid engaging in positive behaviors and remain stuck in depression compression. In Jose's situation, the more he waits for his "old self" to return, the less of his "old self" he becomes. The way out of this trap is for him to choose to engage in valued actions with his wife and children, even if he must do things differently than he used to or do different things altogether. This will give him a chance to reclaim his sense of vitality.

WHAT'S NOT TO LIKE ABOUT REASONS?

As we've seen, the culture of reason giving leads to the tendency to justify behavior rather than accurately explain it. Consider the statement "I didn't go to church because I felt really depressed." In reality, depressed people go to church all the time, so depression isn't the cause of not going to church. It would be more accurate to say "I chose not to go to church, and at the time I was experiencing the feeling called depression." It's not that you're purposely trying to deceive yourself this way. You're trying to live your life and fit into your culture. This is the way you've been trained to respond when things aren't going well and other people want to know how you're doing. The problem is, this type of sense-making is so frequently used that we often begin to buy, rather than hold, our reasons.

Most Causes Are Outside of Awareness

For over three decades, it has been an accepted fact in psychology that humans often are unaware of and unable to describe the causes of their behavior. This fact has been demonstrated over and over again in various laboratory experiments on human thinking (Nisbett and Wilson 1977). Not only do we lack conscious access to important causes, we also often inaccurately describe causes. Think back on the priming experiment with college students described in chapter 5 (Bargh, Chen, and Burrows 1996). Not one single student in that study cited exposure to disguised stimulus words in the fake memory task as the cause of his or her response. They all were completely unaware of how their behavior had been manipulated. The bottom line is that you should be very skeptical of the reasons you give for your behavior, especially important behaviors. Like all humans, you don't have access to the full spectrum of possible causes. This, of course, will not deter your reactive mind from phishing you with simple cause-and-effect explanations; that's all it is able to do. When these explanations take on a negative, self-denigrating tone, allow your wise mind to remind you that these explanations are basically socially conditioned responses rather than scientific truths.

Preconscious Bias

Remember the Racial Implicit Association Test described in chapter 5? There is now a similar line of study looking at implicit self-esteem (Franck, de Raedt, and de Houwer 2007). As the term suggests, implicit self-esteem involves the preconscious priming of negative or positive estimations of self-worth. Think of implicit self-esteem as a knee-jerk reaction you experience about your self-worth or lack of it. It immediately sets the tone for your conscious thinking even though you aren't aware that this has occurred. As with those college students, when you're primed to evaluate yourself negatively, you won't be able to see the tinted glasses you're wearing.

A focus of research on implicit self-esteem has been to examine differences between depressed and nondepressed people. What research shows is that depressed people perform far faster on tasks where they're required to sort through negative self-descriptive adjectives, such as useless, ugly, and worthless, than when they're asked to sort through positive self-descriptive adjectives, such as lovable, kind, and attractive. The bottom line is that when you're depressed, you're programmed to attend much more readily to negative information about yourself. You're also equipped with a filter that makes it harder for you to accept positive information. Not surprisingly, that filter is located in your reactive mind.

The Depressive Skew

A well-researched model of depression, *attribution theory* holds that biased reason giving is a principle factor in maintaining depression (Alloy et al. 2006). An *attribution* is basically the reason given for some type of situation, event, or interaction. One type of attribution is *internal*, which involves citing a personal action or quality as the cause for a particular event. Think of internal attribution as you taking responsibility for an event or outcome. A second type of attribution is *external*, which means the event is described as being caused by external factors, such as the actions of others or simply the luck of the draw. Think of an external attribution as you explaining the event or outcome as being caused by the actions of others.

Now, all life events exist on a continuum ranging from extremely positive to extremely negative occurrences. As humans, we automatically generate reasons for all events on this continuum because that's how we make sense of the world; however, the reasons we generate are often biased. Just as a biased judge has already come to a conclusion about the defendant's guilt before any evidence is heard, a negative bias in reason giving means there's a tendency to assign negative reasons regardless of the facts. Any information to the contrary is either ignored or downplayed.

The research on reason giving with depressed people consistently shows that they tend to assume responsibility for negative events or outcomes while discounting their role in creating positive events or outcomes. In ACT, we call this the "depressive skew." In effect, you unknowingly turn the power of reason giving on yourself. Just to give you a sense of how this operates in daily life, here are a few typical life events, along with interpretations from both the unbiased point of view and the depressive skew.

Situation	Unbiased Perspective	Depressive Skew
Received a promotion at work during a job evaluation	I'm a hard worker and do what I do very well; they recognize that and value it.	If they only knew how many mistakes I make on the job, they would never promote me. They must not have any other people willing to do the job.
Your partner asks you to go to dinner and then watch a foreign film together	My partner wants to spend time with me because I'm fun to be with and I really know film.	She's just being nice to me, probably because her friend didn't want to go to the film.
A person you're interested in getting to know better declines to have coffee with you	He's very busy and probably doesn't have much free time right now. I'll ask again in a month.	What's wrong with me that people don't want to spend time with me? They must be able to see that I'm a loser.

As you can see, the depressive skew can operate in your reactive mind even when something positive happens. Your reactive mind will phish you with the thought that this positive event is a fluke or accident and that you had nothing to do with the outcome. And when a negative event rolls around, your reactive mind will encourage you to consider it as the ultimate proof of how unattractive, worthless, or flawed you are. When you notice this cycle going on, thank your mind for these lovely thoughts, create some space for your wise mind to express itself, and keep moving forward in your life.

EXERCISE: PLAY WITH REASONS

Now that you understand the many drawbacks of reason giving, we want you to do an exercise in which you can practice shifting from the reactive mind perspective to the wise mind perspective. Remember that, for the most part, reasons aren't accurate explanations of events, but rather are just mental products of reactive mind. This means that none of what you write in this exercise is actually true, scientifically speaking; it won't be an accurate cause-and-effect analysis that includes all possible factors. However, you will learn something about the workability of different types of reasons. Since all reasons are arbitrarily constructed, those that produce unworkable outcomes in your life are poor reasons. Conversely, those that produce positive results are sound reasons!

This exercise gives you the chance to entertain the possibility that you're falling prey to the depressive skew of your reactive mind during important moments in your life. The first step is to choose four life situations that are bothering you right now—anything you've done that needs a reason, such as missing work, avoiding intimacy, avoiding a social opportunity, or damaging your health by eating, drinking, or smoking too much. Briefly describe each situation in the left-hand column. If you're at a loss to identify specific situations, go back to chapter 3 and review your responses to the exercise "Inventory of Health, Relationship, Work, and Play Behaviors." Once you've chosen four problematic situations, write them in the first column in the worksheet.

Now, for each in turn, in the right-hand column describe your current set of reasons for why this problem is happening and why you're behaving as you are. Then go to the middle column and describe the situation from an unbiased, wise mind perspective. We like to refer to this as looking at it with "soft eyes." Seeing the problem with soft eyes requires that you detach from your reasons and evaluations, see them for what they are (reasons and evaluations), and approach the situation with compassion and understanding, particularly for yourself. As you do this, notice any phishing lures that your reactive mind throws your way to draw you out of the unbiased, wise mind stance. If you bite on a lure, just notice that and then redirect your attention to letting your wise mind speak.

Play with Reasons Worksheet

Situation	Unbiased Perspective	Depressive Skew

Debriefing. What did you notice as you went through this exercise? Was it easier to come up with and write out the self-blaming reasons? If you noticed this happening, you were directly in touch with your reactive mind phishing you. It wants you to make sense of things in a particular way that may or may not be workable for you. How did you do with seeing the situation with compassion? Did you notice that you felt different when you went the self-blaming route versus the compassionate route? This is one way to assess the workability of the reasons you use to explain your behavior. If your reasons promote your sense of well-being, it isn't dangerous to buy them. If, on the other hand, they seem damaging, buyer beware!

■ *Jose's Journey Toward a Vital Life*

Jose realized that he was trapped in a vicious cycle in which his reasons were promoting his downward spiral into deeper depression, and that many of his reasons were based on rigid rules about how to live a healthy life. He saw that he needed to accept the fact that his knee was never going to be the same as it once was and that he could still function as a husband and father. His kids really liked going fishing with one of his brothers, so Jose decided to borrow some fishing gear from his brother and take his family to a local lake. They had a wonderful time, and Jose found that he enjoyed watching his kids run around even though he couldn't run with them.

Jose also finally agreed to talk with his wife about their financial situation, which both of them had been fretting over. His wife had been a legal secretary before she quit to become a full-time homemaker. She volunteered that since Jose was unable to pursue his former career, maybe she could return to her profession and he could be a "house dad." Jose was intrigued with the idea of being a father in an entirely new way, and they agreed to try it for a year. Jose was on the path to a vital, purposeful life!

BE AWARE—AND WARY—OF REASONS

We've warned you not to trust your reactive mind in certain circumstances. Most of these situations involve events or interactions that can have a negative effect on you. A depressive skew is perhaps one of the most damaging ways the reactive mind can phish you, resulting in a negative and distorted picture of everything: your actions and motivations, as well as the actions and motivations of others. When this bias is at play, the filtering device of your reactive mind is clearly dysfunctional, because everything negative is allowed in and everything positive is discounted. The only antidote for this problem is to detach from your explanations and see them for what they are (phishing lures), not what they appear to be (truth with a capital T).

The same strategy that works to contain the runaway train of evaluation will work when it comes to the depressive skew. Your reactive mind is designed to provide you with plausible cause-and-effect explanations, and it excels at doing so—just as with evaluations. Any time you stop to observe your mental processes, you'll see that you have this type of mental activity going on. However, you have a powerful move you can make in the presence of this process. You can hold your reasons and see them as mental products. You don't have to buy the reactive mind's reasons as being literally true just because your reactive mind gives them to you. As we said earlier, just because your mind thinks it doesn't mean it's real. Simply thank your mind for these reasons and allow your wise mind a chance to express itself.

Secrets to ACT On

☞ You don't have access to the full range of potential causes of your behavior; most of them are hidden inside your mental world.

☞ Reason giving functions to justify your actions or lack of action, but reasons are not the same as causes.

☞ Your depression does not cause you to do anything; you are in control of your actions, or lack of action, independent of your mood state.

☞ Creating space for your wise mind perspective to emerge can counterbalance the biased perspective of your reactive mind and allow you to choose to do what's workable for you.

☞ Don't forget: Just because you think it doesn't mean it's real!

The Coach Says

The bad news is that you can no longer view depression as a reason why you do or don't behave in a way that works for you. The good news is that your depression doesn't run you. You run you! When you learn to step away from your reasons and see them for what they are, you can let your wise mind take over. When you do, you'll step into the life of vitality, purpose, and meaning that's waiting for you.

Sneak Preview

In the next chapter, we'll introduce you to the crown jewel of your reactive mind: your story line. You'll learn that our life stories are often fraught with self-defeating biases and information errors, and learn some skills for neutralizing the destructive effects of your story line—now and in the future.

CHAPTER 11

Step 6: Hold Your Story Line Lightly

The real voyage of discovery consists not in seeking new landscapes but in having new eyes. —Marcel Proust

In the previous chapter, we introduced you to the many problems inherent in our attempts to make sense of our own behavior. We gave this sense-making operation of the reactive mind a name—reason giving—and explained that when reason giving is used to generate cause-and-effect relationships, they are usually inaccurate and illusory. A particularly destructive type of reason giving portrays mood states like depression as the cause of behavior or lack of behavior. This problem is compounded in depression due to the depressive skew, or negative bias, wherein the world is perceived and recalled with an emphasis on the negative. Once again, we propose a familiar antidote: Step back from the chatter of reactive mind and allow a wise mind perspective to emerge.

It's one thing to explain your behavior in a particular situation, such as why you didn't exercise today or why you yelled at your kids this morning, and quite another to do so in compiling a narrative of your life. However, this is precisely what the reactive mind is designed to do. Because of the power of language relations, certain kinds of reasons start to "hang out" together. These reasons collectively form one very basic way we know ourselves, often referred to as self-concept. In ACT, we call this your "story line."

The reactive mind has evolved over the eons to construct this type of self-identify, and it does this job very well. Because we have been socially trained to worship logic, analysis, and cause-and-effect reasoning, we can become very attached to the seeming logic of the story line the reactive mind offers. Unfortunately, when your story line portrays you in flawed and broken terms, you suffer from making contact with the story line—and worse, it functions as a self-fulfilling prophecy. If you think of your story line as accurate and set in concrete, you face a very real danger of fusing with it and making it "you." This allows your story line to intrude into and color your experience of the present and, worse yet, to subtly or not so subtly shape your future. In this chapter, we'll expose the story line for what it is: an inaccurate, biased, and selectively filtered narrative that's full of holes and inconsistencies. Fortunately, if you step back and see your story line as just that—a story—you'll be in a good position to act in ways that will promote the kind of life you want to live.

The warning we issued in the previous chapter also applies here. Your reactive mind is going to be plenty upset about this stuff. We are walking into its castle and taking its crown jewels, so be prepared for a lot of mental chatter as we show you that the emperor has no clothes.

YOUR STORY LINE: A PERFECT STORM OF SENSE MAKING

In a way, your story line is your personal history brought up into the present. Its social purpose is to allow you to explain yourself to others, and because it is so frequently used, it tends to be the dominant form of self-awareness. By dominant, we mean it exerts considerable control over your behavior in the present moment and, consequently, begins to shape your future. Your story line seems credible because you have repeated it to yourself and others so many times. And because of our culture of reason giving, discussed in the previous chapter, it's likely that others find your story line credible too, supporting your belief in its accuracy. This is the toxic aspect of your story line; as you begin to fuse with it, you begin to behave in the ways dictated by the story—and begin to get the very life results that your story says you'll get. We would go so far as to say that fusion with one's story line is a fundamental cause of human suffering and the depression compression that can result.

Fortunately, when you step back and look at how your story line originates and operates, you'll begin to see a lot of holes you hadn't noticed before. The story line is vulnerable to "truthiness mistakes"— mistakes we make in accepting something as fact based on its sounding right or having a ring of truth, rather than it being accurate. Stories that have that ring of truth usually come from mental processing of language rather than from direct experience. As you become more skillful in working with your mind, these stories will continue to show up, but they won't command your attention with the same urgency as when you were indiscriminately buying whatever thoughts your reactive mind offered. For example, the story "I'll always have problems with depression because my parents divorced when I was little, my father was an alcoholic and died when I was a teenager, and my first sexual experience was rape" is less compelling when seen as a part of personal history that is just that—history.

How Story Lines Work

One important property of stories is that they condense a vast array of information into a much smaller number of simple, powerful messages. An example is the New Testament, most of which was written two hundred to three hundred years after the events it describes. What is contained in the various testaments is a highly condensed version of what Jesus said and did, seen from different perspectives. A complete, second-by-second account of the life of Jesus would require a book several thousand times larger than the Bible, if it could be written at all. Some perspectives now known to exist, such as the gospel of Judas, were systematically excluded by high-ranking church officials, highlighting a second important feature of stories: that they exclude information that doesn't fit the story line.

Similarly, your story line is a condensed and simplified version of your life. It would be impossible for you to recall every consecutive moment of your life since you became conscious. That book would be at least a million pages long. So you have to selectively remember information about events, interactions, your emotions, your behaviors, and so on. In order to present a plausible account of who you are, where you are in life, how you got there, and where you're going, your story contains a combination of descriptive elements (objective facts about things that happened) and cause-and-effect elements (your explanation of how these events shaped you). Together, they provide you with a limited set of simple, powerful messages about who you are. When your story line suggests that you are defective or flawed in some basic way, the stage is set for you to enter situations expecting to fail, be rejected, or be disappointed. You may behave like someone who is expecting bad things to happen, and sure enough, bad things happen.

If you're beginning to get it in terms of the ACT approach, you're probably already asking yourself some important questions: "If I can't accurately describe the true causes of my behavior in the present moment, how can I explain cause-and-effect relationships for events that happened years ago?" "How can I recognize when my story line is operating?" "How do I know if my story line is accurate?" "How can my story line be accurate when so much information is left out of it?" In the remainder of this chapter, we'll try to help you answer these important questions and get you in touch with your story line so that you can see it for what it is.

THE PROBLEM WITH MEMORIES

Memory is the core ingredient of your story line. If you didn't have a memory, you couldn't have a story line. Memory has been studied extensively for years, and we actually know a great deal about how it works and about the effects depression has on memory. Let's take a look at what some of that research has revealed.

Rumination and Memory Suppression

One very interesting line of study has looked at the impact rumination has on memory in depressed people. In depression, rumination is the tendency to focus your attention on your depression symptoms, analyze them, and obsess about the impact of these symptoms in your life (Nolen-Hoeksema 2000). Rumination is a very unpleasant mental state, so depressed people tend to try to suppress negative thoughts and memories as a way of stopping rumination. Unfortunately, the attempt to suppress unpleasant memories backfires and the person receives even more negative, intrusive memories. This is sometimes referred to as the *memory suppression effect* (Dalgleish and Yiend 2006). The more you try to suppress negative memories to control your mood, the more negative memories you tend to get. What does this mean in terms of your ability to recall your past accurately? Basically, you will remember more negative events than positive events because of the memory suppression effect. Since your story line is based on memories, it will be biased in the direction of including more negative events than positive events. The trap is that you aren't aware of this filtering bias because it operates behind the scenes.

Autobiographical Memory Deficits

A second line of study has investigated what is called autobiographical memory (Williams 1996), the ability to recall a specific life event with a high degree of detail. Autobiographical memory is necessary for constructing a narrative life story; you have to be able to remember events in order to integrate them into a story line. A typical autobiographical memory experiment asks the subject to look at a set of negative words (such as rejected, helpless, ashamed, and guilty) and positive words (such as excited, friendly, amazed, and hopeful) and then recall and write about a specific memory triggered by each word. So, in this case, you would write eight different stories about real-life events in your past, four negative and four positive.

It turns out that depressed people suffer from a problem called "overly general memory," meaning they tend to retrieve memories that are really life themes, rather than descriptions of a specific life event. For example, when Anna, from chapter 2, tried to recall a situation involving being rejected, she wrote, "My mother was always busy criticizing and rejecting me, and it was particularly bad when we were having friends over for social gatherings. I remember how angry I felt when she would do this and how unfair it was. I could never talk back to her because she would punish me if I did." Notice that Anna has not actually recalled a specific memory of being rejected by her mother; she has lumped many situations involving her mother together into a negative theme, and treats them as a single memory.

What does this mean for you when you're in depression compression? Basically, your recall of events will be blurry and you'll be prone to bringing up memories based on themes they represent. If you aren't able to access the original facts of a life event, how do you know you're remembering it correctly? Here's another interesting fact: When depressed people learn mindfulness strategies (which is the subject of the next chapter, so read on!), allowing them to defuse from the reactive mind, they ruminate less and perform as well as nondepressed people on autobiographical memory tasks (Williams et al. 2000). This means that lack of specific autobiographical memory isn't a defect in your brain or intelligence. Rather, it is a by-product of depression memory bias.

What this line of research implies about your story line is that it's biased toward negative events and at the same time is very lean on specific information that could guide you in the present moment. This is like driving your car with your rearview mirror turned at a 45-degree angle. Although you will see an image of what's behind you in the mirror, the image will mislead you about the real position of your car on the road and make it difficult for you to drive correctly.

EXERCISE: THE LIFE STORY WHEEL

In the popular game show *Wheel of Fortune*, at the end of the show contestants spin the wheel to see what kind of prize they'll win in the final round. This is the big lure and significantly heightens the excitement of the game. In this exercise, we have a similar game in mind, but the prize is a little different. In this game, you get to construct a new story line based on a random word choice. The life story wheel is loaded with evaluative words that are likely to move your mind into spinning a yarn right away.

One way to start the game is to close your eyes, put your finger on the story wheel, and start with the word closest to your finger. Alternatively, you might roll a penny onto the page and see where it lands. Once you have spun the wheel, so to speak, and have a word, begin your story, "I am [whatever word you landed on]" and then let your mind go to work adding details. You're likely to get the best results if you write your story quickly. If your hand stops writing, write the first sentence again ("I am [whatever]") and continue on. Write at least one or two paragraphs before responding to the questions in the following worksheet. When you answer the questions, you may simply say yes or no, or you can elaborate, as Ruth did in the following example. After filling in the worksheet for the first life story, choose another word at random and repeat the process. Do this for four or five of the words.

Life Story Wheel Worksheet

Story Word	Was the Story Easy to Write?	Was the Story Familiar?	How Believable Is the Story?

Debriefing. Were you able to construct four or five stories based upon just a single word? If you're like most people, it wasn't at all difficult, which shows you the power of your built-in storyteller. How credible did each story seem? It's usually possible to construct a story that seems very credible even though it's obviously made up on the spur of the moment. Were the stories based on negative words easier for you to believe than the positive stories? If so, you were probably being phished by your reactive mind. The problem is, you couldn't have completed this game if your reactive mind weren't present, because it is the form of self-awareness that handles explanations, reason giving, and storytelling.

■ *Ruth's Story*

Ruth is a survivor of childhood sexual abuse, and she felt this would always limit her ability to have good relationships with men, a problem compounded by being raped as a teenager shortly after her parents divorced. During college, she had dated a man for several years and had even lived with him for almost a year, but she had never enjoyed intimacy with him. She intentionally discouraged any talk of commitment, and they gradually drifted apart. Following the predictions of her story line, she decided that she just wasn't relationship material and stopped trying to meet men. She had very few other social connections and spent a lot of time alone, often recalling her sexual abuse and rape, and ruminating about the damage this had done to her. She began to experience anxiety at work, where she had to mingle with both male and female coworkers. She knew that the people she worked with were well-intentioned, but she didn't feel safe because of thoughts that she might be exploited again. Gradually, her depression worsened to the point where she had to take a disability leave from work so she could get her life back together.

When Ruth dropped the penny on the Story Wheel, she came up with the words "inadequate," "perfect," "brilliant," and "flaky" and wrote the following paragraphs.

Inadequate

I am inadequate. I don't have what it takes to be in an intimate relationship. My early life experiences cost me big-time. Jim, my long-term boyfriend, was patient and caring, and I believe he loved me. And I messed that up big-time. I just couldn't let go and enjoy the sexual part of our relationship. I was funny, and he liked to hang out with me, but that wasn't enough. I wonder if I could have tried harder, but I don't think so. I just wasn't up to it.

I am inadequate. I am not strong enough to face my fears. I am inadequate. My parents couldn't do it, so how could I expect to? I am inadequate. I was raped, ruined by a thug down the street. I am damaged goods. Who would want me?

Perfect

I am perfect. Right! Well, I would like to be perfect at something. Let's see … I am a clean freak, and I do a great job of organizing. People always compliment my home for its simplicity, cleanliness, and comfort. So that's probably it. I'm in the running for perfect person for cleaning and organizing. On the other hand, I think that might make me an annoying partner because I am uncomfortable with disorganization.

I am perfect. This is hard. I feel very uncomfortable with the phrase "I am perfect." It's as if my mind wants to automatically say, "Oh no you're not!" and tell a story about how not-perfect I really am.

Brilliant

I am brilliant. I am exceptional with colors. On almost every project I undertake, my supervisors and clients compliment me on my sensitivity and creativity with colors. I am brilliant. I am organized at work, and I stay on time with my projects. My performance reviews are consistently good. Brilliant. That's a rather strong word. It means better than average—like at the top, and I'm not sure I'm really at the top, even with colors. This is difficult. Why is it so hard to declare positive things about myself?

I am brilliant. Once, I grew a small flower garden, and everybody loved it. I really didn't know that much about flowers. I just read all winter about flowers, and then I ordered the plants online. Okay, maybe that was brilliant. But I didn't plant a flower garden the next year, after I moved here.

Flaky

I am flaky. Okay, that's a tough word for me. I guess I'm flaky because I can do something brilliant, like the flower garden, and then just drop it. What does that say about me? Maybe I'm flaky in that I don't do everything I could do as well as I could. But in that case, everybody is flaky!

I am flaky. Oh, yes. Here's the story: My friends often want to introduce me to men to date, and I pretend to be interested. However, I often make excuses and don't go to a party or event where I'm supposed to meet one of these men. That's flaky, I think.

RUTH'S LIFE STORY WHEEL WORKSHEET

Story Word	Was the Story Easy to Write?	Was the Story Familiar?	How Believable Is the Story?
Inadequate	Yes, flowed from me. And no, made me sad, so hard to stick with it.	Very familiar	Maybe less than I thought. I think I question it a little more when I see it on paper.
Perfect	No. It's very hard to see myself as perfect.	No	Sort of
Brilliant	In between	No	Sort of
Flaky	No. Flaky is not a word I would use to describe myself.	No	I sort of believe the part about it being flaky to make excuses.

Review. When Ruth reviewed her responses, she noticed it was easier for her mind to tell stories using words with negative connotations. At the same time, she was interested in the fact that even her positive stories (which she rarely experienced in her internal dialogue) seemed plausible as well.

EXERCISE: WRITE YOUR AUTOBIOGRAPHY

The best way to access your story line is to take some time and write a condensed version of your life, an autobiography of sorts. Since a complete autobiography would be too big a challenge, we want you to write a smaller version. Don't do this halfheartedly. Take some time to think about everything that has happened in your life and how you feel these events have shaped you, then take a half hour or so and write a one or two page autobiography. You may find it helpful to first write out specific events before you go on to construct your autobiography. Here's a list of the types of things you might include:

- Formative events in your life and how they've affected you

- Things that stand out as highlights in your life

- Things that stand out as lowlights in your life

- Relationships with parents, siblings, and other family members

- Important intimate relationships and friendships and what they've meant to you

- Specific traumas or negative life events that had an impact on you

■ Gary's Story

Gary, a forty-two-year-old man, has been unemployed for six months. Three years ago, while in the midst of a divorce from his wife of six years, he was laid off from a job he had held for nine years. Gary believes he was laid off because of the stress of his divorce. There was a bitter custody dispute, and Gary ended up being the primary parent for his daughter. Since then, he has been fired from two different jobs because of his attitude toward supervisors and coworkers. He has been very depressed since the divorce, which was initiated by his wife. Here's the autobiography he wrote.

I was the only child in my family. My father was in the military and we moved a lot. I think the longest I was in any school was two years. My dad was strict and didn't have much time for me. I had few close friends because I knew we would move again. I always was the "new kid," so I seemed to attract trouble from classmates. My father taught me to never take any crap from people, so I was in quite a few fights. Once I was suspended from school for fighting, even though I didn't start it. My dad gave me a butt whipping that I still remember. I was a pretty good student, but I never felt I fit in socially. Being alone so much caused me to be very shy and unsure of myself, something I still deal with today. My biggest role model was my mother. She taught me to adjust to being alone because she was alone. She did things by the numbers and had all kinds of routines. I inherited her self-discipline and love of doing things the right way. I can't tolerate doing things in a half-assed way, and I apply those same standards to my friends.

I went to college at eighteen and it was hard on me. I couldn't relate to the other students. None of the women I was interested in were interested in me, so I was pretty lonely. I think my lack of experience caused me to be a little ignorant of how to be a friend or a lover. The biggest highlight of my life was meeting my wife at my first job, at the telephone company. She was the first love of my life, even though I was twenty-six. She seemed to understand me and brought me out of my shell. The biggest blow was when we divorced three years ago. When she had our baby, things seemed to change. She started hanging out with her friends more and more, and some nights she didn't come home. She became more critical of me about almost everything. I couldn't do anything right. I thought she was picking on me deliberately to get my goat.

When she had me served with divorce papers, I was totally bummed out. When she filed papers saying I was unfit to be a father for my daughter, it was like someone had slugged me in the stomach. It was like the only person I had ever been close to decided I wasn't good enough to be a husband and a father. Even though I won custody, I've learned not to let myself be put in the position of being vulnerable. This whole thing taught me not to trust anyone, because they can turn on you for no reason. I have the attitude my father had: I'm not going to take crap like this from anyone.

The first thing to notice about Gary's autobiography is how seamless it feels. The cause-and-effect links just flow together and his story line seems very reasonable. When you read it, it seems logical and reasonable, even though the events and impacts aren't always positive. His current attitude is caused by being rejected and disrespected by the only person he felt close to. He is just putting his foot down and not allowing anyone else to take advantage of him, just as his dad taught him.

With a little assistance, Gary was able to deconstruct his story so that descriptions and cause-and-effect explanations were separated. Below is an example of some of the results of this exercise.

GARY'S WORKSHEET FOR DECONSTRUCTING HIS AUTOBIOGRAPHY

Description	Cause-and-Effect Impact
I was the only child in my family.	Made me learn to be by myself.
My family moved a lot.	I never had many friends because I knew we would move. I learned not to get close to people because you just feel bad when you leave.
My father was in the military and didn't have time for me.	Taught me not to take crap from people and how to defend myself from getting too close to people.
My mother stayed at home and was my main role model.	She taught me how to be alone. She did everything by the numbers and taught me to do things right and use self-discipline.
I went to a lot of different schools, didn't have many friends, and attracted trouble because I was always the new kid.	I never felt like I fit in. I'm shy and unsure of myself because I lack experience with friendship and love.
I went to college at eighteen and was very lonely.	My lack of experience caused me to be ignorant of how to be a friend or lover.
Marrying my wife was the biggest highlight of my life.	She brought me out of my shell even though I was shy and insecure.
I was divorced three years ago and I got custody of our daughter after a prolonged fight.	The only person I was ever close to decided I wasn't fit to be a husband or father, teaching me not to be in a position of vulnerability again and not to take any more crap from people.

Review. When you read Gary's story, did you pick up on how few descriptions of events there are relative to the number of cause-and-effect impacts? Also, did you notice that there are only a limited number of themes appearing and reappearing in terms of cause-and-effect impacts? The main themes are Gary's avoidance of intimacy because people let him down and that he doesn't fit in or belong. This reveals how Gary's reactive mind has selectively recalled events that represent a very simple, powerful set of life messages. He remembers his divorce as the embodiment of his story line: Allow yourself to get too close to someone and they will hurt you very badly.

EXERCISE: DECONSTRUCT YOUR AUTOBIOGRAPHY

Now it's your turn to break down your story line into its basic elements. Just as we did with Gary's story, divide the statements you wrote in your life story into two categories: descriptions and cause-and-effect impacts. Make a copy of the blank worksheet before proceeding, because you'll use it in the next exercise. (Alternatively, make a copy after you've filled in the left-hand column and before filling in the right-hand column.)

In the left-hand column, record statements that are factual descriptions of occurrences—things you did or that happened to you. This might include such things as "My father died when I was twelve," "My parents were divorced when I was two," "I was sexually abused by my cousin at age fourteen," or "I graduated from college with honors when I was twenty-two."

In the right-hand column, record statements that address the impacts of the events contained in your descriptions. These are the cause-and-effect explanations you place on the objective events of your life, such as "After my father died, my mother neglected me emotionally and I stopped trusting people," "I was caught in the middle of my parents' fighting about my dad's alcohol problem and learned to be a peacemaker," or "My sexual abuse made me feel like I was bad and that promiscuity was the only safe way to approach sex."

Worksheet for Deconstructing My Autobiography

Description	Cause-and-Effect Impact

Debriefing. Take a look at the percentage of your story that's description and the percentage that relates to cause and effect. Do you see a similarity between your deconstructed story and the one Gary wrote? Chances are you will discover that your story is focused on two or three main themes, just like Gary's. Storytelling is like that: light on objective facts and heavy on a limited set of simple but powerful (and often destructive) messages.

EXERCISE: REWRITE YOUR AUTOBIOGRAPHY

The themes of your story line are contained in the meanings, or cause-and-effect impacts, you associate with the events described in your story. Let's try an experiment that will involve consciously stepping outside of your existing story line for a few minutes. You'll use the copy you made of the previous worksheet. Without changing the descriptions of actual occurrences, write out new cause-and-effect impacts of each event. We don't care what type of new evaluation you ascribe to it. Your new version can increase the negative impact of an event, decrease it, or offer a different meaning altogether. For example, the statement that the experience of sexual abuse "made me feel like I was bad and that promiscuity was the only safe way to approach sex" could be revised to "made me more sensitive to others who have been victimized in some way and contributed to my interest in social work" or "made me special goods" or "made me a film fanatic."

Debriefing. Were you able to come up with a different set of meanings for the same set of facts? Most people find that this is relatively easy to do, but if you struggled with it, just notice that your reactive mind might have been phishing you so hard that it completely blocked you from considering a different set of meanings. Did you find yourself saying something like "Yeah, I can write these other meanings, but they aren't really true. My original story is the true one!" If you went that route, here's a question to ask yourself: "How do I know that my first story is the most accurate and true?" It's probably the one you've been reciting for a long time, but that doesn't mean it's the most accurate. This is what we mean when we talk about "truthiness errors" in the story line. Just because it's familiar, well practiced, and has a logic to it doesn't mean it's accurate.

HOW MANY STORIES DO YOU HAVE?

If you wanted to, you could write and rewrite your story line using the exact same set of objective events a thousand times, providing different meanings for each event each time. If you don't believe us, go ahead and try this exercise five to ten more times just to see how creative your storytelling device actually is! Notice this important feature of stories: If you take this exercise of rewriting your autobiography seriously, you'll see that each story is somewhat reasonable and logical in its own right.

Is it possible that your reactive mind is similarly arbitrary in constructing your story line, rather than entirely accurate? If your story line is full of being exploited or abused by others, might your reactive mind filter out an event where a person respects you and gives generously to you? If your story line contains one failure after another, could it be that your reactive mind isn't making room for the times you have succeeded?

Stories have a way of taking on a life of their own, and when they do, you can find yourself playing out the prophecies of failure, betrayal, disappointment, or personal inadequacy contained in your story. Living your life with your attention riveted on your story line is a little like trying to drive a car by fixing your gaze on the rearview mirror, not the road; it's ineffective at best and usually downright dangerous. Although you do need a rearview mirror to provide certain types of information, you will never reach your destination if you remain focused on the view it affords. As we say in ACT, the most dangerous thing about the story of your past is that you could make it into the story of your future.

FOUR POISON STORY LINES

While each of us walks the planet with a custom-made reactive mind, certain themes seem to appear and reappear in the story lines of depressed people. Just as there are four poison pills of evaluation, there are four poison story lines you need to be on the lookout for. And just as it is possible to defuse from poison evaluations, you can step back from a poison story line and accept it for what it is: just one among thousands of possible stories.

Victimization

If you were the victim of childhood sexual, verbal, or physical abuse, or some other horrible trauma, your reactive mind may construct a story that tries to make sense of what happened to you. The centerpiece of the story will be the abuse you went through and how it has shaped you as a person. The principal trauma of abuse is that it is a huge breach of trust, often in a situation in which you are both vulnerable and helpless. Children rely on adults to not take advantage of their vulnerability, and when this vulnerability is exploited, a very basic message gets installed in the story. This story line is that you are in the most danger when you are the most vulnerable. As a result, your story line will be operating in high gear any time you are about to develop any type of intimate, close connection with another person, be it a lover, a friend, or a helper. Your reactive mind will tend to filter these situations in terms of the potential for being victimized again.

The danger is that when you fuse with this story, you will tend to enter into situations where you can be victimized, instead of situations where you can experience healthy vulnerability. Paradoxically, people who tend to offer you a "free pass" on feeling vulnerable can end up being the people who later on exploit you. How does this work? In order to avoid unwanted feelings associated with feeling vulnerable, you think you have to enter into relationships that don't elicit these unpleasant reactions. The problem is, there is no such thing as a safe relationship, because healthy relationships require trust, and trust requires a willingness to be vulnerable. We've worked with many depressed people with a history of trauma, and it is distressing to see how many of them bounce from one abusive relationship to another, talking about the need to feel safe with their partners all the while. The story line says that you need to feel safe, but what you get when you follow it is more victimization. The biggest challenge you face in moving on from victimization is to recognize that your vulnerability is not your enemy. It is what makes you a loving and lovable human being, one worthy of a truly balanced relationship. You can have your fear and your images of the past—and enter the present and make yourself vulnerable at the same time.

Silent Martyrdom

Some children are raised in family environments that are so dysfunctional that the child has to act as a caretaker for siblings or parents. Families like this often have a single parent or one or more parents who are addicted to drugs or alcohol. The day-to-day operations of the family are left up to whatever child is able to function as a surrogate parent. To do this, you must learn to anticipate and address the physical and emotional needs of everyone who depends on you. Because no one nourishes you emotionally, you learn to not expect any rewards for your caregiving. You learn to take care of others quietly and without complaint.

The message that gets imprinted in your story line is simple: Your job in relationships and all kinds of life endeavors is to take care of everyone else and not to expect anything in return. You attract people who want to be cared for but don't necessarily want to return the favor. You will be attracted to job settings where you not only do your job, but also do the work of others. Your story line predicts that you will labor in obscurity, so you stay in situations that offer you very little, including relationships that are totally one-sided. Instead of changing things or leaving, you will suffer in silence. The biggest challenge for the silent martyr is to ask to be recognized, appreciated, and cared about. This action announces that you want to enter into the world of real relationships, in which you both deserve and expect to receive your share of consideration.

Self-Imposed Exile

In the course of life, any person can undergo a major emotional trauma, such as a devastating divorce, losing parental rights due to drug addiction, or the death of a child. In such circumstances, people may stop participating in life, like Maria (from chapter 2) did after losing her baby, Martha, to

SIDS. This may take the form of withdrawing from friends and family, avoiding intimacy, or under-performing in both work and play activities. People living out this story line frequently describe the way they live their lives as just going through the motions. You are living, but there is no you in the mix.

The basic message imprinted in this story line is to avoid caring about things because they will be taken away from you if you get attached to them. In order to prevent the pain of being deprived of something that really matters to you, you need to take yourself out of the picture. The irony is that trying not to care about things is a form of caring in its own right. You have to put a lot of energy into trying not to care about what's happening and keeping yourself in exile. It's hard work and it can suck the life out of you. You have to become very engaged with the task of not engaging your life. Your reactive mind will try to convince you that living this way will prevent you from having to suffer more losses. In reality, you are being tricked into the biggest loss of all: losing any possibility of having a vital, purposeful life. The biggest challenge when you're in the midst of this story is to get in touch with the fact that you care about caring. Caring about what you care about is the only healthy way to embrace a life that carries no promises and gives no guarantees of freedom from pain.

Righteous Indignation

There are some events in life that just don't seem fair, such as being excluded from a parent's will even though you were the primary caretaker during your parent's terminal illness. Other examples are being fired from a job for a mistake that a coworker made or losing your parental rights because the judge was biased in favor of your partner. Some life events seem inherently undeserved, and they can have a huge impact, such as losing a limb in an accident or finding out your child has been molested by a relative. These types of life-altering events can trigger a story line that recasts your world in terms of right and wrong.

The primary life theme that may emerge is that your life will never work because of what happened to you. You'll tend to engage in situations and interactions with the idea of ensuring that you're treated fairly. Ironically, the more you focus on whether you're being treated fairly, the less fair everything seems. When you are so on guard for any sign of unfairness, you cast most situations into terms of right and wrong, fair and unfair. Since the world of daily living is inherently gray, rather than black and white, complete fairness seldom exists, so you constantly respond as if you're being treated unfairly. The major challenge when you're stuck in this self-fulfilling, self-defeating cycle is to ask yourself this question: "Is it more important for me to be right, or is it more important to be real?" The fact is that life is not fair—nor is it unfair. Good things can happen to bad people and bad things can happen to good people. This is the human condition.

■ *Gary's Journey Toward a Vital Life*

After Gary did the autobiography exercises, he felt more depressed. He had fused with his story line as he wrote it down. Then he noticed something odd: Right in the here and now, he was doing exactly what his story told him to do, which was to feel alone, isolated, and on guard against the world. He recognized that all he was getting out of his story was a sense of righteousness and that he had taken the same tack in his marriage. When he perceived any criticism from his wife, he overreacted with aggressive statements that resulted in her pulling away. He fused with his story line in such moments and interpreted her reaction as evidence that she was going to reject him. He would then either retreat into his shell or begin accusing her of the very thing he least wanted her to do: falling out of love with him. He saw that this was just the latest installment in what his story had done to him his entire life: He entered relationships feeling as if he wasn't worthy, stayed on guard for signs that this was true, then aggressively defended himself against the hurt when he detected the slightest snippet of criticism or rejection.

Once Gary accepted that his marriage was over and that fusing with his story line played a role in that outcome, he made a commitment to reach out and try to form new relationships so he could practice a new starting assumption: that he was worthy of being loved and capable of being close to someone. When dating, he had to practice stepping back from his story line when something triggered it, which happened quite often at first. Gary didn't always respond in accordance with his values, but he didn't quit trying and he developed a new strategy. He gave his story line a nickname (Scared Little Boy), and when he noticed he was sinking into his fear, he greeted his story with the nickname. This stopped him from fusing with his story line. Since he valued trust, sincerity, and companionship in relationships, he committed to acting in ways consistent with those values rather than following the negative advice of Scared Little Boy. Over time, Gary noticed that, even with the confusing and sometimes unpleasant reactions he experienced in his new relationships, he was feeling healthier physically and emotionally. His old story line didn't go away by any means, and at the same time he didn't fuse with it or react as strongly to perceived criticism or rejection. Despite the pain of coming to grips with the loss of his marriage, he experienced more hope for his future now that he didn't have to live life on the defensive. Gary was on the path out of depression!

Secrets to ACT On

☞ Your story line is a narrative of highly filtered life themes and predictions about the future, not an accurate account of who you are.

☞ Fusion with your story line can have a devastating impact on your behavior in the present.

☞ The very real phenomenon of negative memory bias means that you can't be confident about the accuracy of your story line.

☞ In depression, your reactive mind filters out positive information and focuses on the negative, leading to an artificially negative view of yourself

☞ Your story line is mainly a social creation; it isn't a scientific creation.

☞ If you step back from your story line and see it as a story, you can take action to promote vitality in your life.

The Coach Says

Your story line doesn't run your life, you do! If your story line makes you suffer, play with it, because all stories are just that—stories. While you are at it, consider this idea: If all stories are fabricated, why pick one that sets you up for failure? Why not choose one that's workable, one that portrays you as inherently worthy of love and worthy of a vital, purposeful life, starting today?

Sneak Preview

In the next chapter, we'll introduce you to the permanent antidote for living in your story line: getting into the present moment of your life, free from fusion with the predictions of your story line. We'll show you how practicing mindfulness can open the doorway to the life you want to live.

CHAPTER 12

Step 7: Be Present

Don't let yesterday use up too much of today. —Cherokee proverb

In the previous chapter, we addressed a form of self-awareness ACT regards as the least useful in promoting a sense of vital living: fusing with your story line and its often negatively biased, highly filtered explanations of the past and predictions for the future. The more you fuse with your story line, the less contact you have with more health-promoting forms of self-experience. One major goal of ACT, and the topic of this chapter, is to teach you to access these health-promoting forms of self-experience on a regular basis.

One of the best antidotes for being overly attached to your story line is to return to the present-moment experience that is always available to you as a human. The present moment is the domain of wise mind, and when you learn to spend more time there, vitality, purpose, and meaning are yours for the taking. Consider the following words of wisdom from Agnes Baker Pilgrim, chair of the International Council of Thirteen Indigenous Grandmothers and spiritual elder of the Confederate Tribe of Siletz:

> Yesterday is history,
> Tomorrow is a mystery,
> Today is our gift, and we better use it wisely (Schaefer 2006, 16).

This chapter will focus on a less familiar but highly valuable aspect of being human: the ability to experience life in the present moment. The gateway to present-moment experience is often referred to as mindfulness. In this chapter, we'll describe the core features of mindfulness and look at evidence for its usefulness, particularly in regard to helping you move through depression. We'll teach you various methods for making contact with the present moment in your life by accessing the two health-promoting forms of self-awareness that make up your wise mind: the observer self and the silent self. Some of the exercises in this chapter can form the basis of a daily mindfulness practice in your life. We call it the "practice" of mindfulness because the more you practice mindfulness, the more skill you develop in staying in touch with the present moment. Mindfulness is also a source of vision and insight about what you want your life to be about. Because of this, we will also have you practice exercises designed to help you mindfully envision your goals about health, relationships, work, and play.

THE LONGEST JOURNEY

The process of learning to make intentional contact with the present moment may be thought of as a journey—a journey from the head to the heart, from what should be to what simply is. In Buddhism, when you're able to stay in the present moment, be compassionate to yourself and others, and see mental illusions and attachments for what they are, you are walking the path to vitality. When you are able to experience what simply is, you're much more likely to take actions that propel you in the direction of your "true north"—the values you identified as you developed your values compass in chapter 6. In truth, this journey unfolds in a succession of present moments that span your entire life. If you learn to be in these moments, your experience will be incredibly rich. Unfortunately, learning to live this way isn't simply a romp in the park. Your reactive mind, the relentless phisher, is lying in wait alongside the path, looking for every opportunity to ambush you. It wants to bring you back into its fabricated realm of self-evaluations and unworkable rules for how to live life. Inevitably, you will sometimes become hooked by its lures. When that happens, your job is simply to keep walking, and to understand that no one walks this path perfectly.

MINDFULNESS

Mindfulness is a perfect stance for promoting willingness to experience both positive and negative aspects of your mental life. It's a place from which you can observe mental activity without attachment or evaluation. Although mindfulness does occur spontaneously on a daily basis, we need to practice it so that it can be accessed intentionally when the situation calls for it. Jon Kabat-Zinn offers the following definition of mindfulness: "Mindfulness can be thought of as moment-to-moment, nonjudgmental awareness, cultivated by paying attention in a specific way, that is, in the present moment, and as nonreactively, as nonjudgmentally, and as openheartedly as possible" (Kabat-Zinn 2005, 108).

Think for a moment about your personal experiences with mindfulness. You've probably had moments of effortless mindfulness, as this is a built-in feature of being human. Maybe it occurred as you studied the actions or speech of a child or grandchild while in a state of genuine love and acceptance. Perhaps you had a moment in a garden or forest or on a beach where you suddenly experienced a feeling of peace and well-being. Perhaps you've practiced meditation or prayer and have had the experience of suddenly being relieved of something that was very troubling to you, such as a negative evaluation of an event, situation, or interaction. Think back on such moments and remember the qualities of the experience. These may include feelings of vast awareness and what is often called "radical acceptance," meaning that you can accept everything in the entire field of your awareness exactly as it is. This momentary experience may also provide a profound sense of well-being, purpose, and self-belief.

Benefits of Mindfulness

Not all that long ago, most scientists considered meditation and mindfulness to be wacky new age fads. However, there is now unequivocal scientific evidence to support the benefits of mindfulness training. We can now say with certainty that cultivating mindfulness is an important part of living a vital life. Over twenty studies have looked into the relationship between mindfulness and symptoms of depression. Indeed, British researchers have found that people recovering from depression are less likely to have problems with depression in the future if they receive training in mindfulness after recovering from depression (Teasdale et al. 2000). More recently, a study with a group of primary care patients found that mindfulness training helped people with current symptoms of depression (Finucane and Mercer 2006), with 72 percent of the patients in the mindfulness group showing reduced depression levels. These patients reported that they enjoyed mindfulness exercises, and over half continued to use these techniques after the study ended.

Finally, several recent studies have shown that practicing mindfulness has a generally positive impact on health and well-being, even among patients with serious health problems. A recent review of mindfulness and health showed that mindfulness training helped people with heart disease, cancer, and pain, as well as depression and anxiety (Grossman et al. 2003). Let's take a quick look at some of the theories about why mindfulness practice has such beneficial effects.

INCREASED ACCEPTANCE

Learning to detach from evaluations, reasons, and higher-level sense-making activities and see them as mental processes rather than indisputable truth empowers people with depression symptoms to become more involved in their moment-to-moment lives (Fennell 2004). Since much of the content of the reactive mind serves as a barrier to health-promoting actions, one important impact of mindfulness is that it allows you to accept those messages as mental chatter and engage in health-promoting behaviors at the same time. There's a saying that makes this point well: "Mindfulness is not a means to an end; it is both the means and the end."

DECREASED RUMINATION

As we pointed out in the previous chapter, rumination is one of the most damaging mental processes in depression. Rumination is fueled by fusion with unwanted internal experiences and counterproductive attempts to suppress and avoid them. Applying mindfulness strategies undercuts the cycle of negative rumination that depressed people fall into (Teasdale et al. 2000). When you can simply allow thoughts to be present as thoughts, feelings to be present as feelings, and memories to be present as memories, there is no need to evaluate, control, or suppress them, thus short-circuiting the depression-ratcheting effect of rumination.

INCREASED MENTAL EFFICIENCY

Brain imaging studies have consistently demonstrated permanent, positive structural changes in brain efficiency within as little as two months of beginning mindfulness practice. It appears that practicing mindfulness helps the brain process information more efficiently (Deshmukh 2006; Hankey 2006). Studies of visual-spatial problem solving in people with mindfulness training show that they consistently sort through signal-to-noise information far faster than people who receive no mindfulness training. This directly contributes to your psychological flexibility by allowing you to respond immediately and accurately to the signals that life is giving you without getting hooked by your reactive mind. From the perspective of relational frames (discussed in chapter 5), mindfulness training strengthens the deictic frame of "me and my mind," forging this distinction into an automatic response. As you learn and rehearse the basic "me and my mind" relation in your mindfulness practice, you'll become increasingly able to apply it at will in almost any situation. This is a positive feedback loop: The more you apply it, the more it becomes networked throughout your life. Thankfully, not all cycles are vicious, and not all spirals downward!

LIVING WITH GREATER AWARENESS

Numerous studies of mindfulness have shown that repeated practice begins to change the way the present moment is experienced (Kabat-Zinn 2005). When you learn to drift below the level of reactive mind, you open a pathway into other types of awareness. These expanded states of awareness can be the source of great vitality and clear vision. In religions and cultures that have a meditative tradition, it is the practice of mindfulness, whether through formal meditation, walking meditation, breathing practice, rituals, chanting, prayer, silence, or hallucinogens, that opens the door into a different way of being. In ACT terms, mindfulness practice allows you to slip out of the rigid, preconceived world of your reactive mind and enter into flexible and health-promoting forms of self-experience.

HEALTHY FORMS OF SELF-EXPERIENCE

Throughout this book, we've stressed that reactive mind and wise mind are your companions on this long journey. Although both of them have a role to play in generating self-awareness, that doesn't necessarily mean they both play a health-promoting role in all situations. You must learn to balance the "airtime" of wise mind and reactive mind because, in certain situations, the reactive mind can produce suffering due to its tendency to carve up the world in rigid, provocative ways that trigger unworkable rules about healthy living. The antidote is to access two health-promoting aspects of wise mind: the observer self and the silent self.

Observer Self

When you contact your observer self, you're fully aware of and in touch with the present moment of your life. This form of self-awareness involves being in the immediate moment and aware of, but not fused with, private events, such as thoughts, feelings, sensations, memories, and images. As the name observer self suggests, this is a form of witnessing in which you are nonjudgmentally aware of whatever is in each moment. In Buddhism, this state of instantaneous contact with the present, called *poornata*, is the pathway to full, positive engagement with the here and now, producing an enormous sense of personal well-being. When you're completely in the here and now, there is an entire world of experiences available for you to savor. It is as if the interface between you and your inner and outer world is transformed.

Silent Self

The other form of wise mind is a bit more mysterious and hard to understand via verbal explanations, because it involves being liberated from all verbal constructs and processes that produce a conscious experience of the self as separate from all that you are aware of. This is a state of pure consciousness, often referred to as simple awareness. In ACT, we refer to this as the "silent self." In Buddhism, achieving this state, known as *shunyata*, is the pinnacle of meditation and religious practice. *Shunyata* is the path to enlightenment because it frees you from attachment to all notions of self as distinct from everything that is around you. In a state of *shunyata*, you are everything and nothing all at once.

Of all forms of self-awareness, silent self is most foreign to us in the Western world, and therefore more difficult to make contact with. Because our society is so heavily biased toward verbal intelligence, it's difficult for us to understand or approach the experience of silent self, which is an entirely nonverbal experience. In this book, we will have to use words to help create a picture of the silent self and to guide you in practice, but they will not do justice to the true meaning of this deepest form of self-awareness.

As the diagram below illustrates, the goal of mindfulness training is to help you expand your awareness from the small circle of your story line out to your observer self and, beyond that, your silent self. As you become more capable of expanding your awareness, you'll notice dramatic changes in your sense of vitality, purpose, and meaning. In the rest of this chapter, we'll offer advice and exercises designed to help you gain more skill in moving among the three levels of self-awareness. If you stick with these exercises, within a few months you'll notice that your experience of life looks a lot different than it does right now. It just takes some practice. If you get frustrated, thank your reactive mind for phishing you with whatever thoughts landed you there and then keep practicing!

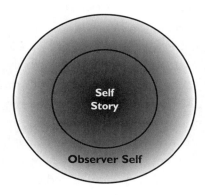

DEVELOPING THE OBSERVER SELF

The observer self is a form of awareness free of evaluation, struggle, and attachment. Ordinarily, developing the observer self is the first step toward expanding the power of your wise mind. A variety of practices can help you develop this form of awareness, and we encourage you to experiment and find those that work the best for you. You may find sitting meditation useful, or you may prefer tai chi or meditative prayer. One of the authors (PR) likes to develop her observer-self awareness by watching the reactive mind as her mind and body participate in a series of yoga exercises in a heated room. The other (KS) prefers to study the sunset while watching and accepting the parade of private events, ranging from familiar disparaging stories about himself to random moments of unexpected laughter. Below, we offer several exercises to help you develop a stronger observer self. Try these and then talk with friends or loved ones about their experiences with the observer self. Putting all of this together, you're sure to come up with a variety of options, some of which can become part of your daily activities in your new and vital life.

EXERCISE: WHERE DO YOU LIVE?

To help you learn how to get into the present moment and stay there as much as possible, we need to do a little diagnostic exercise to find out what time zone you typically inhabit. Think of time as a continuum ranging from your most remote memories of early childhood to future projections that go all the way to the moment of your death—and possibly beyond. As mentioned repeatedly, the reactive mind isn't designed to be in the here and now. Its job is to look backward, try to make sense of what has occurred, and then look forward and make predictions. In moment-to-moment terms, you will notice that your reactive mind darts back and forth along the time continuum. For some people, this darting occurs mostly in the future range of the continuum, while for others it occurs in the past.

In this exercise, we'll help you discover where your reactive mind likes to live. There is nothing good or bad about where your mind ends up living. This exercise simply affords you an opportunity to notice where your reactive mind likes to go when you're trying to be present. If you're like most people, you will find it very difficult to just stay present, because your reactive mind will lure you elsewhere. In the time continuum below, the present moment is in the exact middle. Go ahead and place your index finger there, and then read on. After you read these instructions, close your eyes and try to stay in the present moment for the next five minutes. If you get pulled out of the moment, simply notice where your thoughts go and move your finger to the left—into the past, or to the right—into the future, based upon where your thoughts take you. For a distant childhood memory, your finger would go all the way to the left. For the moment of your death, your finger would go all the way to the right. When the five minutes is up, answer the questions below.

Time Line				
Distant Past	Recent Past	Present Moment	Near Future	Distant Future

How often did you have thoughts about the present moment?

_____

Which place on the time line did you tend to visit when you weren't in the present moment?

_____

Did particular thoughts, feelings, memories, or sensations lure you out of the present moment more than once or on an ongoing basis? If so, describe them:

_____

_____

_____

_____

Debriefing. Did you find it hard to stay in the present moment during this exercise? For most people, this five-minute exercise seems like ten or twenty minutes! In modern society, we hardly ever have or take the opportunity to just sit and try to stay in the present moment. Did you have the experience of suddenly realizing you weren't in the present moment at all, almost as if you woke up and found yourself somewhere else? This is what the process of fusion with the reactive mind feels like. Without knowing it, you're just gone to some other destination. This is why it takes practice and intention to create enough space between you and your reactive mind where you can watch it try to entice you out of the present moment. When you have that space available to you, you can play a much greater role in choosing whether to stay in the present moment or leave it.

EXERCISE: THE BREATH OF LIFE

In order to develop more expansive forms of awareness, you must learn to control and deepen your breathing. The breath is the center of your being. It controls not only your respiration but also your heart rate, your brain waves, your skin temperature, and a host of other basic biological functions. Breathing exercises are the foundation of most forms of mindfulness and meditation practice. The Buddhist term for deep breathing is *pranayam*, which literally means "the breath of life." This isn't just the automatic physical act of breathing; this is deep breathing designed to help you focus and narrow your attention. When you learn to focus your attention on breathing and breathing alone, you are acquiring the ability to do one thing very mindfully. This is a completely different form of awareness than the helter-skelter world of the reactive mind, where your attention is shifting every few seconds. Learning to narrow your attention to something specific, such as breathing, and tune out everything else, is a very important skill for defusing from the distracting activity of your reactive mind. The following exercise is an introduction to the type of deep breathing involved in *pranayam*.

Find a comfortable place to sit and make sure your clothes aren't tight so that you can breathe very deeply. Get your body in a comfortable position and close your eyes for a few minutes. Begin by focusing your attention on your breath. Just notice your breathing for a while without trying to change it in any way. Take your time to get present with your breathing. This is the present moment in your life, and there is no reason to rush through it. Just allow yourself to breathe in and out however your body wants to do it.

Now imagine there's a balloon in your belly that you want to fill with the air you inhale. As you breathe in very slowly and deeply, fill the balloon in your belly. When you are filling the balloon, you will notice that your belly is pushing out and down. When the balloon is full, pause for a second and then gradually let the air flow out of the balloon. When you empty the balloon, you will notice that your belly pulls in and up slightly. As you inhale and exhale, your chest and shoulders should remain almost still. If you notice that your chest and shoulders are rising and falling, try to send your breath into your belly and allow your chest and shoulders to remain still and relaxed.

Now, as you inhale, purse your lips and breathe in through your nose. Notice the sensation of the air coming up through your nose and down into the balloon in your belly. Imagine this flow of air as an upside-down umbrella handle. You start at the crooked end of the umbrella handle, then bring your breath up into your nose and back down the handle into the balloon. As you exhale, open your lips and reverse the umbrella handle. Your breath leaves the balloon, comes up the long, straight handle, then travels over the arch and out of your mouth. Now, as you continue to focus only on your breathing, notice any sensations you experience as the breath goes in through your nose and back down to your belly. Do you notice the temperature of the air as you bring it in? What does it feel like as it goes through your nose? As you exhale, does the air seem warm or moist as it passes your lips? If you notice your attention shifting away from breathing, just gently redirect it to what you have come here to do. Continue to fill and empty the balloon for ten minutes.

Debriefing. What experiences did you have when you practiced this basic breathing exercise? Were you able to consciously fill the balloon in your belly? This is sometimes referred to as diaphragmatic breathing. When you breathe in this way, you provide a lot more oxygen to your brain than when you simply breathe into your chest. Did you notice your mind wandering while you were breathing? Were you able to bring your attention and focus back to the task at hand? Don't get frustrated if this exercise is difficult at first. The simplest things, such as breathing, can seem like a big mental task when your reactive mind tries to get in the way. We strongly recommend that you practice this deep breathing exercise at least once a day, and even better, several times a day, morning, noon, and night. The more you practice *pranayam*, the more interesting things you will see inside the world of your awareness!

EXERCISE: PEEL AN ORANGE

One of the most ancient meditative practices is to use common everyday activity as a platform for mindfulness practice. An old Buddhist koan makes this point: Before enlightenment, chop wood, carry water. After enlightenment, chop wood, carry water. What this form of practice suggests is that present-moment experience is available in even the most mundane daily activities, including eating. For this exercise, get an orange, find a quiet place to sit at a table, then close your eyes for a moment and clear your mind of any concerns or attachments. Place the orange in front of you on the table.

Sit with your hands in your lap and study the orange. Note its color and size. Can you smell it? Notice when your thoughts wander and you think about something you plan to do later or something you wanted to do earlier. Let those thoughts come and go, and return your attention to the orange. You will probably need to keep returning your attention to the orange; your reactive mind is likely to offer numerous instructions and concerns as you move toward the present moment with the orange on the table.

When you're ready, place your hands on the orange. Touch it lightly and feels its texture. What words describe it best? Is it cool? Bumpy? Now hold it more firmly. Does it feel solid? Soft? As you are ready, place a fingernail into the skin to pierce it. Do you feel the oil of the orange skin? What does it feel like? Smell your finger and consider the smell. Notice the thoughts and feelings that come with smelling the orange oil. Look at them and let them go.

Now remove the peel little by little. Notice any urge to finish quickly or "do it right," and simply continue to slowly peel the orange. Once the skin is removed, hold the orange again and study the lines that reveal its sections. Look at their pattern; every orange is slightly different from all other oranges. When you are ready, open the orange at a section line. Look inside, to the center of the orange. Study how the sections are connected to one another inside the orange.

Notice any evaluative thoughts you may be having. Let them be there and let them go. Continue to study the sections, and when you are ready, choose one to separate from the others. Bring it to your nose and smell it. If you like, place it in your mouth. Hold it there for a moment and consider its history—what brought it to this moment. And then, when you are ready, chew the section until you are ready to swallow. When you swallow, feel its movement from your mouth to your throat, your esophagus, and your stomach. You may continue to choose one section at a time to smell, taste, chew, swallow, and follow in its path to your stomach. Finally, take the peels in your hands and hold them for a while as you simply sit and observe.

Debriefing. What happened as you went through this exercise? Did you have moments when you were perfectly present with "orangeness"? Did you notice your reactive mind attempting to pull you out of this exercise? What types of lures did you get hooked on? Were you able to gently redirect your focus and attention back to the experience of an orange? If you like this type of mindfulness practice, you can repeat this exercise with almost any object—a raisin, a cup of tea, a piece of crystal, a flower arrangement, and so on. The idea is to create a place from which you can expand your sense of presence, be it your ability to smell, to experience touch and texture, to appreciate color, to be aware of your own reactions to the object, and so forth.

EXERCISE: CHOOSE EVERY STEP

This exercise, which involves walking mindfully, can be done inside or outside. Before beginning, decide where you want to conduct the exercise and how long you will spend. We recommend ten to fifteen minutes, but even five minutes will help you contact the present moment and move into the observer-self experience. When possible, it's nice to do this exercise barefoot, as this allows you to better sense the contact between your feet and the ground. There are four points on each foot that need to be in contact with the ground to give you maximum stability. The picture below shows these four points. Feeling each of these four points on both feet is your starting point.

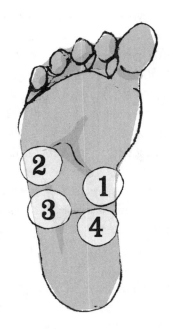

Stand with all eight points in firm contact with the ground. Your task is to choose each step you take and then take that step consciously. Your reactive mind will want to race through this and, in its frustration, might even give you the urge to take a lot of steps quickly. Your reactive mind is not accustomed to having you, the human, observe, accept, and choose rather than allowing it to evaluate, struggle, and avoid!

In addition to choosing each step, you can also choose not to take a step; in so doing, you are choosing to stand in place. Notice how the process of simply standing feels, if that's what you choose to do. It takes conscious choosing on a second-by-second basis to hold still—the same type of second-by-second choosing it takes to walk mindfully.

Choose how many of the four points on each foot are in contact with the ground. Notice what it's like to stand with intention and to make a decision to move or not to move, to have maximum contact between your feet and the earth or less contact. Maybe you'll choose to lift two points off the ground on your left foot. What happens? Does it have an effect on your right foot? Are you going to take a step now? Toward what? Away from what?

Notice any thoughts about this exercise and its value or lack of value to you. Notice how the reactive mind runs on with suggestions and stories. It can be very hard for the reactive mind to accept standing still or moving slowly, feeling the earth, and choosing every step. Notice this sense of tension if it's there and simply make room for it. Notice if there are unpleasant or pleasant sensations in your body. Where are they? What are they? What do they feel like? Are they hot, cold, flowing, pinching, itchy, or something else? Make room for those sensations and continue to choose to stand or step.

Notice how many points on each foot are on the ground at any moment. Can you feel each point as it leaves the ground and touches the ground when you take a step? Do you notice a thought about needing to get someplace? That's okay; just notice it and choose your next action in the moment.

Debriefing. How did you do with this exercise? The interfering effects of the reactive mind can make it extraordinarily difficult to make even simple choices. We're used to walking toward something, and in daily living that's why we walk. This is a reflection of our driven, mindless lifestyle. It's all about results, not about the process of living that happens along the way.

EXERCISE: REVEILLE REVERIE

The minute we surface from sleep, the reactive mind is at work. It is like the 5:30 a.m. reveille call in military barracks. You go from being soundly asleep to hearing the blare of a bugle in your ears. It seems as if the reactive mind is already active before other forms of awareness appear. And if this is the case, you have to learn to greet your reactive mind without immediately getting hooked by its contents. This exercise will help you take present-moment experience and observer-self awareness into your daily life. It involves waking every morning with the intention to stay in bed and allow yourself to move into observer-self awareness as you wake up and remain there for a while, in reverie, before starting your day.

When you first wake up, take ten deep, slow breaths and stretch for a moment. Then remain in bed, lying down, and simply observe yourself and the operations of your reactive mind. What shows up? Are there negative thoughts? Positive thoughts? Memories? Feelings? For most people, both negative and positive private events are present in roughly equal numbers, even on a good day!

The next part of this exercise involves thinking through your day and what you plan to do or what you anticipate will happen. Perhaps you can notice three or four things that your reactive mind brings up about your day. For example, you may plan to go to work or clean the house or go to a meeting. Notice what your mind says about any given activity. Will it go well or not so well? Do you fuse with this vision? Is it possible to just notice it? If you have a negative vision, can you let it be there without doing anything about it? Do you have a more positive vision at some point? Can you let this be there without doing anything about it? Continue observing your thoughts in this way for about five to ten minutes.

After five to ten minutes, return to your regular awareness and fill out the following worksheet. It's best to make several copies and use them, so you'll always have a blank form available. (Alternatively, you can print out fresh copies from the CD.) In the left-hand column, write what your reactive mind was looking ahead to for the day. In the middle column, record what your reactive mind predicted would happen if you engaged in this activity. In the right-hand column, assess your response to this vision from the stance of your observer self. Seen from that perspective, how believable was your reactive mind's prediction? Describe anything you experienced or thought in regard to the believability of what your reactive mind offered.

Reveille Reverie Worksheet

Observed Plans	Vision of What Will Happen	Believability

Debriefing. How did you do in terms of letting your reactive mind in for a visit? After considering what your reactive mind offered you, were you able to go back to present-moment experience and your observer-self stance? What about your response to your reactive mind's predictions for the day? How believable were they? If believability was high, you probably fused with something your reactive mind was phishing you with. What was it? If believability was low, what allowed you to stay detached and nonjudgmental? Continue experimenting with this exercise for several weeks to establish a pattern of starting off your day by contacting your observer self.

DEVELOPING THE SILENT SELF

Learning to move from the observer self to the silent self requires that you let go of any attachment to verbal knowing. Silent self doesn't exist in the land of thoughts, words, and descriptions of things. It is the place from which you can simply be aware that there is a "you" here. You can be aware of your immediate experience in the here and now (observer self), and notice that there is a bigger you that is the source of awareness. This is the "you" that you have been since you first became conscious. When you practice exercises that help you access the silent self, you will notice that this is a place that cannot be disturbed, even when you are being assaulted by your reactive mind.

A famous Buddhist story describes the silent self better than we can. But first a little background: The Bodhi tree is a common symbol of Buddha because Buddha first meditated for forty days under a Bodhi tree on the question of human misery before coming to enlightenment. So, references to the Bodhi tree in Buddhist writings mean approaching things with Buddha nature.

In the seventh century AD, Hung-jen, a departing senior monk, challenged his followers to construct a verse to show their mastery of the Buddha's teachings. The monk demonstrating the best understanding would be appointed the new patriarch of the monastery. Hung-jen's foremost student, Shen-hsiu, who was expected to demonstrate the greatest mastery, wrote the following verse:

> The body is the Bodhi tree,
> The mind is like a clear mirror standing.
> Take care to wipe it all the time,
> Allow no grain of dust to cling.

A poor kitchen helper, Hui-neng, saw a flaw in this understanding of enlightened mind. By describing the mind as a mirror, it was made into a thing. By insisting that no dust be allowed to cling to the mind (a metaphor for fusion), the objective appeared to be to keep the mind empty. But to keep the mind empty means there has to be a mind that has to be kept empty. Over the objections of the junior monks, Hui-neng submitted this verse:

The Bodhi is not a tree,
The clear mirror is nowhere standing.
Fundamentally, not one thing exists;
Where then, is the grain of dust to cling?

Based upon his understanding of enlightened mind, Hui-neng was appointed senior patriarch (Merton 1961).

EXERCISE: INSIDE AND OUTSIDE

This exercise will let you practice simple awareness using a visual and kinesthetic experience. When you practice this exercise, you develop the ability to direct your attention and awareness from the inside to the outside and back again. This will help you appreciate the contact point between what you are conscious of inside your skin and what you are contacting in the external world. You may listen to this guided exercise on the CD or record it in your own voice and play it back. Sometimes listening to your own voice is particularly powerful in these types of experiences.

For this moment, simply breathe in and out, filling your lungs and emptying them slowly. Notice the sensation of air flowing through your nose and throat and into your lungs, slowly and effortlessly. Feel your chest and abdomen rising and falling with each slow inhalation and exhalation, creating the feeling of a wave endlessly ebbing and flowing over your body. In and out goes the wave, and upward and onward goes the energy outside the skin of your chest and abdomen as it moves to accommodate the rhythmic flow of your body in response to the flow of air in and out of your body.

Notice your heart. Can you feel a pumping sensation? Can you feel a pulse? If you like, place your fingers lightly on one of the carotid arteries in your neck or on the inside of your wrist. That's your pulse—the rhythm of your heart's moving the oxygen in the air you breathe to all parts of your body, your blood's flowing like a river with many tributaries, all so perfectly designed, all of this happening with your awareness and acceptance.

Now shift your consciousness to the edge between your body and what it is touching. Feel your clothes on your skin, your shoes on your feet. If you are lying down, notice the places of contact between your body and the floor, bed, or couch. If you are sitting, notice the places of contact among your body, the chair, and the floor that supports your feet and the chair. Describe these points of contact to yourself.

Now focus your awareness on the space you are in, the room that holds you and the things that surround you at this moment. Listen for small sounds in this space—a fan, a bird just outside the window. Hold these in your awareness and then move beyond them to the larger physical space around you, the entire house or building that holds the room that holds the chair or bed that holds your clothes and you. What is this building like? What are its sounds and smells? Are there cars passing by? If so, notice them and hold them in your awareness—their noise, their smell, the people they carry. You can be aware of this, and so much more, as you pay attention to the points of contact between you and the objects and events occurring in your awareness.

Now, if you are willing, shift your attention to the city, town, or geographic area that holds the building where you are. See it from an eagle's-eye view. There it is below you, the building; the other buildings; and the parks, dogs, cats, and people—young and old. They are there, and you are watching, allowing all of this as you continue your approach to a larger and larger experience of the context of your experience. Now you are seeing the entire world and looking deep into space, where many stars look back at you. Stay here as long as you like and see the edge of your consciousness.

When you become aware of something smaller, like a thought or sensation in your physical body, say hello and let it go. Allow yourself to expand back to the edge of your consciousness, where your experience is inclusive and accepting. And when it is time for you to return, allow yourself time to retrace your path of expanding awareness. Go from the galaxy slowly and take in the beautiful colors of Earth as you approach your hemisphere, your city or town, and then your building and your room. When your attention is back to your body, connect again with your pulse and feel the rhythms of your body. Feel the movement of your body as it takes in the air needed to sustain it.

Debriefing. What happened when you allowed your simple awareness to roam free, as this exercise encourages you to practice? Typically, you will be shifting back and forth between observer-self and silent-self experiences. Notice the serenity that is contained in these transitions and how easy it is to escape attachments.

EXERCISE: MOONRISE MOUNTAIN

According to Native American thought, the sun is a symbol for male energy and the power to make an effort. Alternatively, the moon represents female energy and the ability to relax, perceive, imagine, and allow. Balance in living comes from having both sun and moon energy present in our lives. There is a great deal of conflict in the world today, and a tendency for us to push ourselves to action. When life presents contradictions to us, we need to create a space that is large enough to hold them and, from that space, take action.

In preparation for this meditation, take a moment to reflect on contradictions in your life. What is it that you want to fight or get away from? Is it an injustice at work? Is it some type of social inequity? Do you want to fight or get a break from worrying about problems with your health or the health of the planet? Is it a relationship problem that brings you a lot of pain but also love? The silent self can help you with this, as it has the ability to find a still place where a new perspective can emerge. Before starting this exercise, write out your questions or concerns and put them in a place where you can access them after the exercise. We recommend that you use the recorded version of this exercise, available on the CD accompanying this book.

Take a moment to focus on your breath. Allow it to slow and deepen naturally and easily. Follow it and feel the rhythm and the ease of its motion, in and out, up and down. It is a constant, a foundation, and place from which you can travel. Now focus on using your attention to create a dream, a dream that can help you better understand yourself. With better understanding, you will have more compassion for yourself. With the ability to care for yourself and trust your wise mind, you can perceive new possibilities in your life and say yes to them. This is the spirit of this, the "Moonrise Mountain" meditation. In and out, your breathing continues effortlessly as you begin to imagine a warm summer day.

Yes, days are long now and you've been walking with friends. They go on ahead to pursue another trail, and you choose to stay by a creek. You like the way you feel as you stand beside the creek and breathe. You are tired from your walking and you sit down. You take off your shoes and walk into the creek. The cool water is refreshing, and you reach down and cup your hands to draw the cool water to your face and neck. Then you lie down on a flat, warm rock beside the creek and listen to the movement of the water, the rustling of the leaves in the trees, and the birds. They sing for you, and you listen and breathe.

You are aware of the transitory nature of your experience, and this makes it all the more precious for you. The birds, the trees, and you—all have a beginning and an end. Only the rock you lie upon will live forever. You consider the warm rock and the strength it offers as it holds you lightly, confidently, and endlessly. Perhaps you doze off for a few moments, knowing that you don't have to hold yourself now; the rock will support you.

Rested, you are drawn to walk back into the forest you came from. You're filled with new energy and your senses are heightened. You smell the forest—the rich earth and the green trees. You come to a fork in the trail, and you decide not to take the path back to your car. You are drawn to take a new path, a path to Moonrise Mountain. You quicken your pace in anticipation of being there for sunset. Your legs move easily and effortlessly, and your breathing is slow and deep.

You pause for a moment in your walk because something catches your eye. You understand that the forest is offering you something to help you remember this moment and the trust you feel in your future. Look closely. What is it? Go ahead and pick it up; it's yours and you can take it with you. It will help you remember this moment and your ability to be fully present and connected—connected with your silent mind, the rock, the water, and now the forest.

You arrive at the foot of the mountain at sunset. You see a steep path that will take you up to a good viewpoint, and you take it. Again, it is amazingly easy to walk this path, and you breathe in and out, slowly and deeply, as you climb up and up and up. You arrive at a large red rock with a smooth, warm surface, and you sit down. You watch the sunset and reflect on your life, what you have done, and what you wanted to do. You understand the things that have impeded your actions. You accept your fears, your sadness. The sunset is long and beautiful, and the clouds make it all the more interesting and unpredictable. There's really nothing to control or avoid, no problems to solve as you consider your life and this precious sunset. It just is.

Now darkness is falling upon you and the mountain, and you decide to look around for a place to stay the night. You walk a little farther along the trail, and you notice a cave in the side of the mountain. You go there and find a bed of pine needles. It is soft and warm. Someone has stayed here recently, and it is an inviting place to rest. You feel protected and ready to rest. Before you lie down, you step outside and look toward the sky. There it is—the rising moon. It is full, and it is huge. You look at the moon, and the moon looks at you. You look for the edge between your looking and seeing, between the moon and you, and this edge blurs. You are the moon, and the moon is you. You feel a pulsing, and with this pulsing a sense of rising or falling. Your silent self has something for you, something to help you with the conflicts and contradictions that concern you at this time in your life. What is it? Pay attention. It might be an image, a thought, a verse. Listen and learn. If you experience strong emotions at this time, allow them. Remember your gift from the forest and continue to pay attention.

When you are ready, go back into your cave and rest. Your understanding of what your silent self offers you may deepen as you descend into sleep. Caves are special places for dreaming, and your dreams here may be particularly helpful for you. And soon, the morning light wakes you slowly. Although you have not slept long, you are rested and ready to see the sunrise. You walk to the entrance of your cave, and you see the moon setting and the sun rising. A butterfly rests on a nearby tree that grows from a small indentation between the rocks. It spreads its wings so that you can enjoy its colors. You are ready to return, and you walk down the mountain path and through the forest. You remember the secrets that silent self revealed to you, and your gift from the forest. You know you can return here whenever you want, and you thank your mind for allowing this.

Debriefing. Take a few moments to make notes on your experience during the "Moonrise Mountain" meditation. There is a great deal of variability in what people experience with this meditation, and if you repeat this exercise, your results are likely to be quite different from what they are today. You might consider creating a Moonrise journal, as this can encourage continued practice of this exercise for accessing silent self.

■ *Leslie's Experience*

Leslie, a hardworking and proud single mother, had raised her son, Sam, without support from his father, and Sam was the center of her life. He was accepted into a good college with some financial aid, but attending would still involve considerable expense. Leslie took a night job to support Sam in getting the best education possible, and he moved to a distant town to attend college. Leslie missed Sam and tried to call him daily during the break between her jobs. If she didn't reach him, she had trouble sleeping.

Sam was ambivalent about his mother's frequent calls; he missed her and only felt more down after they talked. Although he maintained average grades, he started hanging out with a group of students who drank excessively on weekends. Halfway through Sam's second semester, Leslie received a call from the emergency room. Sam was being treated for an alcohol overdose. In an effort to calm herself and find direction in this difficult situation, Leslie used the "Moonrise Mountain" meditation, asking, "How can I help my son and support him now that he no longer lives with me?"

In the forest, Leslie discovered a rare blue butterfly; she'd read about this type of butterfly but had never seen one. At moonrise, Leslie had an image of a beautiful horse racing around a track. The horse was wet with sweat and gasping for breath. She saw herself mounting the horse and slowing his pace to a canter, a trot, and then a walk. Finally, he relaxed and then stopped altogether. She dismounted and began to groom him, and he allowed this. In fact, he accepted her attention lovingly, as it was offered freely and without reservation, and Leslie began to cry.

After the meditation, Leslie felt as if a burden had been lifted. Although she wasn't sure what she would do differently, she knew she was better prepared to perceive her own needs, as well as her son's. She understood that being in the present moment was as elusive as a rare butterfly and that if she relaxed her grip on Sam, he would settle in and find his way in life. She saw that she couldn't control him and didn't need to. If she simply expressed the fact that she loved him and would be there for him, that would be enough.

WISE MIND AND VITAL LIVING

When you cultivate your observer self and silent self through daily practice, you increase the ease with which you can move from reactive mind to wise mind. This will allow you to access the aspect of your mind best suited to the moment. As your wise mind grows stronger, the predominance of your reactive mind will decrease, making it easier to shift gears. These skills pave the way for more creative and meaningful experiences in key areas of life.

Once you learn how to defuse from your reactive mind and access the life space of the wise mind, you can pursue health and vitality in your physical health, relationships, work, and play. Without changing or ignoring your history, you can engage in new life activities, or in familiar activities in new ways, from the wise mind space of present-moment experience and intuition.

EXERCISE: MYSTERY, HISTORY, GIFT

In the spirit of Siletz elder Agnes Baker Pilgrim, remember that yesterday is history, tomorrow is a mystery, and today is a gift to be used wisely. In this exercise, we'll help you bring a wise mind perspective to the four key arenas of life we've been examining: health, relationships, work, and play.

We'll begin with mystery questions, as this will help you create a space where something new can arise more easily and where your history can be held gently. When you focus on your history, you may miss gifts that life is offering in the here and now. Mystery questions are designed to provide you with some clue as to the direction you're taking in life and the strategies you're using along the way. We ask that you allow yourself to be confused, to wonder, to be unsure, to marvel, and to be open to unexpected revelations. To help you get into the spirit of this, imagine that you are a student at the feet of a life master and you are allowed to ask the most important questions you carry about your health, your relationships, your work, and your play. You may get some answers, although they might not come in a conventional form.

The history questions concern your past experience and reveal your stories about those experiences. There's no need to provide a lot of detail as you answer these questions, as you have done this previously in other exercises in this book and will probably quickly recognize the story lines that surface. In this exercise, the point is to hold your story line lightly. Think of your responses as simply volumes in a set of books, all of which you have read many times.

Finally, we ask you to think about the gifts you'd like to take with you as you pursue your values in each of the four areas of life. A gift can be a present from someone you're familiar with or a donation from the universe that is out of the blue. Or your gift might be some new and even confusing perspective given to you in an oblique way by the life master. You might realize that you have a talent, skill, or flair for doing something well. When you're ready to receive a gift, you may discover that you had it all along but didn't see it. Accessing your wise mind in this exercise might facilitate seeing your old situation in a completely new way, making many gifts possible. Be open to the possibility that you might receive something that opens a new door in your life, even if your reactive mind or your history tells you it isn't possible for you.

Think of this as an extended mindfulness exercise that will help you connect with what you want to be about in your life and what skills and talents you are going to bring along with you to accomplish these life outcomes. In some ways, this exercise is the crux of the book, helping build a foundation for the work in the next chapter—creating a life vision and plan that will set you firmly on a path toward a vital life. For this reason, avoid rushing through this exercise, or your results won't be as meaningful as they could be. Consider working through the questions over the course of four days, working through each life arena on a separate day. We recommend that you answer the mystery and history questions in the morning, and then practice a wise mind exercise in the afternoon or evening prior to answering the gift questions. When you respond to the gift questions after warming up your wise mind, sit quietly and wait. Wise mind doesn't always express itself immediately (like you-know-who), and it's less bound to words, so look for images or symbols that represent gifts that can transform your efforts to live vitally in all areas of your life. Consider writing complete responses to each question on a separate sheet of paper or in your journal and then summarizing your responses in the worksheets below. If you have difficulty with this exercise, take a look at the example from Charlie, which follows the worksheet.

Health

Mystery questions about health

1. How do you see your health in the future?

2. How far into your life or how close to your death do you think you are?

History questions about health

1. In the past, how well have you promoted your physical health in terms of diet, exercise, habits such as smoking and drinking, stress, and spirituality?

2. Do you have any health concerns? If so, are you doing what is necessary to optimize your health?

Gift questions about health

1. In a world where anything is possible, how would you use the gift of being alive to create good mental and physical health for yourself?

2. What might other people, such as loved ones or coworkers, see you doing differently to promote your mental and physical health?

Health

Mystery	History	Gift
1.	1.	1.
2.	2.	2.

Relationships

Mystery questions about relationships

1. What puzzles you about your most important relationships?
2. What most intrigues you about the role relationships could play in your life pursuits?

History questions about relationships

1. What's been your best relationship experience so far?
2. What's been your worst relationship experience so far?

Gift questions about relationships

1. In a world where anything is possible, how would you use the gift of being alive today to create better relationships?
2. What might others, such as loved ones or coworkers, see you doing differently to create better relationships in your life?

Relationships

Mystery	History	Gift
1.	1.	1.
2.	2.	2.

Work

Mystery questions about work

1. What puzzles you about your approach to work or being of use on a day-to-day basis?

2. What themes about the role of work and creating a better balance between work and other activities are surfacing for you right now?

History questions about work

1. What has come easier for you in your life thus far, work or engaging in other activities?

2. How does your story line influence your approach to work?

Gift questions about work

1. In a world where anything is possible, how would you use the gift of life today to create joy in the work you do?

2. What might other people, such as loved ones or coworkers, see you doing differently in terms of work or your balance between work and play?

Work

Mystery	History	Gift
1.	1.	1.
2.	2.	2.

Play

Mystery questions about play

1. What puzzles you about how you approach play as an important part of your life?

2. What types of play have intrigued you, but you've never let yourself explore them?

History questions about play

1. What comes easier for you, work or play?

2. How does your story line influence your approach to play?

Gift questions about play

1. In a world where anything is possible, how would you use the gift of life today to create joy in your play?

2. What might other people, such as loved ones or coworkers, see you doing differently to create a balance between work and play?

Play

Mystery	History	Gift
1.	1.	1.
2.	2.	2.

Debriefing. How did you do with this exercise? Did you see some new possibilities for yourself as you considered the gift questions? As you envisioned these possibilities for yourself, did you feel more optimism and less attachment to your reactive mind's negative chatter? This exercise helps you go deeper into understanding and embracing your values. Think of it as turning a corner and setting your compass sights firmly on "true north." In the next chapter, we'll help you chart out a plan for traveling in that direction.

■ *Charlie's Story*

Charlie spent the first twenty years of his adult life struggling with addiction to various drugs and a series of failed relationships. While he felt loved by his parents, his childhood had been difficult. He had been diagnosed with attention-deficit/hyperactivity disorder (ADHD) and was never able to succeed at school without a tremendous amount of structure. He grew up in a military family and they moved frequently, so he never felt he fit in with his peers. His father was in and out of his life, and Charlie worried from a young age that his father would leave one time and never return. When Charlie was in his early twenties, his father returned from a tour overseas with significant injuries, and Charlie, who had been experimenting with drugs, lost his footing completely. At age thirty-eight, he started trying to put a sober and straight life together. While he was a talented musician and dancer, and had a loving family, he had many obstacles to overcome, especially his tendency to be "scatterbrained" and to depend on the women in his life to keep him focused. He worked through the four life arenas on four consecutive days, doing the "Moonrise Mountain" meditation before responding to the gift questions in the evening. Some of his responses follow.

Health

Mystery	History	Gift
1. My health is a gift; I find it hard to practice good self-care habits on a day-in, day-out basis. I tend to put myself last on the list. How do I avoid falling into the temptation of relying too much on others to help me, and learn to help myself?	1. I abused my mind and body for a long time and I feel guilty about what I've done to my body. I probably have less life to live because of my hepatitis.	1. I would limit my availability to others and give myself more time to learn about relaxation and sleeping well.

Relationships

Mystery	History	Gift
1. My relationships with women don't last; they tire of me. I don't know what to do.	1. I've been married five times. The best was when I remarried my fourth wife.	1. I can forgive myself, grieve, and try again. I can pay attention and learn.
2. I want a lifetime companion, but I'm finding the opposite—lots of relationships, none of which last.	2. The worst was when we divorced again. She said I wore her out, and I don't want to do that to someone else.	2. Image of a turtle; I'm able to protect myself and can also choose to make myself vulnerable—and to go slow!

Work

Mystery	History	Gift
1. I'm a drummer, and when I perform I feel as if I'm working and playing at the same time. I feel that there's not a big difference—maybe just that I get paid when I'm working. The mystery for me is about how to rest, to not be "on" all the time.	1. My wives have complained that I'm a workaholic, and several have said I ask for help too much. It's just that I need help organizing so that I can succeed with my music.	1. I had an image of a beautiful woman. As I watched she kept putting more and more clothes on. Soon, she couldn't move naturally, and her beauty disappeared. I think the gift would be that I see women as beautiful whether they help me with my career or not.
2. Simply this: How do I stop working too much and resting too little? Things seem out of balance to me right now.	2. I spent so much time failing in the first part of my life; I have to do double time to make up.	2. Image of my sitting and playing the flute for a whole show. I think others would see me as a more relaxed performer—not always intense.

Play

Mystery	History	Gift
1. I don't think I know how to play. I did as a kid, but then drugs and alcohol became my sole approach to play. I don't really do anything to relax per se—watch TV, I guess. I need help to find some new ways to play.	1. Work, for sure! My reactive mind says I'm okay, worthwhile, etc., if I'm working.	1. I would create time to play every day—outside of music and dance. I would try different things other people do to play and see what I liked.

Review. Although he struggled with his reactive mind over the seeming illogic of this exercise, Charlie found the experience worthwhile. Once he freed himself from the demand for linear thinking, he discovered new perspectives on his struggles in all four arenas of life. He felt apprehensive about the changes suggested by his response to the gift questions and noticed an urge to discredit the idea of learning new behaviors to cope with his ADHD. He had viewed his ADHD as an obstacle that would forever prevent him from succeeding or force him to be dependent on others. This exercise helped him see that freeing himself from his story line and his cause-and-effect rules about his ADHD was a gift that could open new doors for him in relationships and in his efforts to create a more balanced life.

■ *Charlie's Journey Toward a Vital Life*

Charlie realized that, despite the limitations imposed by his ADHD, his scatterbrained nature was also the source of his musical creativity. He also admitted to himself that he had never really tried to harness his thinking by practicing organizational skills. He purchased a self-help book on living with ADHD that gave him lots of practical strategies for organizing his day and keeping track of his commitments. He began writing jazz music on a daily basis and pulled together a group of musicians to start a band. He noticed that his urge to work long hours at his day job was being replaced by a desire to enjoy himself musically.

One night during a gig at a local club, Charlie met a woman who was really into jazz and they started hanging out together. Charlie's reactive mind went into overdrive when he started to have romantic feelings for her, but this time he was aware of what was happening. He resisted the temptation to make excuses for his scatterbrained nature and didn't ask her to help organize his life, as he had done in his previous relationships. Instead, he used his new organization skills to help him stay on track with his relationship commitments, and when he did forget something, they would joke about it being part of what made him lovable. Charlie was on the journey toward a vital life!

Secrets to ACT On

☞ Mindfulness is the antidote for the dominance of reactive mind.

☞ Mindfulness has a direct link to psychological flexibility and is known to reduce or prevent depression.

☞ Getting in the present moment and learning to stay there is the path to a more vital life.

☞ When you learn to be in the present moment, you expand your awareness.

☞ There is nothing more basic to your experience of a vital life than your silent self, because it is a place from which you can look at all things with understanding and compassion.

☞ Living mindfully can involve practicing with day-to-day activities, such as eating, walking, or breathing.

☞ Since mindfulness is an acquired skill, you can use daily practice to get better and better at it.

☞ Through mindfulness practice, you'll be better able to recognize and use gifts, or opportunities, that support living in ways consistent with your values.

The Coach Says

Your wise mind is the source of true knowledge—about the richness of your life on this planet in each moment as it unfolds, and about the bigger role you play in the universe. From the space of wise mind, you can begin calling the shots in your life for the rest of your life.

Sneak Preview

In the next chapter, we'll help you use your wise mind to construct a vision for your life based on your values and your dreams about how life could be for you. We'll help you create a plan and use it to set goals in the four arenas of life we've been discussing: health, relationships, work, and play. Armed with this plan, you'll be fully prepared to embark on your journey to a life worth living!

CHAPTER 13

Step 8: Create a Life Vision and Plan

Vision without action is a daydream. Action without vision is a nightmare.
—Japanese saying

In the previous chapter, we introduced you to mindfulness as an important alternative to fusion with your reactive mind. Being squarely anchored in the present moment of life allows you to see the world as it is, not what your reactive mind says it is. You can then clearly see what's working and what isn't from the viewpoint of self-compassion rather than evaluation and reason giving. You can be aware of your story line without being dominated by it, allowing yourself to pursue your values in the here and now. Indeed, learning to live mindfully will become a powerful weapon in your campaign to move through depression and reclaim your life.

In this chapter, we'll introduce you to another very important quality of mindfulness. Mindfulness often is experienced as a dreamy quality of knowing something without being able to explain how you know it. This kind of nonverbal knowing has such names as intuition, premonition, preconscious awareness, vision, and inspiration. All of these words speak to a kind of awareness that allows you to see the future not in the rigid, evaluative terms of your reactive mind and its story line, but rather in an idealistic, positive, and intriguing way. In contrast to the quest for sameness that is the hallmark of the reactive mind, the visions, intuitions, and premonitions of the wise mind draw us into the future with a sense of curiosity and eagerness.

In this chapter, we'll help you envision the life you want to live, first at the level of basic qualities and then at the level of planned actions. The first level involves developing a life vision based upon intuition and inspiration with the aim of defining the themes for the rest of your journey through life. The second level involves planning the actions you intend to take to realize that vision. This type of planning requires you to hold your story line lightly, to be present in the moment, to set goals consistent with your values, to monitor your progress, and to make revisions in plans as needed. Taking specific steps to live out your vision is done with full knowledge that your reactive mind will undoubtedly attempt to stop you in your tracks with those all-too-familiar emotional barriers. When it does, the question life is asking is whether you're willing to accept these barriers for what they are and keep moving toward your "true north." You've heard the expression "two steps forward and one step back." Indeed, life is a process of ups and downs; however, honing your mindfulness and planning skills can help you improve on this ratio.

As you work through this chapter, we have an important request: The vision exercises we will take you through require you to leave the familiar, day-to-day world and to let your mind travel to places not of this world. We'll ask you to be open to visiting this metaphorical world, where you can pick up pieces of wisdom to help guide you on your life journey. Accept any of these gifts the same way you would an unexpected birthday present. Be amazed and thankful for the gift the universe has given you and consider how it can help you in your journey.

WHAT IS A LIFE VISION?

A life vision revolves around a clear image of your overall purpose in life. While it doesn't usually include a step-by-step guide, it does provide a sense of continuity and direction as you proceed through the typical stages of life: birth, childhood, emancipation from your parents, formation of a family of your own, old age, health problems, and death. In contemporary society, we often develop a life vision in a haphazard way, if we develop one at all. A variety of factors may contribute to this clouding of life vision, including messages received from relatives, teachers, and other authority figures. As we grow up, most of us receive a mixture of optimistic and pessimistic predictions from various authority figures, and many of these people are less than intentional in their delivery of these messages. Various personal qualities may create an imbalance in feedback that favors negative predictions about what a child can expect from life, often creating a self-perpetuating cycle. For example, children who struggle with focusing their attention or controlling activity levels often receive more negative than positive messages, repeatedly hearing things like "You'll never amount to anything because you don't listen" or "You drive me and everybody else crazy with your endless questions." This unfortunate experience makes forming a vision of a meaningful life particularly challenging.

Common cultural notions about how to live "the good life" often inform people's life visions, but the messages originating in the culture of feel-goodism are fraught with peril. Children and teens absorb this information from the media, as well as from relatives and friends. These notions are often delivered as rules about how to live and the rewards that are sure to come if we live according to these rules. We recently asked several college students about their visions for their life. Here are some of their responses:

- I don't know what to do. I know I have to go to college because everyone in my family does, and I know that I'd better get good grades.

- Go to school, get good grades, and then get a job being the boss.

- Get a degree in business, then get a good-paying job and buy a nice car.

Rules about acquiring things that symbolize success are common in modern society. However, a nice car, a nice house, and a good job may not translate to a vital, purpose-driven life. Even with the trappings of "the good life," many young people feel empty and wonder why their lives lack substance and a deeper sense of purpose and meaning.

If you developed a vision about your life when you were young, think for a moment about that vision. Would the people around you now recognize that vision being actualized in your daily activities? If you didn't have a life vision when you were younger, do you have one now? If you do, who in your life supports your efforts to live according to that vision? Has your vision for your life changed over time? How? Why? All too often, people climb a long ladder in pursuit of a vision only to find that the prize at the top isn't really what they set out to attain. Don't worry if a vision for your life has not yet come to you. You aren't alone. Many other people are seeking a life vision, while others are seeking to clarify, refine, or revise their visions. Life takes many unexpected twists and turns, creating a need to evaluate and update our visions. In truth, pursuing your life vision is something you'll do every day for the rest of your life. The fact that you're reading this now means you're ready to come closer to a more meaningful and deeply experienced vision; it means you're preparing yourself to live the life you want to live.

EXERCISE: VISION PLATEAU

This exercise invites you to use your imagination to clarify your life vision at this point in your life and to generate information that will help you make plans that support that vision. Find a quiet place to lie down and do the following visualization. You can record the script in your own voice or play the version on the CD.

At this moment in time, you are going to take a journey to Vision Plateau. Inhale deeply and allow yourself to relax as you exhale slowly. As you breathe, prepare yourself to receive something important. Breathe in the air you need to sustain you and breathe out any reservations. Feel your body as it warms and becomes heavy and soft. This is the nature of relaxing and a helpful way to prepare to receive something you need. Breathe in and out, and know the breath for what it is—a bridge between your body and mind. Walk that bridge and strengthen the connection. Be here and be now.

As you are ready, begin to imagine that you're walking on a path. Everything is new on this path, yet it seems familiar. It is as if you've been here before, but you have no conscious memory of it. The path goes through the woods and comes out at a river. The river is wide and the current swift. You sit down to watch the water. You wait and watch and breathe. The sun is high in the sky and it warms you. The sunlight plays on the water and the current takes the light, and together they create shapes. While you don't understand this, you sense that the sun and the water are working together to give you something, something to take with you. It may be a shape, a texture, a sound, or a color. You will know it when you see it. Name it and take it, because it is for you.

When you're ready, you can leave the river. It will be time to move on. Now you're going to Vision Plateau, where someone is waiting for you—a special person who has known you all your life. This person has heard every affirmative statement made to you. This person knows your strengths, your vulnerabilities, and your values. Breathe in and out, and know that you will soon shake hands with a person who understands and loves you.

The plateau is only a few hundred yards ahead. Take your time. There's no need to rush as you climb to your final destination. When you reach the top, you sense the presence of another being. You sit down on the plateau. It feels good, solid and warmed by sunlight. This is a good place to rest and wait. Your back is straight, and you feel relaxed, almost as if you're floating. You can see a long way in every direction from Vision Plateau. You stand up so that you can turn in all directions to appreciate this extensive view. You look to the east, to the south, to the west, and then to the north.

Having taken in so much, you are satisfied and you sit down again, now facing the north. You close your eyes, and you can easily see moments from your life, from the beginning of your consciousness to this very moment. Some are pleasant, some less so. They are all just moments, memories, and images. Take them in and let them go. Breathe in and breathe out. Walk the bridge of the breath, connecting mind and body.

As you watch the picture show of your life and breathe, someone approaches you. You sense the presence of a friend and feel no need to open your eyes or stand. You wait for this friend's touch, and you know that it will be a loving, gentle touch. You feel soft, warm fingertips on your forehead, and you know that this person is here to help you see your life vision clearly.

Remember the gift the sun and river gave you, and tell your wise friend about it. This will strengthen the work you do together now. Talk it over. Breathe in and out. Allow silence. Pay attention closely. What does your friend do with the shape, sound, or image you were given? Does your friend change it or simply mirror it back for you to see? How does this relate to a vision for your life? Accept anything your mind says about your vision—good or bad, desired or not desired. Accept it as mental activity, then accept your evaluation of mental activity and return to the moment and your friend and your work together on Vision Plateau.

When your friend is ready to leave, stand and express your gratitude. After your friend departs, look to the east and imagine a future that includes your past. Then look to the south and imagine a future that includes the present and the courage to pursue to your life vision. Then look to the west and imagine a future that includes the present and the ability to plan activities that fulfill that vision, even when there is no specific reward for doing so, and perhaps no end to the suffering of pursuing your vision. Finally, turn to the north and see that wise people are there to help you now and always with your life vision. Look into their eyes and thank them.

You can now prepare to leave Vision Plateau. This is a place you can return to. Your experiences will differ each time you go. Say good-bye and take the path down and around, back into the forest, past the river, and back to the place where you live day-to-day and where you are resting and using your powers of imagination to create a vision for planning a vital life. Breathe in and breathe out, walk the bridge between your body and mind, and when you are ready, open your eyes. You are seeing a new world now—seeing a new world with new eyes.

Debriefing. As soon as you complete the "Vision Plateau" visualization, make some written notes about your experiences and answer the following questions. You can answer these questions on a blank sheet of paper or in your journal, or you can print out a worksheet on this topic from the CD. Save your responses and review them from time to time. You may find that you understand them differently as you go further with planning directions and changes in key areas of your life.

- What did the river and sunlight offer you? Was it a shape, an image, a group of words, or something else? What does this mean to you?
- What did you see from your past as you waited on Vision Plateau?
- What did you feel when your friend touched your forehead on Vision Plateau?
- What happened to your life vision as you talked with your friend about your gift from the river and the sun?
- What did you say in expressing gratitude to your friend?
- What did you see when you looked to the south and saw courage to pursue your life vision?
- What did you see when you looked to the west and saw the ability to plan activities consistent with your life vision?
- Who did you see when you looked to the north and saw wise people ready to support your life vision?

Ruth's Experience

Remember Ruth from chapter 11? A survivor of childhood sexual abuse and then rape as a teenager, she had struggled with forming a close and lasting relationship with a man. While she wanted a lifetime partner, she eventually concluded that this simply wasn't in the cards for her. After all, her parents spent most of their relationship in a cold war and finally ended their marriage when she was fourteen. Even if she could get over the trauma of the abuse and assault, how would she ever learn the skills needed to have an enduring intimate relationship?

Ruth's life vision involved being an artist, a person who could arrange colors and objects in ways that were aesthetically satisfying. As a child, she had shown talent and also found that drawing helped her escape from the silent suffering she sensed in both of her parents. From the larger culture, she had learned that artists often have significant personal problems— relationship struggles and perhaps health issues as well. She downplayed the fact that she drank a little too much in the evenings when she was feeling particularly blue and reasoned that it was okay because she went to an exercise class several times a week. Ruth was a little apprehensive about the "Vision Plateau" exercise, but she truly wanted to deepen and expand her vision for her life. She decided to take a walk to the park to settle her mind and connect with nature before doing the meditation and answering the questions. Here's what she came up with in response to the questions on the previous page:

- What did the river and sunlight offer you? Was it a shape, an image, a group of words, or something else? What does this mean to you? *I saw a rainbow, and this means good luck to me. It also means diversity and unending transitions.*

- What do you recall seeing from your past as you waited on Vision Plateau? *I saw Jim, my old boyfriend, laughing at me when I was joking around. Then I saw him cry because I froze when we were making love.*

- What did you feel when your friend touched your forehead on Vision Plateau? *I felt surprised and then afraid, but then I relaxed a little and the fingertips felt warm and caring.*

- What happened to your life vision as you talked with your friend about your gift from the river and the sun? *I saw myself being in the present moment with a man, comfortable and truly interested in him.*

- What did you say in expressing gratitude to your friend? *I said namaste, meaning peace for both of us, and told him I would return.*

- What did you see when you looked to the south and saw courage to pursue your life vision? *I saw a little girl who could make pretty pictures, even when she and the people around her were unhappy.*

- What did you see when you looked to the west and saw the ability to plan activities consistent with your life vision? *I saw myself showing up when I said I would go to an event to meet a man a friend thought I might like, instead of making excuses at the last minute. I also saw myself going to group activities that I like just by myself—like going on a group hike or joining a dinner club.*

- Who did you see when you looked to the north and saw wise people ready to support your life vision? *I saw people who didn't shame me for using alcohol to escape my pain, but instead wanted me to treat my body as if it were sacred. They wore blankets the color of golden corn, and they offered one to me.*

Ruth felt that the exercise did help her expand and clarify her vision. She felt more optimistic, and she decided to spend a few minutes every morning drawing a rainbow and considering her life vision further. She bought a new journal with a warm yellow cloth cover and named it her "Rainbow Journal." In addition to drawing, she planned to make notes each morning about her life vision and her plans for that day.

FROM A LIFE VISION TO A LIFE PLAN

Next, we'll help you create several life vision statements from the information you received in the "Vision Plateau" exercise, and also help you identify the underlying values that form the foundation of your vision plan. Before we get started, take a bit of time to review the work you did on your values compass, in chapter 6, and your responses to the "Mystery, History, Gift" exercise, in chapter 12.

Elements of your life vision often come from your wise mind, and may appear in the form of images and pictures, as well as words. Similarly, values originate in your wise mind. They aren't derived logically; rather, they are more like intuitive ways of knowing where you want your life to head and what you want to stand for in your life. When you link your values with words, the words are typically action oriented; for example, to be a *loving* partner, to be a mother who really *listens*, or to be someone who *shows up* for the underserved, not with pity but with unwavering hope for their future. Values establish the general direction you'd like to move in the course of living, and exist independently of your story line. The act of valuing can be thought of as self-generating, meaning your values would continue to drive you even if no one supported your efforts. Because values reflect what we want to care about, valued actions give us a feeling of vitality and imbue our lives with deeper meaning.

EXERCISE: LIFE VISION TO LIFE PLAN

This exercise will help you apply your vision to your core values about health, relationships, work, and play. For our purposes, health has a broad definition, being a state of physical, mental, social, and psychological integrity supported by skills that help you deal effectively with the ongoing stresses in life. The arena of relationships involves the way you interact with people and your ability to be present, honest, and authentic. Engagement in work activities looks at the specific qualities you bring to the process of working; for example, a strong focus, the ability to persevere, respect and support for team members, or a conviction to do your best. Engagement in play activities concerns qualities you bring to the process of play; for example, an immediate presence, gusto for the activity, or spontaneity.

Life vision and values are highly personal, reflecting your unique life space rather than being driven by social expectations or norms. Keeping this in mind, if you're having difficulty with these concepts, take a look at the following examples, and the sample worksheet on the next page. We offer these examples not to tell you what would be appropriate for you, but rather to help you grasp the spirit of the exercise.

Health

- *Using the gracefulness of the bird I saw in my vision to surrender to sleep so that I approach life with more rest and better balance*

- *Using my cane to help me dance and play at the park with my grandchildren*

Relationships

- *Listening with all my senses, just like my wise friend on Vision Plateau*

- *Accepting my lack of control over my husband's struggles (the man with the rope I couldn't reach in my vision) and filling that space between us with love*

Work

- *Being mindful in my work activities (like the sun on the water in my vision, which always found a new place to connect)*

- *Connecting and cooperating with my coworkers (accepting that we can't all be like the monarch in my vision)*

Play

- *Taking my pain with me into my play (knowing it for what it is, hot and heavy like the piping hot biscuit offered in my vision) and letting it, too, be a teacher*

- *Laughing with abandon like my great-aunt, now passed on, but present in the group of wise people I saw when I looked north*

Before filling out the worksheet on the next page, spend some time contemplating your responses. You may wish to write out detailed answers before distilling them into concise statements in the worksheet.

1. In the first column, "Life Vision Gift," describe what you saw or received on Vision Plateau that gave breadth or depth to your vision for your life in each key arena of life.

2. In the second column, "Life Vision Statement," use one sentence to describe your vision for your life in each arena.

3. In the third column, "Values," describe your values in each of the arenas at this point in time. This statement need not be comprehensive; just write a concise statement that's representative of your current perspective on what's important in each arena.

4. In the fourth column, "Vision and Values Statement," integrate your vision and values into one statement of purpose and intention.

Life Vision and Values Statements Worksheet

Core Arena	Life Vision Gift	Life Vision Statement	Values	Vision and Values Statement
Health				
Relationships				
Work				
Play				

RUTH'S EXPERIENCE

Ruth recorded the following responses on her worksheet. Her answers helped her better understand the gifts she received in the "Vision Plateau" exercise.

Ruth's Life Vision and Values Statements Worksheet

Core Arena	Life Vision Gift	Life Vision Statement	Values	Vision and Values Statement
Health	A gold blanket from wise, accepting people	Other people love and support me.	I value recognition of support from others.	I will treat my mind and body with the same attitude of caring that others have shown me.
Relationships	A rainbow	Many kinds of people come into my life. I respect their differences and the impact those differences have on me.	I value courage.	I value courageous, bold moves in relationships, even without knowing the outcome.
Work	A rainbow	I will always have meaningful work opportunities.	I value creativity and respect.	I will bring respect and creativity to my work and the work of others.
Play	The little girl	I have a gift for making beautiful things.	I value peace of mind and self-expression.	I value peace in expressing my gifts as an artist, and it's okay for work and play to overlap.

Review. When she reflected on the exercise, Ruth felt motivated to address the health and relationship issues in her life. She also experienced greater acceptance of her quiet nature and her preference for a solitary form of play.

VISION AND MYSTERY: THE WILLINGNESS TO PLAN FLEXIBLY

The purpose of this section is to suggest a strategy for finding a balance between imagining and doing, between seeing possibilities and executing various actions. While being able to see life possibilities is important, only by planning can you identify the skills needed and the steps you must take to engage in effective action. Conversely, taking action without planning can have disastrous results, as suggested by the quote that started this chapter. That said, it's important to be flexible in implementing any plan, no matter how worthwhile or well thought out it is.

Most of us have had the experience of pushing ourselves too hard to implement a specific plan. In pushing, and especially in pushing to adhere to the details, we lose some of our flexibility and can overlook important feedback from the external world. For example, we might not realize that the plan, however well-intentioned, isn't moving us closer to our values. Or we might develop tunnel vision and fail to see other opportunities that might be more consistent with our values. The following exercise offers a strategy for becoming more flexible and mindful in planning and living a vital life.

EXERCISE: "YES AND..."

This exercise involves making a plan to do something that's consistent with the vision and values statements you came up with in the preceding exercise. If you have any difficulty with this exercise, take a look at the example from Ruth that follows.

1. Copy your vision and values statements from the previous exercise into the first blank column of the following worksheet.

2. Now plan something you can do this week that supports your vision and values statement in each arena and write it in the next column.

3. Imagine that you're implementing the plan and things are going well.

4. Next, imagine that something negative and unsupportive happens as you implement your plan, and you feel discouraged. Visualize the details and watch what your mind has to say about them.

5. Now, and this may be the most difficult part of the exercise, imagine again that something happens after the negative obstacle show up, and this time it's positive and supportive of your vision and values statement and your plan. It may be subtle, and you may only recognize its potency after redirecting your attention away from the chatter of your reactive mind. When you see it, say yes to it and explore its ability to support your vision and values.

The "Yes, and…" Worksheet

Core Arena	Vision and Values Statement	Plan	Negative Event	Positive Event
Health				
Relationships				
Work				
Play				

Debriefing. What was your experience with imaging something unsupportive of your plan and something supportive of your plan? Was one easier to imagine than the other? Were you able to watch your reactive mind go to work on the negative event? Did a lot of old phishing lures start to show up? Did your wise mind intervene with some kind of positive or reassuring image or inspiration? We encourage you to use this exercise on a regular basis, as it can help you develop greater levels of willingness as you pursue values-driven plans.

RUTH'S EXPERIENCE

Ruth started this exercise with a great deal of enthusiasm. Having clarified her vision and values, she was ready to start making changes in her life. Here's what she came up with.

Ruth's "Yes, and..." Worksheet

Core Arena	Vision and Values Statement	Plan	Negative Event	Positive Event
Health	I will treat my mind and body with the same attitude of caring that others have shown me.	Go to a beginning yoga class on Saturday morning.	I feel panicked when I get there and just want to leave.	After the class, the teacher invites us to come to a picnic later that day, and I say yes, I'll be there.
Relationships	I value courageous, bold moves in relationships, even without knowing the outcome.	Go to a jazz concert alone on Friday night.	A man starts talking to me at intermission, and I want to leave.	He invites me to have coffee with him on Sunday, and I say yes.
Work	I will bring respect and creativity to my work and the work of others.	I'll say thank you whenever someone does something helpful at work.	Someone says, "What's up with you? You're, like, all positive," and this irritates me.	My supervisor asks if I want to be on the employee recognition committee, and I say yes.
Play	I value peace in expressing my gifts as an artist, and it's okay for work and play to overlap.	I'll volunteer to help with some type of art-related project at my church.	I go to a planning meeting, and people can't agree. I'm bored and frustrated.	I visualize the project and draw while I listen. They ask me to share my sketch with them, and I say yes.

Review. While this exercise was more difficult than Ruth thought it would be, it helped her anticipate the negative thinking that often appeared when she began to implement an important change in her life. It also helped her stretch her imagination in the direction of seeing unanticipated positive events that could support her efforts. She decided that this exercise would be worth integrating into her weekly Sunday afternoon routine.

PLANNING A VITAL LIFE

Developing a life plan and actually implementing it on a short-term basis will immerse you in a process of learning to live intentionally. Many of the skills you've learned in this book will be helpful, even essential, in living vitally and intentionally, especially clarifying your values, practicing acceptance and mindfulness on a daily basis, and engaging in specific actions that push you in the direction of the life you want to live. In the next exercise, you'll consider how on the mark you are in living in accordance with the values that have surfaced as important in your life vision planning process. When you combine your life vision, personal values, and commitments to specific actions, you are truly embarking on living the life you want to live.

EXERCISE: YOUR VITAL LIVING PLAN

Because of the importance of flexibility in planning and in acting, we recommend that you do this exercise every three months. This will help you gauge the effectiveness of your plan and your actions. Use the results of these periodic self-assessments to make course corrections so that you continue traveling toward your "true north." Each time you do this self-assessment, select just one or two life arenas to focus your work on, based on your priorities. You will undoubtedly notice that your priorities shift over time; this is to be expected when you live life flexibly. However, we do recommend that you address all four of the life arenas at least once a year, as each usually has an important role to play when you're living in a balanced and vital way. Make copies of this blank worksheet so you'll always have a fresh copy. (Alternatively, you can print out fresh copies from the CD.)

1. Choose one or two life arenas you plan to address in the next three months.

2. For each, write your vision statement where indicated. You may simply copy the vision and values statement you generated in this chapter, or you may want to revisit the work you did with your values compass back in chapter 6. And, of course, you may wish to revise or overhaul these statements when you do this exercise in the future.

3. On a scale of 1 to 7, where 1 is not at all consistent and 7 is entirely consistent, rate your consistency in living in accordance with that vision statement. At this point in time, you'll record a rating next to "Today," based on how consistent your day-to-day behavior has been with your vision and values during the past month. It wouldn't be surprising or unusual if your present rating is a 1 or a 2; that's probably why you've chosen to address the arena. Even if your rating is low, it indicates that you have a clear picture of your vision and values and that you're paying attention to the way you live. For this, we hope that you're proud of a 1 or 2. You'll come back to the worksheet and rate your consistency every month for the next three months. The trend in your monthly ratings is more important than the actual numbers (not to say that you shouldn't aim high!).

4. Now you're ready to make a three-month action plan. Choose up to four activities you plan to pursue to improve your consistency ratings. For example, if you value having a body that can hike in the mountains, you may plan to walk thirty minutes daily at a brisk pace to develop your endurance. When you describe your planned activities, be specific. Set a time and place for doing each action and set a goal for how many times you'll engage in this action weekly or at whatever time interval makes sense. For example, a plan to eat breakfast by eight o'clock each morning is specific, whereas a plan to eat better isn't. The more specific you are, the better you can assess whether you're acting as planned—and the better you can evaluate how your actions are impacting your sense of vitality.

5. At one month intervals, review your plan and rate your consistency over the course of the previous month. Use this as an opportunity to review the effectiveness of your plan. Is your score going up, even slightly? If so, your plan is bringing you closer to your values and you are probably experiencing more vitality in life. If your score stays the same or gets lower, consider whether you need to change the plan. You can't always be sure how a plan will work out when you're creating it, but you can have an open mind and change the plan when your experience tells you it isn't working. This review is important, so record it on your calendar, just as you would any important activity. If you've chosen a particularly challenging arena to work on, you may want to review your plan more often at first— perhaps once a week.

Vital Living Plan

Health

Vision statement: _____

_____

Consistency ratings (1 = not at all consistent; 7 = entirely consistent)

Today: _____ Month 1: _____ Month 2: _____ Month 3: _____

Action plan

1. _____

_____

2. _____

_____

3. _____

_____

4. _____

_____

Relationships

Vision statement: _____

_____

Consistency ratings (1 = not at all consistent; 7 = entirely consistent)

Today: _____ Month 1: _____ Month 2: _____ Month 3: _____

Action plan

1. _____

_____

2. _____

_____

3. _____

_____

4. _____

_____

Work

Vision statement: _____

_____

Consistency ratings (1 = not at all consistent; 7 = entirely consistent)

Today: _____ Month 1: _____ Month 2: _____ Month 3: _____

Action plan

1. _____

_____

2. _____

_____

3. _____

_____

4. _____

_____

Play

Vision statement: _____

_____

Consistency ratings (1 = not at all consistent; 7 = entirely consistent)

Today: _____ Month 1: _____ Month 2: _____ Month 3: _____

Action plan

1. _____

_____

2. _____

_____

3. _____

_____

4. _____

_____

Debriefing. We recommend that you ask someone you trust to support you in following your plan. (If this is challenging for you, go ahead and take some time to read chapter 16, which offers a lot of guidance on enlisting social support.) This might involve scheduling a monthly get-together to update the person about your monthly consistency ratings and review your plan. When you discuss your successes and troubleshoot any setbacks with someone supportive, you're likely to reap greater benefits from the entire process.

At the end of three months, go through the entire process again, choosing one or two life arenas to work on, restating your vision and values in that area, rating your consistency, and choosing up to four actions you'll engage in to support your vision and values. Continue this for at least a year. You'll be amply rewarded for your efforts—so much so that you may want to make this exercise a lifelong process.

Secrets to ACT On

☞ The journey to reengage in your life begins with developing a clear vision of the direction you want to head in, based on your values.

☞ Using your imagination to envision the life you desire activates your wise mind, reduces the dominance of your reactive mind, and allows you to see new and different opportunities.

☞ Pursue your vital living plan with flexibility and with your eyes open to possibilities you might miss because of being too single-minded or habitual in your thinking.

☞ Conduct a review of your vital living plan on a regular basis so that you can assess the results you're getting and change your direction depending on your success, and as your priorities change.

☞ Limit your vital living plan to one or two life arenas during any particular period, as this will increase your focus, energy, and chances of success!

The Coach Says

All great journeys begin with a vision of what lies at the end of the journey and what will be experienced along the way. Your wise mind is your best guide on such a journey. Allow it to lead you in your quest for a vital, purposeful life. Pay attention to its messages, whether they come in the form of images, premonitions, hunches, dreams, or reveries. When your bliss calls you, follow it!

Sneak Preview

In the next chapter, we'll help you develop the essential skill of making commitments to yourself and keeping them. We'll help you appreciate both the joys of making commitments and the obstacles that your reactive mind will put in your way. You'll learn the importance of compassion and forgiveness in allowing you to fulfill your commitments.

CHAPTER 14

Step 9: Make and Keep Commitments

Life is what you make of it. Always has been, always will be. —Grandma Moses

Before we introduce you to the nuances of making and keeping commitments, we want to congratulate you for getting to this point in the book! Give yourself a big pat on the back for sticking with it—and recognize that this indicates you have what it takes to make and keep commitments, even when the going gets tough. All of the strategies presented in this book have provided you with a strong foundation for making changes and living purposefully: When you know what your values are, you have a compass heading you can follow. Knowing how to accept things that cannot be changed allows you to better focus your efforts on changing what *can* be changed. As you learn to separate yourself from your ever-present reactive mind, you have more success with noticing old rules—and more freedom to not follow them blindly. When you learn to step outside of your story line, you can make choices in living that reflect your values, rather than being controlled by your life story. Using mindfulness skills to fully experience the present moment in your life supports flexibility in responding to the challenges that life presents day to day. Identifying specific goals and actions that embody your personal values primes you to take action to improve the quality of your life. There's just one remaining skill for vital living we want to help you with, and as it turns out, it is the most important in many regards: making commitments to yourself and following through on them.

THE C IN ACCEPTANCE AND COMMITMENT THERAPY

At its heart, ACT is a therapy for behavior change. Its goal is to help you use behaviors that work to promote your sense of vitality, purpose, and well-being. This result isn't achieved in the world between your ears; it's a process that unfolds in the field of play of your life, and particularly in behaviors related to your health, relationships, work, and play—arenas of living that ultimately determine your life satisfaction. Making and keeping commitments to engage in valued actions in these arenas, even with the ever present temptation to avoid difficult emotions and the situations that trigger them, takes courage. Your reactive mind will work overtime to get you to stop. You'll have to stare down your demons and keep moving in the direction you want your life to go, even if you still see those demons on the sidelines. Your desired life is out there waiting for you, and you can claim it. However, it won't be handed to you on a silver platter. You'll have to do some difficult work to get there, but the rewards more than compensate for the challenges.

■ Luke's Story

Luke, a twenty-six-year-old single man, lives by himself. He's been chronically depressed since childhood, and as an adolescent, he slipped into a pattern of substance abuse. He entered drug treatment two years ago, and although he's had a few slips, he basically hasn't been using drugs or alcohol since starting treatment. His depression has steadily worsened since he stopped using drugs and alcohol, and he admits to thoughts of suicide on an almost daily basis. He works part-time as a night janitor and frequently gets to work late because no one is there to know whether he arrived or not. He enrolled in a local trade school to study computer repair but dropped out because he was failing. While he liked the classes and was academically and intellectually capable of doing the work, he didn't complete required assignments.

Luke hasn't been on a date for several years and avoids any activity that might lead to that, having convinced himself that he probably couldn't follow through on even the simplest commitments in a relationship. While he purchased a health club membership three months ago to get in shape, he has yet to go to the club. He has a few friends from his drug rehabilitation program, but he doesn't get together with them often. Some of them are using drugs again, and he doesn't want to relapse. He smokes about a pack of cigarettes a day and doesn't exercise. He doesn't attend church, but he is interested in Buddhism. Luke wants to follow through on things that are important to him, but so far his only success has been in staying off drugs.

WHAT IS A COMMITMENT?

Luke hasn't kept many of the commitments he's made to himself in recent years. Consequently, his life lacks the meaning he desires, and he easily fuses with a story about his life that includes never being able to stick to an important commitment over time. Living this kind of story line is inherently depressing because it precludes taking risks in the pursuit of vitality. Luke is so sold on this sad story of defeat that he has voluntarily withdrawn from the world of relationships. This is the poison story line of self-imposed exile that we discussed in chapter 11. Luke's life is going nowhere fast, and although he believes his depression is what keeps him from a better life, in reality the problem is his inability to make and keep commitments.

In ACT, we use the term "committed action" to describe a pact you make with yourself—a pact to take a specific action in a specific situation regardless of what shows up inside your head. In all likelihood, your reactive mind will show up and make its best effort to get you to stop. Even as you read this, your reactive mind might already be telling you that this approach will never work for you, that you're too weak to pull it off, or that it will just provide you with another opportunity to fail in life. Your reactive mind is probably feeling fairly threatened right now, because committed action is to the reactive mind what the sunlight is to Dracula. Committed action spells the end of your reactive mind's reign of terror and opens the door on a new day, where your wise mind can prevail. Committed action allows you to stop following rules and instead do what works in your life. So, if you noticed any kicking and flailing on the part of your reactive mind as you read any of this, simply thank your mind for these thoughts and come back into the present moment with us so we can get to work on banishing that vampire who's been sucking you dry.

Committed Action Is a Choice

One important aspect of committed action is that it is a *choice*—an action taken for no other reason than to take it. A choice means you are free from having to choose an action because of social expectations or the programming of your reactive mind. This creates a very powerful tool in your campaign to reclaim your life. Choices aren't a matter of logic and decision. In fact, many choices are made in situations where there are good reasons for any number of actions.

It's like making a choice to be a nonsmoker. There are many good reasons to continue to smoke (smoking relieves tension, helps you avoid angry outbursts, keeps you from overeating, and so on), and there are many good reasons to stop (better health, better breathing, better body odor, saving money, and so on). Approaching this as a logical decision is dicey because the relative importance of various reasons may change. If you have a stressful day at work, the importance of smoking to reduce stress may shoot through the roof. People often stop smoking based on a logical decision rather than a commitment, and shortly after stopping, they start again. Choosing to quit is different from deciding to quit. Choosing to quit means making a choice with full awareness that your mind will come up with compelling reasons for smoking (and not smoking) over and over again, and each time you will make the choice to be a nonsmoker.

Committed Action Is Consistent with Your Values

Another important aspect of committed action, as opposed an action you decide to do, is that committed action is rooted in and brings life to your values. When you value your personal health, continuing not to smoke, even in situations where you're tempted, embodies that value. And caring about your health supports other actions consistent with that value. For example, Susan stopped smoking because she valued her health and wanted to coach her daughter's soccer team. This value motivated her to give up smoking and kept her on track in sticking to it. She was successful this time around, which she hadn't been a few years ago, when she quit just to keep her husband off her back.

The *action* of caring about your health is different from mentally caring about your health. Taking an action consistent with caring about her health led Susan to explore other behavior changes consistent with a passion for creating and preserving her health. In sharp contrast to her previous pattern of using food as a substitute for cigarettes when she tried to stop smoking before, this time she began to make time for a thirty-minute walk every day.

EXERCISE: QUALITIES OF COMMITTED ACTION

A committed action is measured not by the size of the action, but by the qualities of choosing (rather than deciding) and how consistent the action is with the person's values. An action need not be heroic in order to be committed. You don't have to face your biggest fear as the first step in a campaign to reclaim your life, and you don't need to turn your life around overnight. A choice to act, no matter how small the action, is a commitment. While the impact of an action on your life may be small or large, every committed action shares the quality of being chosen in accordance with your values. This exercise (based on Hayes, Strosahl, and Wilson 1999, 241) provides an illustration of the point that committed actions of any magnitude, small or large, have a great deal in common. For this exercise, you need a piece of paper; a large, thick book; and a chair.

1. The first step is for you to make a commitment to do this exercise, which involves jumping. Do you commit? (If for some reason you're physically unable to jump, simply commit to imagining the exercise.)

2. Okay, next you can stand solidly on both feet atop the piece of paper. Ready? Jump off the paper and onto the floor!

3. Now you're ready for the next step: put the book on the floor and stand on it with both feet, then jump off the book and onto the floor!

4. Finally, stand on the chair with both feet, and then jump off the chair and onto the floor!

Debriefing. What did you notice as you went through this simple exercise? You probably noticed that there are differences among jumping off a piece of paper, a book, and a chair. There's a difference in height, and jumping off a chair feels like a bigger act than jumping off a piece of paper. If we asked you to jump off your roof, you would probably say no, correct? Notice something else though: The act of jumping is always the same, regardless of the height you jump from. You always have to bend your knees and use your muscles to propel you up and forward. That is the essence of jumping. The differences among the paper, the book, and the chair have more to do with the size of the commitment and, as often occurs in the real world, the things your mind presents (for example, "Be careful; you could hurt yourself," "This is stupid," or "You've never been good at sports")—and perhaps your physical preparedness. Jumping is jumping, and committed action is committed action, or action you take even with your reactive mind yammering at you. The size of the act is of less importance than the quality of the act.

In fact, smaller circumstances are ideal for practicing committed action. As you get comfortable with these small actions, you can take on bigger challenges in a stepwise fashion. Lisa, a single woman in her thirties, was painfully shy and wanted to have an intimate partner. Her first committed action was joining a book club that included men and women. Jumping from staying home where she felt safe (and lonely) to going to the book club is jumping, just as jumping from having no dates to asking a male acquaintance to have coffee together is jumping. There's no "jumping if I feel like it"; there's only jumping—up and forward without an effort to control or avoid internal thoughts, sensations, or feelings. Jumping off a piece of paper can be a huge step toward vital living! There's a Zen Buddhist saying that makes this point far better than we can: "You can't jump a canyon in two steps."

Committed Action Is a Process, Not an Outcome

Another ingredient of committed action is that it is an ongoing process, rather than a single achievement in your life. When you're striving to act in ways that are consistent with your values, you never reach the end of this process. If you value being a loving, devoted parent, you don't finally reach a place called "loving and devoted parent." You don't get a certificate from the universe announcing that you have achieved this value and can now stop being a loving and devoted parent! There is always more love and devotion to do. As long as you are alive and hold this value, acting on this value is an important part of your life. You will want to be as loving and devoted a parent at age eighty as you were at age thirty.

Vitality and meaning in life originate from the act of making and keeping commitments, not from the outcomes of actions or commitments. In many life endeavors, it is what you learn along the way that's important, not whether you obtained the outcome you set your sights on. At times, when you're very close to achieving a goal based on a value, such as getting a long-sought promotion or quitting smoking, you may notice that the journey has changed you and that the goal no longer seems to be an end point at all; rather, it's just a milepost on the path toward your values.

Committed Action Is Never Perfect

Because committed action is an ongoing process, you can never do it perfectly. You will make mistakes, and you will behave in ways that aren't consistent with your values. This happens to everyone; it's the human condition. The bright side of this is that after every choice to act comes another choice to act. If you choose to act in a way that isn't in accordance with your commitment or your values, just notice that and then turn your attention to the next choice that awaits you. Just as in the purposeful walking exercise in chapter 12, every action you take is a choice, and each moment in time presents the opportunity to make a new choice.

EXERCISE: COMMITMENT IN THE PRESENCE OF BARRIERS

Another characteristic of committed action is that you expect your mental barriers to be present along the way. This is why acceptance and mindfulness skills are necessary. Your reactive mind will come along for the ride and will present any number of obstacles, including those same old rules for living that put you in the depression trap in the first place. In the many case examples we have given you throughout this book, there is a consistent course of action that suggests a pathway out of depression. This path involves taking valued actions and being willing to face potentially distressing private experiences along the way. Pursuing the path on an ongoing basis requires a commitment to continue even with the inevitable mental barriers. Walking this path requires you to be willing to fail, be accountable to yourself, and then affirm the commitment once again. There is no easy way around your barriers. You must go through them. Here's a little mental exercise that will help you see this point. You will benefit from it more if you listen to it on the accompanying CD as an "eyes closed" experience.

> Imagine that you've been set on the river of your life and are asked to float the river to its end. You haven't been given much instruction on how to do this; all you have is the assurance that this river will end in the ocean. Soon after you begin your trip, the river begins to meander back and forth, almost coming to a standstill at times so that you stop making progress. You begin to wonder whether the river is somehow coming to an end. It doesn't seem to be going anywhere, it just meanders back and forth with hardly any force. It's frustrating and you feel you have to walk in the river just to make the kind of progress you think you need to make.
>
> A little while later, the current quickens and all of the sudden you are in very shallow rapids. You are bouncing along with the river and hitting rocks and boulders. You're splashed in the face, and then

splashed again repeatedly until you're soaked through. The rapids go on and on, and you begin to feel tired, bruised, and disheartened. After one particularly hard jolt, your raft flips and you frantically swim over to the riverbank and begin cursing the river. If life were fair, this river would go straight down to the ocean—no meandering, no rapids. If the function of rivers is to deliver water back to the ocean, why are there so many rocks and twists and turns? What do rocks have to do with getting water to the ocean? It isn't fair that rivers are made the way this river is made! You decide that if this river doesn't change its character immediately, you aren't going to float in it. But as you stare at the river in disgust, you notice that the water didn't decide to go ashore and complain about its journey. It simply does what water knows how to do. It understands what the nature of a river is. How can you get to the ocean if you stand on the bank looking at the water flowing by?

Debriefing. What went though your mind during this mental exercise? Could you relate to the outrage of being asked to float on a river like this? You didn't ask for these boulders. You didn't ask for your life to be hard like this. Even so, what committed action is required to get you to the end of your journey? Yep, you have to get back on the river and start floating again. You have to accept that this is how rivers are. They don't follow your mind's specifications. Rivers have their own nature and you can't change that. Your job is to reaffirm your commitment to floating the river of your life, and let the river take you where it will.

EXERCISE: MAKING CONTACT

This exercise (based on Hayes, Strosahl, and Wilson 1999, 244–45) reveals how difficult even a seemingly simple committed action can be. We strongly recommend that you use the version of this exercise on the CD, because it will make the experience more powerful for you. This exercise involves eye contact, so you need to ask a friend or partner to do it with you. You'll also need an alarm clock or timer.

Start by sitting very close to each other in a face-to-face position. You should be within two feet of each other. Set the alarm clock or timer to go off in five minutes.

Here is the committed action we're asking you to engage in: Spend the next five minutes looking directly into each other's eyes, making room for any private events that show up in your head. If you notice yourself looking away, bring your eyes back onto the other person's eyes. Notice anything that shows up for you and make room for it. If you feel anxious, notice your anxiety and bring your attention back to your partner's eyes. This isn't a stare down, so you can blink your eyes as needed. If you feel the need to laugh nervously, just notice that urge and return your gaze to your partner's eyes. Try to see that there is a real human being sitting across from you. This is a person with a unique history and a life force, just like you. Let yourself connect with the simple fact that you are here with this person, right here and right now. Whatever comes into your mind, just notice it and return to your commitment.

Debriefing. What happened inside your head as you did this exercise? Did you get flooded with different kinds of feelings? Did you laugh nervously? Did you notice your mind trying to take you away from your commitment? Were you able to return to your commitment if that happened? Did you engage in the committed action for the full five minutes, or did you break it off? Did you see this person in a different light when you had five minutes to completely take in that person's face? Take a few moments to discuss this exercise and your reactions with your partner.

HIDDEN BARRIERS TO COMMITTED ACTION

As the previous exercise suggests, a commitment to act is made with the understanding that you will encounter barriers. Throughout this book, we've helped you identify some of these barriers: life issues you might be avoiding; the thoughts, feelings, memories, and sensations that are scary to you; and mental tricks that your reactive mind might play on you. So, at this point, you're quite clear about what some of the barriers will be; unfortunately you can't anticipate all of the barriers that your reactive mind will give you once you start to act. We'd like to help by alerting you to some hidden hazards that could surface in the journey down the river of your life.

The Feeling of Confidence vs. Confident Action

One of the nastier tricks of the reactive mind is to get you into a dialogue about whether you feel confident enough to engage in a committed action. The reactive mind tells you that to take a confident action you have to have a confident feeling, and that if you aren't sure of yourself, you're not ready to act. To the extent that you do feel confident, your reactive mind is capable of giving you all kinds of bogus intelligence to undermine that feeling. It will remind you of other times when you made promises to yourself and didn't follow through on them. It will remind you of times when you acted and got negative results. It will try to get you to doubt your ability to follow through. You might find yourself saying something like "I would do that valued action if only I felt more confident in myself." Unfortunately, because you've struggled with depression in the past, you're prone to having feelings of low confidence, and this could keep you stuck in not making commitments at all or not following through on the ones you have made.

The word "confidence" hails from Latin and literally means "acting with fidelity to yourself." When you act with confidence, you take valued actions even when you aren't feeling confident. You aren't sure what will happen, and your reactive mind might even be giving you negative predictions. Acting with fidelity to yourself means you stay true to your values even in the midst of uncertain thoughts and feelings. Ironically, this is the only way you can ever acquire confident feelings: by entering situations where you're uncertain, and still acting in ways that are consistent with your beliefs. The goal isn't to acquire the feeling of confidence; the goal is to learn to act confidently even if you don't feel confident.

Trauma and Forgiveness

If you experienced a traumatic childhood involving sexual, physical, or verbal abuse, you will have to come to grips with a difficult issue: If you start living a vital, purposeful, committed life, someone who has done you wrong might be let off the hook of blame and responsibility. If one of your parents was physically abusive, and you overcome that injustice and reclaim your life, that parent might go around telling people that you were a willful child and needed to be punished more than other children. Your parent could point to how well you're doing now and claim that this is a result of his or her having been so strict with you when you were little.

What if you were sexually abused as a child, but no one in your family ever acknowledged that someone did you wrong? What if a parent or sibling did this, but no one is willing to fess up? Would you be willing to reclaim your life, knowing that the person responsible for this outrage is still at large? Often, a life story of victimization has a secret clause in it: You cannot be or act in a healthy way until the person responsible for what happened to you is singled out and punished. You have to be the victim until the crime is avenged in some way. This means that your spirit must remain broken so that you can continue to point to your abuse as the cause of your brokenness.

If your reactive mind has latched onto this powerful story line, it will be a major obstacle on the journey to a vital, purposeful existence. Fortunately, there's an equally powerful antidote to this poison story line: forgiveness. The modern meaning of this word is actually a distortion of its original meaning; it suggests that to forgive someone is to let that person off the hook, so to speak. In ACT, we don't view the action of forgiveness in this way. This isn't about freeing someone who hurt you from responsibility for such horrible actions. That person will have to face the universe eventually, and it won't be pretty when it happens. But that isn't your job; that's the universe's job. Your job is to live your life as best you can and in a way that reflects your values. One of your values might be to stop the cycle of abuse in your family by being a loving and devoted parent to your children. Why not take this stance, which is positive and points you toward your "true north," instead of a stance that you are broken and someone needs to be brought to justice?

When you consider the original meaning of the word "forgiveness," you can instantly see another course of action available to you. The Latin root of the word "give" means "grace," and the prefix "for" means "that which came before." Thus, the act of forgiveness can be viewed as giving yourself the grace you had before you were victimized. When the Bible talks about turning the other cheek, this doesn't mean inviting someone to strike you over and over again. It refers to an act of cleansing yourself of a transgression. It's a metaphor for the power of forgiveness in leading a spiritual life. Forgiveness is the highest form of committed action, and one that restores the grace you were born with and that resides in you even as you read this book. You can take back your life and reclaim your grace with this simple, powerful action!

"I've Wasted My Life"

Another way the reactive mind can trick you into abandoning your commitments is by getting you to blame yourself for not having figured out all of this stuff earlier in your life. As the ACT approach begins to work, some depressed people get more depressed because they think they should have known how to do this all along! In truth, months if not years of your life might have been subject to the reactive mind's reign of terror. You can't rewind the videotape of your life and start over ten years ago with a clean tape. Your life is what it is, and you *can* live with it.

Another way of thinking about this dilemma is that you are in the perfect spot you need to be in at this very moment in your life. Everything you have gone through, including your suffering, has prepared you to break free of the depression trap at this point in time. The forces in your life that led you to pick up this book are exactly what needed to happen for you to pick up this book. When you think of what you've been through in life and where you're going, there is no such thing as wasted life or wasted time. Every element, including the difficult ones, is precious. You only get to do this once (unless you believe in reincarnation), so don't look backward; look forward!

DEALING WITH FAILED COMMITMENTS

We can tell you a hundred times that no one keeps commitments perfectly, that clarifying and living your values is a process, and so forth. No matter how many times we say it, that doesn't mean your reactive mind will listen and get on board with the program. When you fail to live up to a commitment, your reactive mind will go on the attack and present you with a wide array of clever phishing lures. If you take the bait, you'll be tempted to take your focus off your commitments. Don't ruminate about past failures or buy the thought that you're fated to fail. This can cause you to break commitments and eventually stop making commitments in an effort to prevent the entire cycle of failure from occurring.

Can't vs. Won't

When you choose to stop following through on a commitment to yourself, you can be certain that your reactive mind has somehow phished you into stopping. You might notice thoughts like "I just can't do this; it's too hard," "I don't have the time to do this the way I want to do it," or "I can't make any more commitments like this because I feel like a failure when I don't follow through." When this happens, your reactive mind is creating the impression that you lack the ability to engage in the committed act.

Notice the word you ordinarily use in such circumstances: "can't," which literally means that you don't have the ability to engage in the act. While it may occasionally be true that you lack the skills to live up to a commitment, normally this isn't the cause of the problem. Usually, you will have the skills needed to stick to your commitment, but your reactive mind will create the impression that you don't have what it takes to follow through. You might notice its all-too-familiar trick of using reasons as causes, as discussed in chapter 10. In all likelihood, what has happened is that you aren't willing to engage in the committed action when certain barriers are present. The word "won't" means you "will it not," and since willingness is a voluntary action involving choice, you are actually *choosing* not to engage in committed action. Thus, when you find the word "can't" showing up in your reason giving about a failed commitment, we want you to replace it with the word "won't." This will signal you that you've encountered some barrier that you aren't willing to confront and move through.

We want to make it clear that not living up to a commitment isn't a matter of blame or failure. It's a matter of choice. Choosing, and being conscious that you're choosing, is what ACT is all about. At the same time, you can't let your reactive mind phish you with an inaccurate and self-defeating vision of what you're capable of.

Recommit

Instead of beating yourself up for not following through, and making this into yet another trigger for more depression, we want you to try another strategy. When you first make a commitment to act, we want you to make another commitment to yourself. If you violate a commitment, we want you to commit to bringing this forward in nonjudgmental terms. Essentially, you are a person who started the day committed to a certain action in the service of a personal value, and you instead chose a different action that wasn't consistent with your values. Then we want you to express whatever value you have about being true to your word, both to yourself and to others. You might say or write something like "I am a person who values following through on my commitments to myself and to others. Today, I engaged in a behavior that isn't consistent with what I stand for in terms of my values about making and keeping commitments."

Notice that all you are doing is holding yourself "response-able." You aren't blaming yourself, but you are holding yourself accountable for your actions. The next step is to restate your original commitment, because each moment presents a new opportunity to follow through and, as such, you have an endless number of opportunities to make choices about keeping or not keeping commitments. The great thing about choosing is that you get to choose again within a matter of seconds, minutes, or hours. If something is valuable enough for you to make a commitment to it, it's probably still going to be valuable in the next moment of your life. Not keeping a commitment does not change your values!

■ *Luke's Journey Toward a Vital Life*

Luke did a lot of work on clarifying his values, and he didn't like the results, which revealed a big gap between those values and how he was living his life. He discovered that he had several important values in life. He wanted to get into an interesting, fulfilling line of work that would challenge him. He wanted to have a family, and he really wanted to be a devoted, caring father. He wanted intimacy in his life. He valued taking care of his personal health. The problem wasn't that he lacked values; the problem was that he was way off the bull's-eye in terms of his actions. Luke realized that his story line of ultimately failing at anything meaningful wasn't useful and that buying it had probably planted the seed for most of his failures.

Luke created a plan for a vital life by committing to several seemingly small actions. The first was to go to his health club and exercise once a week. The morning of the day he had planned to go the gym, he felt lethargic and had the thought that he should put off exercising until he felt better. Luke thanked his reactive mind for that thought and went to the health club anyway. As it turned out, the exercise really helped his energy level and mood. Luke's next step was to apply for admission to the trade school he had dropped out of. Despite the predictions of his reactive mind, he was accepted. He next made a commitment to attend all of the project meetings in a course he was taking. Within the first week, he missed a project meeting. But rather than throwing in the towel, as he might have done before, he simply owned up to missing the meeting as something he didn't value and recommitted to attending all project meetings.

Before long, his instructor noticed how gifted Luke was and asked him to tutor students who were having trouble. Luke noticed that he enjoyed tutoring and that he had a knack for it. He decided to apply to a local community college and work on getting a teaching certificate. In his first class, he met a woman he was instantly attracted to. His reactive mind kicked in big-time and reminded him that he would eventually disappoint her and violate his commitments. Luke pushed right back and made a commitment to continue dating her despite these predictions, and soon their relationship became serious. He also learned to participate in social activities even if his mood wasn't perfect, and a lot of times it wasn't. However, he also noticed that his mood was less of a factor in his daily activities than it had been for a long time. The more Luke engaged in committed actions, the more motivated he was to engage in other activities. Luke was on the pathway out of depression!

Secrets to ACT On

☞ The secret to reclaiming your life is to make and keep commitments to yourself and others.

☞ A commitment is a choice to act in a valued way regardless of the advice you get from your reactive mind.

☞ You make commitments knowing that engaging in valued actions will involve encountering your mental barriers; you make a pact with yourself to stay the course anyway.

☞ A committed action is a quality of responding and isn't defined by how big the action is. Small committed actions have the same impact as big ones.

☞ A commitment is an ongoing process that provides you with vitality over time.

☞ Forgiveness is the single most powerful committed action.

☞ Life is never wasted; wherever you are in your life is where you are meant to be.

The Coach Says

You have the tools you need to live a vital, purposeful life. When you make and keep your commitments, you'll notice that even painful events are healthy. If you don't keep a commitment, don't stop being committed! Just notice what your reactive mind did to trick you, thank it, and reaffirm your commitment.

Sneak Preview

The next part of this book is designed to help you continue taking committed actions in the four key arenas of your life: health, relationships, work, and play. In part 3, the last section of the book, you'll learn how to use the ACT strategies discussed in part 2 on a daily basis. We'll help you create a new, ACT lifestyle and develop a network of social support for it.

Make a Commitment to Vitality

We are what we repeatedly do. Excellence, then, is not an act but a habit. —Aristotle

In this part of the book, we'll teach you how to keep the journey of your life moving in the direction set by your values compass. This is not going to be easy; like life itself, the road to living a vital life is full of unexpected twists and turns. You will come to forks in the road where the signage is confusing, incorrect, or perhaps entirely absent. You'll have to use your gut instincts and exercise your ability to choose a valued course of action without knowing in advance what the results will be. In short, you'll have to let your wise mind be your travel guide. The lack of certainty and constant change involved in valued living is scary and can stop you in your tracks. The antidote for situations like this is to develop habits that allow you to ACT (accept, choose, and take action). The following diagram illustrates where you're heading on this journey: to a life in which you promote your personal health, develop rich and fulfilling relationships, and approach your work and play with gusto.

Good Personal Health

Healthy Relationships

Satisfying Work

Fun and Relaxation

Spiritual Satisfaction

Mindful Lifestyle

Depression Risk

You have been on a mission since you started working on this program: a mission to step out of depression and get back into a life worth living. On the next page, you'll find a worksheet to help you keep track of your intention to use the ideas presented in the next two chapters. After reading each chapter, come back to this worksheet and use a scale of 1 to 10 to rate your intention to practice the strategies in your daily life. Note that we use the verb "practice." We don't expect that you'll apply any of these strategies perfectly. As the saying by the great philosopher Aristotle suggests, vital actions are not isolated moments of excellence; rather, they are the result of habits you create through repeated practice. You never arrive at a vital life; it's a direction you head toward each and every day.

PART 3 INTENTION WORKSHEET

Not Likely to Practice				More Likely to Practice				Extremely Likely to Practice		
1	2	3	4	5	6	7	8	9	10

	Chapter	Intention Level
15	Maintain Your Life Direction	
16	Give and Take Support	

Debriefing. If your intention level is at a 5 or less after reading either chapter, we recommend that you consider sharing that chapter with a friend or partner. Ask the person to read it and discuss it with you. Having another person to bounce ideas off of might give you some fresh ideas about ways to put ACT into practice on a daily basis. If you find you're having trouble sticking with these strategies, consider increasing your support level, perhaps seeking an ally in a health care professional; a therapist; or a priest, minister, or rabbi. You can also contact us with specific questions about how to apply these strategies at our website: www.actondepression.com.

CHAPTER 15

Maintain Your Life Direction

Nobody trips over mountains. It is the small pebble that causes you to stumble.
Pass all the pebbles in your path and you will find you have crossed the mountain.
—Author unknown

Congratulations on reaching the point where you can go out and build the kind of life you want to live! It has a taken a lot of time, persistence, and energy to get to this point. Take a moment to feel proud of yourself for doing this. We give you complete permission to fuse with any positive thoughts and feelings that arise!

In part 2, we taught you the skills necessary to reverse depression compression and expand your life space. Applying these skills and living a valued life is a journey that will never end. No matter where you are in your life right now, there is more life to go. In this chapter, we'll teach you how to be on the lookout for depression-producing behaviors, how to make your new healthy-living habits permanent, and how to embrace rather than struggle with setbacks.

LIFE IS A MARATHON, NOT A SPRINT

When it comes to stepping out of depression and into life, think of the journey you are on as a marathon, not a sprint. In a marathon, you must conserve your energy because you have to run for many, many miles. It isn't a matter of speed; it's a matter of strategy and endurance. Experienced marathoners know that there will be a point in the race where they hit the wall; a point of physical pain and mental exhaustion that they must go through in order to finish the marathon. Most long-distance runners will tell you that, as painful as it is, going through that wall is the most satisfying part of running a marathon.

Likewise, you're bound to hit the wall several times in your life, whether that means being laid off, losing a life partner to death or divorce, being diagnosed with a chronic illness, being in a bad accident, or any number of countless other personal setbacks. It isn't a matter of whether this will happen in your life, just when it will happen. Your job is to anticipate this and even see it as part of the reason you're running. The most satisfying part of being alive is looking back on your life and feeling a deep sense of satisfaction about how you handled the obstacles that life placed in your path. To enhance your success in this, you need to have a game plan for your life journey, just as a marathoner has a game plan for each race. The first step is to anticipate what kinds of stumbling blocks you're likely to encounter as you pursue a vital life.

The Honeymoon Trap

You're probably familiar with the honeymoon phase of relationship: that period of time at the beginning, when everything seems to be going right and each person sees the other as perfect. As wonderful as it feels, that phase is time-limited and eventually must give way to the working phase of the relationship. Daily life isn't nearly as easy or fun at this point, because things are starting to get real. Conflicts arise over dirty laundry, dirty dishes, and how to spend money. The long-term success of the relationship depends upon how persistent each person is in trying to work through these issues of daily living. As it turns out, being in a long-term relationship is hard work, and it's never-ending. When the honeymoon's over, you hit the wall in the relationship. The question is whether you'll go through it or just give up.

You can find yourself enjoying a similar honeymoon with ACT. The strategies may be working fabulously well for you right now because they're new and, in some ways, easy to use; you may even feel you've been given a new lease on life. If so, fantastic! Just understand that almost anything new, including ACT, will have a honeymoon aura to it. When you get into the working phase of your relationship with ACT strategies, it might not seem as easy as it was at the beginning. Life keeps throwing you curveballs, and you're likely to get tired of the need to practice acceptance, commitment, and taking valued actions on a daily basis. You might even notice thoughts like "This isn't working as well as it used to" or "Following this value in my life doesn't seem to be getting me anywhere."

Reactive Mind Is a Relentless Phisher

Remember, your social training is so ingrained that you can't expect your reactive mind to roll over and let you live the life you want to live; instead, it will try to barge in and dominate you. One way it does this is by co-opting ACT principles and putting them into your old system of rule following. In other words, ACT will become a new belief system that's supposed to make you feel happy all the time. When you run into the inevitable setbacks life has to offer, your reactive mind will use this as proof that ACT can't help you live a good life. It will offer some attractive new phishing lures, and you may not recognize them, precisely because they're new:

- You've lived according to your values, and look what you're getting in return!

- You're never going to become present in your life because you don't have the character it takes.

- These strategies are just bandages; the real problem is that you are screwed up inside.

- ACT might help other people, but it clearly isn't helping you.

- Being willing to make yourself vulnerable just leads to being rejected again.

Your reactive mind will offer an endless stream of negative thoughts like these, and you'll have to be careful not to fuse with them each and every day.

Turning Your Back on What Works

If you understand depression as something you do rather than something you have, depressive behaviors clearly put you at risk for becoming depressed again, especially if those behaviors are habitual. Although most depressed people understand that there's a risk of becoming depressed again, the experience they have gone through is so unpleasant and humbling that they just want to put the entire experience out of mind. Unfortunately, they so desperately want to forget the depression era in their lives that they also jettison the very strategies that helped them step out of depression in the first place! If new ACT strategies have not yet become habits, old depressive behaviors can reappear and put you back in depression compression.

There's an old saying we use regarding this: "You have to dance with the one that brung ya." You have to remember the strategies that allowed you to step out of depression and take them along with you for the rest of your life. You can't turn your back on the very things that allowed you to move forward in your life. You need to put these tools in your bag so that if you fall into another hole in your life journey, you'll have what you need to extricate yourself—not just that old, ineffective shovel.

DEVELOPING HABITS FOR VITAL LIVING

So, let's get down to the business of developing habits that, practiced over time, can replace the behaviors that leave you vulnerable to depression compression. Notice two key phrases here: "developing habits" and "practiced over time." You have to build daily habits that embed ACT strategies in your life. And you have to approach this with compassion for yourself, understanding that practice makes permanent, not perfect.

The ACT Habit

When you make a behavior into habit, it becomes automatic and almost immune to external or internal barriers. Psychologists have studied the way habits are formed for nearly five decades, and we know a lot about the process. It is clear that habits are created through repeated practice in different settings and circumstances. The more you practice various ACT strategies in different settings and life circumstances, the more likely they are to become automatic responses. The term "habit strength" refers to the degree to which a learned behavior is likely to occur across different situations. A negative example of habit strength is tobacco addiction. Smokers have practiced smoking so often and in so many different situations that the behavior of lighting and smoking a cigarette is almost automatic. It just happens. We want you to take the positive side of the habit strength idea and apply it to your use of ACT strategies.

Another important aspect of learning habits is the process of shaping—practicing parts of a larger habit and then beginning to piece the parts together. When smokers quit, they don't just stop smoking, they gradually become nonsmokers. Most people who eventually quit smoking have tried four or five times. In little bits and pieces, they develop specific thoughts and behaviors that are the opposite of the smoking habit. Instead of instinctively reaching for a cigarette after eating, a person might take a five-minute walk to relax. This is but one of many different behaviors the nonsmoker will have to learn. The more these small behaviors are practiced, the more habit strength they have in the situations in which they're practiced. Similarly, if you find many little ways to practice ACT strategies, you will notice over time that they begin to link together in a network of ACT living strategies. You can do this one step at a time. It's like putting ten dollars into an investment account every week. It might not seem like much, but if you keep it up for ten years, at a normal rate of return you would have over ten thousand dollars! The key here is that little steps and strategies do add up to bigger results than you might expect, particularly if you keep it up over time.

A final concept in developing habits is the process of generalization—spreading a habit to other situations that share some common elements with the original situation where you first learned the habit. As you practice a specific behavior that might include accepting certain challenging thoughts and feelings (for example, in regard to your physical appearance while dressing for a party), your ability to use these acceptance skills will spread to other situations involving similarly challenging private events (for example, dealing with a difficult interaction at work).

Developing an ACT Lifestyle

Think of the task at hand as building a new lifestyle that uses ACT principles as a basis for healthy living. Although we've focused on depression in this book, practicing acceptance, mindfulness, commitment, and positive action on a daily basis is a healthy move for anyone. If you connect ACT strategies to routine activities in your life, you'll develop substantial ACT habit strength and reap the benefits of this simple but powerful process as you go about the activities of your daily existence.

The more mental processes you use to trigger ACT habits, the more ingrained they'll become. Here are some mental processes that can act as cues for the ACT habit:

- **Reciting:** using chosen phrases or quotes as simple reminders

- **Mental rehearsal:** mentally practicing ACT strategies for specific situations

- **Visualizing:** imagining positive life outcomes, such as getting a college degree

- **Recalling:** remembering previous positive experiences using ACT strategies

- **Pairing:** using a daily event, such as lunch, to trigger specific ACT strategies

The neat thing about cues is that you can take them with you anywhere, and they can trigger an ACT response even in novel situations. In general, the more ways you practice ACT strategies, the more likely they are to feel natural and automatic in troublesome situations. The reverse is also true. If you don't practice these strategies very often, you will find it much more difficult to apply them in emotionally charged situations. Instead, you'll find that the behaviors you've practiced more often, such as avoidance, escape, or fusion with rules, tend to take over and dictate the outcome.

EXERCISE: FAVORITE ACT HABITS

To make ACT strategies the basis of your lifestyle, you need to know which habits you want to form. Not every ACT strategy works for every person. As you've worked through this book, you may have noticed that some of the strategies fit your personal style and seemed easier to use. These strategies will probably be easier to make into habits. Some of these strategies might be variations on behaviors you already practice in your life. This exercise will help you think over your experience with this book and identify specific lifestyle strategies you see as useful. Take some time to think about the ACT strategies you've found the most useful and write them in the following worksheet. You may find it helpful to review the exercises in part 2 to remind yourself of everything you've learned. To make this easier for you, the worksheet presents the core ACT skill areas in the same sequence as they were presented to you in part 2.

Favorite ACT Habits

Clarifying my values:

_____

_____

Practicing willingness and acceptance:

_____

_____

Staying detached from my reactive mind:

_____

_____

Holding my thoughts rather than buying them:

_____

_____

Being skeptical of my explanations for my own behavior and that of others:

_____

_____

Holding my story line lightly:

_____

_____

Being present and expanding my wise mind:

_____

_____

Creating a vision and plan for my life:

_____

_____

Making and keeping commitments:

_____

_____

Debriefing. What did you find as you completed this exercise? Did you find it difficult to identify specific strategies for one or more areas? That might suggest that you focus on developing ACT habits in the areas where you found more strategies useful. Alternatively, you could go back to the chapter on that strategy and review your work to come up with some ideas. If you wrote down quite a few ideas in one area, you could concentrate your ACT habit-building efforts in this area.

EXERCISE: CREATE AN ACT PRACTICE PLAN

As mentioned, creating a habit requires practicing the behavior in as many situations as possible and developing cues you can take with you anywhere you go. If you create a specific plan for how you'll practice an ACT strategy on a daily basis, it's much more likely that you'll follow through. In this exercise, you'll identify specific situations in which you'll practice your ACT strategies and the mental cues that will trigger them. This could be as simple as practicing being present for ten minutes every morning right after you wake up. It could be saying the ACT mantra ("Accept, choose, and take action") ten times while driving to work. It could be reading over your values for personal health each evening before you go to bed.

Notice that we are asking you to identify both a time and a place for practice, and a specific habit you want to practice. It's best to practice daily, as this will increase your ACT habit strength more quickly and effectively. Feel free to list any number of habits; more than three is great, and even just one is a good start. You may wish to make copies of this blank worksheet so you'll always have a fresh copy. Alternatively, you can print out fresh copies from the CD.

My ACT Practice Plan

I. Desired ACT habit:

_____

Time, setting, and cue:

_____

_____

2. Desired ACT habit:

_____

Time, setting, and cue:

_____

_____

3. Desired ACT habit:

_____

Time, setting, and cue:

_____

_____

EXERCISE: IDENTIFY YOUR REWARDS

Developing a habit depends in large part on the rewards that come after the behavior has occurred. This is because all forms of human behavior are organized and maintained by the rewards that follow them. If cigarette smoking didn't offer any rewards, no one would become addicted to cigarettes. The smoking habit develops because of the many physical and mental rewards tobacco offers. Similarly (but more healthy!), if you provide yourself with rewards for practicing ACT strategies, you'll strengthen the habit of practicing them. Of course, there are many rewards inherent in practicing ACT strategies, both in the external world and in the world between your ears. But we also want you to reward yourself for remembering to practice in the first place!

This exercise helps you identify various ways you'll reward yourself for practicing your ACT habits. Rewards can be as simple as going to a movie, taking a warm bath, eating a favorite snack, or going out with a friend. Generally, we want the reward to be a positive experience, so you'll be even more motivated to practice your ACT habits and experience more vitality! Link your rewards to specific ACT behaviors and habits, and to specific goals. For example, if the target behavior is mindful eating to slow yourself down after a hard day's work, you may have a goal of eating at least five meals mindfully each week. When you accomplish your goal, you've earned your just desserts!

My Rewards Plan

Target Behavior	Goal	Reward

EXERCISE: EXPAND YOUR ACT HABITS

Once you've begun to develop ACT habits in the situations identified in your ACT practice plan, it's time to expand them into other situations. This is one reason why we've focused on having you develop mental cues to trigger particular ACT responses. You take your mind with you everywhere you go; therefore, you always have access to cues that can trigger ACT responses in any situation. It's helpful to identify targets for expanding ACT strategies in advance of actually being in those situations. This exercise asks you to take each ACT habit you've been practicing and pick two new target situations to expand that strategy to. Be patient as you do this exercise. Take time to imagine your daily routine and the types of situations that tend to pop up. This will help you identify areas of daily living that are good candidates for expanding your new habits.

My Plan for Expanding ACT Habits

Expanding my practice of clarifying my values:

1. _____

2. _____

Expanding my practice of willingness and acceptance:

1. _____

2. _____

Expanding my practice of being present and staying detached from my reactive mind:

1. _____

2. _____

Expanding my practice of holding my thoughts rather than buying them:

1. _____

2. _____

Expanding my practice of being skeptical of my explanations for my behavior and that of others:

1. _____

2. _____

Expanding my practice of holding my story line lightly:

1. _____

2. _____

Expanding my practice of being present and expanding my wise mind:

1. _____

2. _____

Expanding my practice of creating a vision and plan for my life:

1. _____

2. _____

Expanding my practice of making and keeping commitments:

1. _____

2. _____

Debriefing. The process of expanding habits is like a pyramid scheme; the formula isn't 4 + 4 = 8, but rather 4 x 4 = 16. This is because you acquire habit strength faster when you practice the same habit in a variety of situations. The more situations you spread ACT strategies to, the more they will become an automatic part of your lifestyle.

EXERCISE: CREATE A PLAN FOR REVIEWING YOUR RESULTS

Any time you set out to change your lifestyle, you need to periodically review the results to see if your changes are delivering the goods. The best way to do this is to periodically do the "Workability Yardstick" exercise, in chapter 5. We suggest doing this assessment at least once every three months to determine whether your score is going up or down, or staying about the same.

Your numerical score is, of course, important, but equally important is to look at the words you circle to describe qualities of your life. Are you circling different words to describe your life? Hopefully you'll find yourself circling fewer words in the low workability column. Each time you do this exercise, view it as an opportunity to step back from your daily routine and look at how your life is really working. Making this type of life review a strong mental habit will put you in a great position to pursue the life you want to live.

Following is a worksheet to help you keep track of your results. Use it to record the date of your workability assessment, your overall score (noting whether it's gone up or down), and insights about the low and high workability words you've circled.

Workability Yardstick Tracking Sheet

Date	Workability Score	Trends in Low and High Workability

MONITORING DEPRESSION COMPRESSION EXPERIENCES

The fact that you've struggled with depression means you have an increased risk of falling into the depression trap again in your life. There are some aspects of this risk that can be controlled and others that can't. As discussed in chapter 7 (and as the Serenity Prayer suggests), your job is to accept the things you cannot control and channel your energy into things you can control.

There's an old saying that makes an important point: "Life is one damn thing after another; your job is to make sure it isn't the same damn thing!" You will hit walls in your life journey; this is an inevitable part of the process of living. The key is what you do when that happens. ACT is not a new strategy for avoiding walls; it's a set of strategies for moving through the walls you encounter. Just because you're being present, using acceptance, following your values, and following through on commitments doesn't guarantee you immunity from setbacks in life. If your reactive mind phishes you with the evaluation that ACT must not be working because of the setbacks you encounter, remind your mind that life is one damn thing after another. ACT is a way of living with such events and allowing them to be part of your long-term quest for personal meaning and vitality. Even the most dreaded life event offers an opportunity to live out your values and commitments. In fact, it is when you experience setbacks that using ACT strategies becomes critical. Otherwise these challenging events can trigger old, unworkable behaviors that spring the depression trap again, which is exactly what happened to Andy.

■ Andy's Story

Andy, a forty-one-year-old man who's married and has three children, works as a branch manager at a local bank. He started having problems with depression at twenty-five, when his father died suddenly of a heart attack. They had been very close, and Andy held him up as a role model. His father was very ambitious and driven at work, and taught Andy to excel by outlasting his competitors on the job. As a result, Andy arrived at work before everyone else and left after everyone else. This created quite a bit of tension in his marriage, because his wife felt he was always preoccupied with work. He tended to get irritable with his children when his job stress was high. He had also developed a smoking habit, which his wife really disliked.

ACT helped Andy see that his depression was a signal that he was expending too much energy in his work life, to the detriment of other important areas of life. He felt unhealthy, he had trouble relaxing and playing, and his relationships weren't going well. Andy made a commitment to limiting his work hours and scheduling fun activities with his wife and children at least three times weekly. He also made a commitment to staying present during these activities rather than thinking about work issues. Over a six-week period, Andy noticed that his sense of vitality was steadily increasing. He and his wife began talking about taking a long road trip with their children, which would require Andy to take an extended vacation. Andy was enthusiastic about this idea and put in for a three-week vacation that would occur in six months, when his kids were out of school. At the urging of his wife, Andy also made a choice to quit smoking and, with the aid of his family doctor, set a quit date. Andy was on the path out of depression and into vital living!

Four months later, Andy was informed that his bank had been purchased by a much bigger regional bank and that he was being laid off with only one month of severance pay. Andy was devastated. He felt betrayed and was extremely angry about the way he'd been treated. Buying his father's messages about work, Andy ruminated for hours on end about not being a success unless he could find a job with the same status. However, job options at that level were extremely limited and he couldn't find a similar position. He stopped going out with his wife and children and started smoking again, and he snapped at his wife and children when they tried to bring him out of his shell. His depression level steadily increased as weeks went by without any job opportunities. Andy fused with thoughts that he was a failure, that he had let his family down, and that life had treated him unfairly. Andy was back in the depression trap!

EXERCISE: IDENTIFY YOUR RISK SITUATIONS

As Andy's story demonstrates, life is going to give you setbacks. When this happens, you have an important choice to make: intensify your commitment to practicing ACT strategies or use familiar but unworkable avoidance and escape tactics. In Andy's case, he reverted back to the very strategies he had used after his father's death and that had led to his first depression compression experience—believing unworkable rules about his value, withdrawing from the people he loved, and treating his body in uncaring ways. While you can't predict every act of fate that will occur in life and you certainly can't prepare for devastating losses, you can learn to identify situations that trigger your risk for depression.

One easy way to approach this is to look back on your depression history and identify events, situations, or interactions that have increased your depression. An event is a specific occurrence, such as being fired from a job. A situation is an ongoing process that poses emotional challenges, such as having a child with severe behavior problems. An interaction is an emotionally challenging relationship between you and one or more people, such as a spouse, several family members, or a group of friends. Take a moment now to reflect on this, and then write down potential depression risks in each category.

My Depression Risks

Risky life events:

_____

_____

Risky life situations:

_____

_____

Risky interactions:

_____

_____

Debriefing. What did you come up with in the way of depression risks? Were these primarily specific life events that could set you off, or are you more prone to being triggered by difficult interactions with people? Did you identify some life situations that would pose an ongoing risk to you? The key to staying on top of your situation is to make sure you anticipate the setbacks that life is going to offer you.

EXERCISE: MONITOR DEPRESSIVE BEHAVIORS

Although being laid off was the triggering event for Andy's slide back into depression compression, he didn't become depressed again overnight. It took weeks for Andy's depressive behaviors to take hold, and this made it difficult for him to see what was happening to increase his depression risk. He didn't stop going out with his wife and children all at once; he started by begging off a few outings and slowly ended up stopping altogether. This is a key characteristic of a developing depression compression: Each depressive response tightens the compression a little bit. You can get stuck in this trap little by little without realizing what's going on.

To prevent this from happening, regularly take inventory of your depressive behaviors in the four major arenas of life—health, relationships, work, and play—using the "Inventory of Health, Relationship, Work, and Play Behaviors," in chapter 3. (You can print out a fresh copy from the CD accompanying this book.) Go ahead and review your previous responses to this inventory, then fill it out again and score it. In the first row of the worksheet on the next page, write today's date and record how you scored today in each category: health, relationships, work, and play. Since the greatest risk for becoming depressed again occurs in the first year, we ask that you do this inventory once each month for the next year and record your scores on the worksheet. Post this worksheet in your home to serve as a reminder to do the inventory each month.

Depressive Behaviors Monitoring Worksheet

Date Inventoried	Health Score	Relationships Score	Work Score	Play Score
Baseline:				
Month 1:				
Month 2:				
Month 3:				
Month 4:				
Month 5:				
Month 6:				
Month 7:				
Month 8:				
Month 9:				
Month 10:				
Month 11:				
Month 12:				

EXERCISE: CREATE A DEPRESSION PREVENTION PLAN

Andy's story illustrates something that occurs all too often: He stopped using ACT strategies at the time when they would have been most useful to him. In his case, keeping his commitment to spend time with his wife and children and practicing being present would have helped buffer the stress of losing his job. Remaining a nonsmoker would have preserved his sense of commitment to his personal health in the midst of this stressful life transition. Staying in an accepting, mindful posture with respect to his reactive mind's chatter about being a failure would have allowed his wise mind to guide him through the transition. Andy didn't have a prevention plan in place to help him activate ACT strategies in the midst of challenges.

To avoid this pitfall, you need to develop a personal depression prevention plan. This is a written description of the actions you'll take if you sense your depression is increasing, or if you score more than 3 points higher than your baseline score in any life arena during your monthly inventory. In the following worksheet, describe specific ACT strategies you will use in each life arena if you're getting more depressed.

My Depression Prevention Plan

Core Area of Life	Specific ACT Strategies I Will Use
Health	
Relationships	
Work	
Play	

Debriefing. Post your depression prevention plan in a conspicuous location in your home, perhaps on your refrigerator, on a mirror, by your computer, or on a toilet seat. Choose a place where you'll make visual contact with your plan daily. Also consider posting your depression risks worksheet from earlier in this chapter in the same location. This will help you be vigilant for high-risk situations and prime you to use ACT strategies in those situations.

SPRING INTO *ACTION*!

As we've stressed, many people have depressive experiences, but they usually bounce back after a few days. You need not be overly concerned about short-term depression experiences; they are part and parcel of everyday existence. Just notice what's happening, step back, and consider whether you're fusing with some provocative thought, emotion, memory, or sensation and have accidentally slipped back into using avoidance behaviors. If you notice this happening, don't get down on yourself. Instead, accept this for what it is, access your wise mind, look at what your values are, and take action in a direction consistent with your values.

What you want to be on the lookout for are more pervasive, long-term patterns of depressive behavior. The purpose of the monthly self-inventory is to give you an objective view of your depression behaviors over a longer time span. If your score in one or more areas starts moving up, that's a sign that you may be at risk for sliding back into depression compression. Ask yourself the following questions:

- Has anything happened in my life recently that might be responsible for this higher score?

- How have I been feeling over the last several weeks?

- Is there anything that I'm avoiding dealing with in my life right now?

- If I'm experiencing depression right now, what might be out of balance in my life?

- What does my wise mind have to say about the situation I'm in right now?

- Am I being phished by my reactive mind in this situation? If so, what's the lure?

The next step is to spring into action and implement the strategies in your prevention plan. Once you're operating under the influence of depression compression, it's harder to come up with solutions. This is why it's important to have a specific, written plan of behaviors you intend to engage in if you notice your depression is on the rise again. And, just as when you first acted on your depression, you need to follow through on these strategies regardless of your energy level and how you feel. Following your prevention plan can reverse the downward spiral of depression. If you spring into action as soon as you see the signs, depression doesn't stand a chance!

DEVELOPING INTENTION

The word "intention" literally means "to lean toward or lean on." As commonly used, it means that you are primed to respond to some event, situation, or interaction. As we mentioned earlier, mentally rehearsing your responses to specific depression risk situations imprints these responses in your mind and makes it more likely that you'll actually use the behavior you've been rehearsing. This will help you develop behavioral intention—a specific mental image of how you intend to respond in a certain type of situation. The intention becomes stronger if you're very specific about the situation that poses a risk to you, and even more specific about the behaviors you intend to use in that situation. You can also strengthen your behavioral intention by mentally rehearsing the response and by saying it out loud to yourself and to others who want to support you.

EXERCISE: TAKE A HIKE!

In this exercise, we'll help you prepare for that inevitable time when you're faced with an event, situation, or interaction that poses a depression risk. This will usually be a situation that evokes strong feelings in you, triggers past memories, or triggers a surge in phishing by your reactive mind.

We want you to take a walk to a location that's about fifteen to thirty minutes from your home. Before you start, make a copy of the depression risk events, situations, and interactions you identified earlier in this chapter. Get some 3 by 5 index cards and write one risk item on one side of each card as specifically as you can. On the other side of the card, write down the specific behaviors you intend to use in that situation. Once you have completed your cards, tuck them in a pocket or purse and start your walk.

Your goal is to walk to the destination you have selected with your depression risk items along for the ride. During your walk, stop periodically, take out one of your index cards, and create a vivid mental image of the risk item. Imagine you're actually in that situation and try to create as much detail as you can in terms of your emotions, memories, thoughts, and physical sensations. Then flip the index card over and read aloud the behaviors you intend to engage in. Create a vivid mental image of actually engaging in that behavior. Imagine you're using this response even while in the presence of unpleasant feelings, memories, or thoughts. Imagine that your response also produces a sense of healthy, vital living, even if the situation is difficult for you. After completing this card, clear your mind as you walk for a few minutes more, then stop, pick another card, and repeat your mental rehearsal. Continue with this exercise until you've worked your way through all the cards.

Debriefing. What experiences did you have while taking this walk with your depression risk items in tow? People often notice that some depression risk events, situations, or interactions lead to a fuzzier mental picture of the strategies they intend to use. If this happened to you, go back to your written strategy and make it even more specific. Then, on another walk, take out the cards with fuzzy images and rehearse them again. The more complete your mental image of both the depression risk and the responses you will use, the stronger your behavioral intention will be if you actually encounter that situation.

■ *Andy's Journey Toward a Vital Life*

When Andy reflected on his situation, he realized that events involving being turned down for a job were a major depression risk for him and that he needed a depression prevention plan for times when he felt discouraged about finding a job. Since he had experienced being rejected for a job several times, he was able to generate some specific scenarios for his walking exercise. What he had noticed from studying his new depression compression was that he wasn't allowing his wife and children to support him emotionally and he wasn't engaging in family activities that he valued. He generated a depression prevention plan in which he would seek out his wife when he was discouraged and ask her to go to dinner and a movie with him. When he went on his walk, he mentally rehearsed a variety of job rejection events and then stated his intention to immediately go to his wife and ask her on a date.

In the following weeks, Andy had a few more unsuccessful job interviews, but this time he had a plan and followed through on it. He noticed that his thoughts about being inadequate and a failure didn't get to him nearly as much when he was involved in activities with his wife and children. Granted, he was concerned about his family's financial security, but that seemed to be balanced by the fact that he had a loving relationship with his wife and enjoyed being around for his children. Andy resolved to continue his job search but to begin looking for jobs that were less competitive and demanding of his time. This took a lot of mental pressure off of him, and he realized that he had been searching for a job that would prove his worth according to his father's standards. Instead of insisting on a job that would prove his worth, Andy decided to go for jobs that he found enjoyable and challenging. He accepted the fact that this might take some time and require further personal adjustments, but he felt this would move his life in the direction of his values. He noticed that his depression, irritability, and sense of isolation were no longer the dominant experiences of each day, and he found a job that would support his lifestyle after a couple more months of looking—and it wasn't even in the banking industry. Andy was back on the path toward a life worth living!

EXPRESS YOUR GRATITUDE

As the old saying goes, "What doesn't kill you makes you stronger." Although we've encouraged you not to mindlessly fuse with such sayings and we don't want you to take this saying too literally, it does offer some wisdom about embracing life's challenges. It acknowledges that tough times are indeed difficult and painful, but at the same time, they allow you to learn a lot about who you are as a person.

You can put this perspective on life's difficulties into practice by expressing your gratitude to life for giving you the opportunity to learn something new about yourself. This is what living a vital life is all about: taking the good, the bad, and the ugly in stride and using each life situation as an opportunity to choose actions that reflect your values and allow you to grow as a person. You don't have to do this perfectly either; you can make mistakes. When you do, the most workable response is to get back on your feet and resume your journey. That's where all of the life learning is—in the journey.

One way to express gratitude is to start each day by thanking life for something specific that you're grateful for. You can write a thank-you note to life or perform some kind of ritual to welcome each day and whatever it may bring. Here are some examples of the kinds of things you might thank life for:

- Thank you, life, for giving me the opportunity to learn to live with the money I have.

- Thank you for helping me learn to bounce back from arguments with my spouse.

- Thank you for helping me learn how important my friends are.

- I'm grateful for the opportunity to seek a vital life today.

- I'm grateful for the opportunity to promote good health today.

- Thank you, life, for helping me learn how to accept the loss of someone I love.

Expression of gratitude is also a great way to get into the present moment of your day-to-day living. It prepares you for the path you'll travel each day and allows you to stay in a mental space where you expect to learn something new about yourself each day. In ACT, we often speak of setting a daily goal to end each day as a new person. This type of ongoing growth happens when you're in direct contact with the results in your life and how those results are changing your understanding of who you are.

Secrets to ACT On

☞ Life is a marathon, not a sprint. You need to build a lifestyle that uses ACT strategies on a daily basis to help you deal with the challenges that life has to offer.

☞ The more specific you are about the ACT strategies you intend to use, the more likely it is that you'll make them into habits.

☞ You can build a healthy lifestyle through practicing ACT habits in small ways and then linking them together to form a daily routine.

☞ To reduce your chances of future depression, identify depression risks and specific ACT strategies you intend to use to offset each depression risk.

☞ Mental rehearsal of depression risk situations and your responses in those situations will help you build a strong intention to ACT!

The Coach Says

A marathoner doesn't look forward to hitting the wall in a race but knows it will happen. Life will throw obstacles at you, and learning to navigate them will help you grow as a person. Even the tough times can promote your health and vitality when you accept that this is a part of the race you are running.

Sneak Preview

In the next chapter, we'll help you identify and rally your social support to help you succeed in your quest to build an ACT lifestyle.

CHAPTER 16

Give and Accept Support

Each friend represents a world in us, a world possibly not born until they arrive, and it is only by this meeting that a new world is born. —Anaïs Nin

In the previous chapter, we helped you develop a plan not just for preventing another episode of depression but also for incorporating ACT strategies into your life on a daily basis. The formula for healthy living and preventing depression involves accepting what is there to be had, living each day with a mindful and values-based vision, and choosing to act in ways that are consistent with what you believe. Because this entails long-term changes in your lifestyle, you'll be much more successful if you look for people who can support you in your quest. In turn, you can support them by sharing what you've learned from this program.

Ultimately, we live in an interpersonal world. It's hard to go anywhere or do anything without running into other humans. Even when approaching the very summit of Mount Everest, climbers often find themselves in a long string of people with the same goal in mind. Reaching the summit requires each individual to summon the will to persevere, but in most cases it also involves teamwork and compatible climbing partners. Ultimately, we are social beings, and you can use your social connections to help solidify your lifestyle changes. In this chapter, we'll help you identify people who can support you in your quest for a life worth living. We'll also help you develop strategies for reaching out to these people in ways that will make them want to help you.

CREATE A CIRCLE OF SUPPORT

One of the effects of being in depression compression is that you can lose contact with the social world that surrounds you. Depressed people tend to become very self-focused and preoccupied with managing their moods. This often leads not only to a sense of being isolated but also to isolating behavior. As depression compression deepens, that sense of isolation moves quite literally closer and closer to home. The last people you isolate yourself from tend to be those who are closest to you.

Building a strong, vital social foundation that will help you ward off a recurrence of depression requires that you first imagine the social world you want to construct. Remember, part of your values compass involves acting in ways that are consistent with what you want your relationships to be about. This might mean renewing relationships that have weakened over time, forming new relationships with people who are kindred souls, looking to an existing relationship to bolster your efforts, or inviting the help of professionals who might be able to support you. As you approach the tasks in this chapter, remember that the broader and more varied your base of social support, the more beneficial it will be. The goal of this chapter is to help you build a community of social connections that will support your new lifestyle. Before we work on identifying the people in your life who might provide support, let's take a look at what social support is, what it isn't, and qualities to be on the lookout for as you seek to create your own community.

What Is Competent Social Support?

Not all kinds of social support are created equal. We use the term "competent social support" to describe a healthy form of social connection characterized by a nonjudgmental and empathic stance. It doesn't involve criticism, lecturing, giving advice, or comparing how you're doing to how that person (or anyone else) dealt with a similar problem. When you're struggling and your morale is sagging, the last thing you need is someone who criticizes you, lectures you, or makes you feel like a failure.

■ *Kay's Story*

Kay, a thirty-nine-year-old single lesbian, has struggled with depression since she was a teenager. She had a long-term love-hate relationship with her mother, a very strong-willed woman who was deeply disappointed about Kay's sexual orientation. The family lived in a conservative rural community, and Kay was discouraged from coming out of the closet because her mother was sure it would disgrace their family. Despite the challenges in the relationship, Kay admired her mother and sought her approval, only to receive one criticism after another, whether about her grades, her friends, or her appearance. As Kay's problems with depression worsened in her teenage years, her mother frequently declared that Kay's sexual orientation was responsible. Kay was dragged into therapy on more than one occasion to see what could be done about the underlying "problem" of her sexuality.

After Kay left home, she experienced a multitude of problems, including drug abuse, dropping out of college, failed relationships, and escalating depression. The one person who remained constant in Kay's world was her mother. They talked several times a week, but their conversations were often marked by heated disagreements about Kay's failures and her sexual orientation. Kay generally felt much worse after talking with her mother about her problems. When Kay began to use the ACT approach, she realized that her mother wasn't providing competent social support. She wasn't positive and accepting; on the contrary, she was demanding, judgmental, and critical. When Kay began to track changes in her depression experiences, she discovered that talking with her mother was a major trigger for increased depression.

Kay realized she needed to form a more complete and competent circle of social support. She made a commitment to join a local hiking club, and on one of the first outings, she met a same-sex couple she really connected with. They seemed to accept Kay for who she was and offered to be there for her if she needed support or someone to talk to. The relationship was mutually rewarding; they enjoyed hiking with Kay because she was very athletic and had a great sense of humor. They scheduled a variety of hikes as a trio, and Kay began to meet some of their other friends. Kay soon noticed that she was feeling much less isolated and didn't have the desire to talk with her mother on such a frequent basis. She also decided to limit the length of phone conversations with her mother and quickly end the conversation if she noticed her mother was getting prickly with her.

Like-Minded People

As Kay's situation demonstrates, the best social support is often provided by people who have a similar view of the world or share a common interest. For example, if you go to church, other members of the congregation probably share many of your religious or spiritual views. If you take a yoga class or go on a meditation retreat, you'll probably be surrounded by people who are interested in acceptance and mindfulness as a way of living. Even something as simple as a reading group or a gardening club can help you connect with kindred souls.

EXERCISE: IDENTIFY LIKE-MINDED PEOPLE

This exercise will help you to identify possible social connections in a variety of venues. Take some time to think about the types of people you might meet in one or more of the areas listed below and the types of relationships and support they might offer. Church and other organized spiritual activities are fairly self-explanatory. The range of hobby and special interest groups is almost endless, encompassing everything from arts and crafts to games to vintage cars. Health and wellness activities also run the gamut, from yoga and tai chi to aerobics to a healthy cooking class. Volunteer activities can be a great choice; if you get involved with a cause that really matters to you, you'll be taking action that reflects your values while also forging social connections with others. Of course, some social opportunities, such as a dinner group, won't fit any of these categories, and others, such as a meditation group or a dance class, might fit into several categories. The categories here are provided simply to get you thinking about the possibilities. In the middle column, write down activities or groups that seem like a good fit for you, and in the right-hand column describe how each can support you in living an ACT lifestyle.

Inventory of Like-Minded People

Social Resource	Activity or Group I Could Join	How It Can Support Me
Church or other organized spiritual activity		
Hobby or special interest club		
Health and wellness activities		
Volunteer activities		
Other		

Debriefing. Look over the answers you came up with. Do any of these possible sources of social support seem immediately available to you? What would it take for you to make contact with that particular group or activity? Did you list any activities or groups that used to be enjoyable or beneficial for you? Any such activities would be an excellent initial goal for you. Are there any areas where you couldn't think of anything to list but are still intrigued with the idea of doing something in that area? You might want to look in your local newspaper or on community bulletin boards for opportunities in these areas.

FIND A VITALITY PARTNER

Normally, people value their privacy and are reluctant to share their deepest, darkest secrets with others. One of the most powerful forms of social support is having a person you can share your most private feelings and yearnings with. This person might be a very close friend, a sponsor in a self-help group, or a spouse or life partner. This person can help you stay accountable to your ACT commitment to live a vital, valued life; hence the term "vitality partner." To help you stay accountable, this person will need to know about your struggle with depression and how you intend to use the ACT approach to create a vital life. In most cases, people who are likely candidates to be your vitality partner will already know you've been depressed, but they may not really understand the ACT approach. You may have to educate them about the essentials of the ACT model. A natural result of this process of education is that your vitality partner might get interested in using ACT as well. This is a great outcome because you can then support each other in sticking to your new lifestyle and commitments.

Despite the obvious benefits that a vitality partner provides, your reactive mind is going to try to phish you out of doing this by creating emotional barriers. Don't buy any thoughts that discourage you from reaching out. Let's take a look at some of the obstacles your reactive mind is likely to present.

Not Wanting to Be a Burden

One typical barrier to being willing to enlist the aid of a vitality partner is the thought that you're burdening this person with your problems. Further, your reactive mind will try to hook you with feelings of guilt for doing so. A wise mind view of social support is summed up in the old saying "One hand washes the other." There will be times when you need the support of your vitality partner, and there will be times when your vitality partner needs you. As you go through life, there is a constant give-and-take, and things tend to even themselves out in the end.

This phishing lure is suspicious in other regards too. The ACT lifestyle doesn't involve commiserating about how lousy life is and how bad you feel. That type of behavior is burdensome not only for your vitality partner but also for you. ACT involves focusing on where you want to go and taking positive actions that produce a sense of vitality and well-being. You won't be burdening your vitality partner; rather, you'll simply be asking to be held accountable for following through on actions you've committed yourself to. As your vitality partner begins to see some of the positive effects of ACT strategies in your life, it's likely that he or she will also begin to use these strategies and benefit from them. What better gift to give to someone who is going to be there for you over the course of months, years, or a lifetime!

Humiliation and Stigma

Another barrier to enlisting the aid of a vitality partner is a sense of shame, stigma, or humiliation about being depressed in the first place. Your reactive mind will try to hook you with the belief that you lack character or are weak or mentally ill, that others will surely see this in you, and that the best strategy is to keep your problems to yourself. All of these phishing lures are designed to keep you silent in the presence of people who would be glad to help you, if only you would ask. In reality, you might discover that your vitality partner has struggled with some of the same life issues as you have. A wise-mind approach to this issue might be summed up in the phrase "We're all in this stew together." To be human means to confront life challenges and the pain and suffering that go along with them. In all likelihood, your vitality partner will have experienced life setbacks too, and will be able to understand where you're coming from.

Not Wanting to Ask for Too Much

Another phishing lure is the idea that asking for help and support proves you're selfish, self-centered, and asking too much of your partner. If you bite on this lure, you might not involve your vitality partner at a critical time because you think you've already asked for too much support. Just remember, your vitality partner isn't a mind reader and won't know how to help you if you don't speak up and say what you need. A wise mind approach is to trust your vitality partner's ability to set limits. If you ask for more than your vitality partner is willing to give, your vitality partner will tell you. Don't be devastated if this occurs. Again, it probably isn't about you; everyone has his or her own priorities. Maybe tomorrow your vitality partner will be ready to provide the support you're asking for.

EXERCISE: IDENTIFY AND ASK

In this exercise, you'll identify one or more potential vitality partners and develop a plan for talking with them about your ACT goals. Remember, a good vitality partner is someone who can support you, not judge you, and who will hold you accountable rather than criticize you for failing to keep a commitment. Try to identify people who are clearly on your side and who can motivate you. List the names of one or more such people here:

Vitality partner 1: _____

Vitality partner 2: _____

Vitality partner 3: _____

Next, we want you to describe the specific kind of support you'll request from each vitality partner. Try to describe this in very specific terms, such as "Check with me weekly and ask me if I've practiced mental images of acceptance at least three times that week" or "At the beginning of each month, ask me if I've completed my inventory of depressive behaviors." You could also elicit support by having your vitality partner join you in some valued action, such as swimming laps on a regular basis. It's perfectly fine to ask your vitality partner to actually join you in some activity that you value. The more specific you can be about the support you are seeking, the more likely it is that your vitality partner will be able to meet your needs. List the support you'll ask for here:

1. _____

2. _____

3. _____

4. _____

5. _____

Now consider each potential vitality partner you identified and ask yourself, "Is this person likely to be emotionally supportive and nonjudgmental? Can this person motivate me?" If the answer is yes, you have a very good candidate for your vitality partner. If you hesitated, go back and rethink this choice. What caused you to hesitate? You can still choose this person after reconsidering; we simply want to make sure there are no red flags that might argue for another choice.

Now, look at the specific types of support you're going to request. Are you asking for something clear and specific? Have you indicated when and how often you'd like each form of support? If you wrote something like "Be positive and support me in my ACT program," that's too vague. What kind of positive support would you like your partner to engage in? For example, you might ask your partner to call you on Saturday mornings and ask how your ten-minute morning mindfulness practice is going and what you've been learning from it. If one or more support requests seem vague, go back and rewrite them in more specific terms: what you would like the person to do, and when and how often you would like him or her to do it.

Now that you've identified a potential vitality partner and have developed a list of specific support activities, it is time to meet with this person and discuss your request. The best way to follow through with this is to develop it as a behavioral intention, as recommended in the previous chapter. If you frame this request as something you intend to do in a very specific way, it's more likely that you'll do it. Complete the little statement of intention below as a way of making this commitment to yourself.

I intend to meet with _____ [possible vitality partner]

on _____ [date], at _____ [location]. In

this meeting, I intend to ask _____ to be my vitality

partner and provide me with the specific types of support I just listed.

ENLIST SUPPORT FROM PROFESSIONALS

Another important form of support involves discussing your situation with a health care professional, such as your family doctor or a nurse practitioner or physician assistant. These people provide health care to patients experiencing depression compression every day. Your doctor might already be aware of your situation, and may be prescribing antidepressants for you. Although most health professionals are very familiar with the use of antidepressant medications, they may not be familiar with the ACT approach. Either way, it will be to your advantage to initiate a brief discussion with your doctor about your goals in the ACT program. Medical professionals are usually very busy and may not have the time to get a full history of your depression and your use of ACT. You can facilitate the dialogue by giving your health care provider a copy of your depression prevention plan and requesting that it be put in your medical chart. This way, if you do start to slide back into depression compression, your health care provider can review the plan and support you in following it. Often, this is all that is needed to stop depression compression from developing.

Obviously, any mental health professional you work with is also an important source of support. Perhaps you've been working with a therapist to get on top of your depression. You might want to take this book with you to your next appointment and go over the structure of the program together. When we use this program with depressed people, we organize therapy goals so that they correspond with the structure of the book. For example, the goal between sessions may be to complete the values compass work in chapter 6 and bring the results in for review and discussion. If you aren't currently working with a therapist but have had good results with one in the past, you might want to schedule several visits now to talk about your plan for preventing future depression compression experiences.

INTERNET RESOURCES

With the seemingly endless expansion of the Internet, people now have access to all kinds of resources for better understanding depression and what to do about it. Unfortunately, the same characteristics that make the Internet so beneficial can also make it harmful. Since depression is such a common problem, there are literally hundreds of websites, blogs, and other resources on this topic. Not all of them offer accurate or helpful information. For example, some sites use depression as a lure to encourage people to buy a particular herbal product or a specific religious doctrine. Other sites make exorbitant claims about the benefits of a treatment for depression that they offer. Here are some simple rules to help you surf through these resources:

- Beware of sites that portray depression strictly as a medical illness or a disease. Instead, look for sites that seem to balance the role of biology with psychological and social factors.

- Beware of sites that seem to say depression can only be treated with medication or one specific medication.

- In general, avoid websites sponsored by pharmaceutical firms because of an inherent conflict of interest. Their goal in educating you is to convince you to buy one of their products.

- Beware of sites that use depression to hook you into trying untested treatments or to promote an unrelated type of product, such as joining a new age church or buying a nutritional supplement.

- The best and most trustworthy sites are generally those that provide free information about depression and its treatment.

- Beware of sites that make exorbitant and unrealistic claims, such as how you can cure your depression overnight, the secret treatment that scientists don't want you to hear about, or the way to completely turn your life around in seven days.

SELF-HELP GROUPS

Another great way to rally social support from like-minded people is to participate in a self-help group for depressed people. Most communities have groups like this. They might be sponsored by a local church, hospital, mental health agency, or wellness center. You can usually locate these support groups by calling a local information and referral line or by looking them up in a community resource directory, which most municipalities offer for free. Here's what to look for in a self-help group for depression:

- The group is based in some recognized form of treatment for depression, such as ACT, cognitive behavioral therapy, interpersonal therapy, or problem-solving therapy.

- The group is focused on finding solutions for depression rather than allowing members to ventilate excessively about the pain of depression.

- The group has an atmosphere of all members being equal.

- The group practices competent social support tactics (nonjudgmental, accepting, positive, and affirming of you as a person).

It's a good idea to test out a support group a couple of times before committing to it. If it seems that the group is dwelling on the negatives, that only a few members seem to be doing most of the speaking, that there is an informal leader who is telling others what to do, or that the atmosphere of the group doesn't feel supportive, try other groups until you find a good fit.

Secrets to ACT On

☞ Rallying your social support will be a crucial part of your success at achieving your personal goals.

☞ Focus on identifying competent forms of social support—support that's nonjudgmental, accepting, positive, and motivating.

☞ Look for opportunities to link up with like-minded people in your community who can support you.

☞ Find a vitality partner who will help you stay on track in sticking to your ACT commitments and lifestyle goals.

☞ Consider enlisting the support of your health care provider or, if you are seeing one, a therapist.

☞ Internet websites can provide useful information and referrals, but you need to be on guard for sites that are trying to get you to buy something you don't need.

☞ Self-help groups can be useful if they have the qualities characteristic of competent social support.

The Coach Says

Coming out of your shell and reaching out to people who can help you is never easy, particularly if you have been in depression compression. Know this: you have what it takes to create the social world you have always dreamed of living in! If you have a clear vision of what you want, you will notice that life often has a way of giving it to you.

Sneak Preview

This is the end of the book but not the end of your journey, so we'd like to offer a sneak preview of the path that lies before you. You've learned a lot of strategies in this book that will be very helpful as you reengage your life. You understand and accept that life has its many challenges—that there will be good times and bad times. By accepting and participating in both the good and the bad, you will be able to experience both in a healthy way. You'll be able to show up and stay present in your life on a daily basis, and your stance of mindfulness will put you into direct contact with the immense richness and vitality life offers. Because you are in touch with your closely held values, you'll have a compass bearing to follow when things get difficult or confusing. You will persist in pursuing your dreams no matter what obstacles life puts in your way. You will be flexible enough to revise or abandon strategies that aren't working and to sense new opportunities that you may not have been aware of before. In short, you will be an unstoppable force in the world, free from self-defeating attachments and focused on what matters most. As fellow travelers, we wish you all the best and pray that you will have the rich and fulfilling life that you deserve.

References

Alloy, L. B., L. Y. Abramson, W. G. Whitehouse, M. E. Hogan, C. Panzarella, and D. T. Rose. 2006. Prospective incidence of first onsets and recurrences of depression in individuals at high and low cognitive risk for depression. *Journal of Abnormal Psychology* 115(4):145-56.

Bargh, J. A., M. Chen, and L. Burrows. 1996. Automaticity of social behavior: Direct effects of trait construct and stereotype activation on action. *Journal of Personality and Social Psychology* 71(2):230-44.

Campbell-Sills, L., D. H. Barlow, T. A. Brown, and S. G. Hofmann. 2006. Acceptability and suppression of negative emotion in anxiety and mood disorders. *Emotion* 6(4):587-95.

Dalgleish, T., and J. Yiend. 2006. The effects of suppressing a negative autobiographical memory on concurrent intrusions and subsequent autobiographical recall in dysphoria. *Journal of Abnormal Psychology* 115(3):467-73.

Demyttenaere, K., R. Bruffaerts, J. Posada-Villa, I. Gasquet, V. Kovess, J. P. Lepine, et al. 2004. Prevalence, severity, and unmet need for treatment of mental disorders in the World Health Organization World Mental Health surveys. *Journal of the American Medical Association* 291(21):2581-90.

Deshmukh, V. D. 2006. Neuroscience of meditation. *Scientific World Journal* 16:2239-53.

Ekman, P. 1992. An argument for basic emotions. *Cognition and Emotion* 6:169-200.

Fennell, M. J. V. 2004. Depression, low self-esteem, and mindfulness. *Behaviour Research and Therapy* 42(9):1053-67.

Finucane, A., and S. W. Mercer. 2006. An exploratory mixed methods study of the acceptability and effectiveness of mindfulness-based cognitive therapy for patients with active depression and anxiety in primary care. *BMC Psychiatry* 6:14.

Franck, E., R. de Raedt, and J. de Houwer. 2007. Implicit but not explicit self-esteem predicts future depressive symptomatology. *Behaviour Research and Therapy* 45(10):2448-55.

Grant, B. F., D. A. Dawson, F. S. Stinson, S. P. Chou, M. C. Dufour, and R. P. Pickering. 2004. The 12-month prevalence and trends in DSM-IV alcohol abuse and dependence: United States, 1991-92 and 2001. *Drug and Alcohol Dependence* 74(3):223-34.

Greenwald, A. G., D. E. McGhee, and J. L. Schwartz. 1998. Measuring individual differences in implicit cognition: The implicit association test. *Journal of Personality and Social Psychology* 74(6):1464-80.

Grossman, P., L. Neimann, S. Schmidt, and H. Walach. 2003. Mindfulness-based stress reduction and health benefits: A meta-analysis. *Journal of Psychosomatic Research* 57(1):35-43.

Hankey, A. 2006. Studies of advanced stages of meditation in the Tibetan Buddhist and Vedic traditions I: A comparison of general changes. *Complementary and Alternative Medicine* 3(4):513-21.

Hayes, S., D. Barnes-Holmes, and B. Roche, eds. 2001. *Relational Frame Theory: A Post-Skinnerian Account of Human Language and Cognition*. New York: Plenum Press.

Hayes, S., K. D. Strosahl, and K. G. Wilson. 1999. *Acceptance and Commitment Therapy: An Experiential Approach to Behavior Change*. New York: Guilford Press.

Hayes, S., K. G. Wilson, E. V. Gifford, V. M. Follette, and K. Strosahl. 1996. Emotional avoidance and behavioral disorders: A functional dimensional approach to diagnosis and treatment. *Journal of Consulting and Clinical Psychology* 64(6):1152-68.

Kabat-Zinn, J. 2005. *Coming to Our Senses: Healing Ourselves and the World Through Mindfulness*. New York: Hyperion.

Kelly, M. A. R., J. E. Roberts, and J. A. Ciesla. 2005. Sudden gains in cognitive behavioral treatment for depression: When do they occur and do they matter? *Behaviour Research and Therapy* 43(6):703-14.

Kessler, R. C., P. Berglund, O. Demler, R. Jin, K. R. Merikangas, and E. E. Walters. 2005. Lifetime prevalence and age-of-onset distributions of DSM-IV disorders in the National Comorbidity Survey Replication. *Archives of General Psychiatry* 62(6):593-602.

Last, J. M. 1988. *Dictionary of Epidemiology*. Oxford: Oxford University Press.

Lundgren, T. March 2006. Personal communication.

Marcks, B. A., and D. W. Woods. 2005. A comparison of thought suppression to an acceptance-based technique in the management of personal intrusive thoughts: A controlled evaluation. *Behaviour Research and Therapy* 43(4):433-45.

Merton, T. 1961. *Mystics and Zen Masters*. New York: Dell.

Mynors-Wallis, L. M., D. H. Gath, A. Day, and F. Baker. 2000. Randomised controlled trial of problem solving treatment, antidepressant medication, and combined treatment for major depression in primary care. *BMJ* 320(7226):26-30.

Nisbett, R. E., and T. D. Wilson. 1977. Telling more than we can know: Verbal reports on mental processes. *Psychological Review* 84(3):231-59.

Nolen-Hoeksema, S. 2000. The role of rumination in depressive disorders and mixed anxiety/depressive symptoms. *Journal of Abnormal Psychology* 109(3):504-11.

Paykel, E. S. 2006. Cognitive therapy in relapse prevention in depression. *International Journal of Neuropsychopharmacology* 10(1):131-36.

Robinson, P. 1996. *Living Life Well: New Strategies for Hard Times*. Reno, NV: Context Press.

Schaefer, C. 2006. *Grandmothers Counsel the World: Women Elders Offer Their Vision for Our Planet.* Boston: Trumpeter.

Segal, Z. V., J. M. G. Williams, and J. D. Teasdale. 2002. *Mindfulness-Based Cognitive Therapy for Depression: A New Approach to Preventing Relapse.* New York: Guilford Press.

Schotte, C. K., B. van den Bossche, D. de Doncker, S. Claes, and P. Cosyns. 2006. A biopsychosocial model as a guide for psychoeducation and treatment of depression. *Depression and Anxiety* 23(5):312-24.

Teasdale, J. D., Z. V. Segal, J. M. Williams, V. A. Ridgeway, J. M. Soulsby, and M. A. Lau. 2000. Prevention of relapse/recurrence in major depression by mindfulness-based cognitive therapy. *Journal of Consulting and Clinical Psychology* 68(4):615-23.

Wakefield, J. C., M. F. Schmitz, M. B. First, and A. V. Horwitz. 2007. Extending the bereavement exclusion for major depression to other losses: Evidence from the National Comorbidity Survey. *Archives of General Psychiatry* 64(4):433-40.

Williams, J. M. G. 1996. Depression and the specificity of autobiographical memory. In *Remembering Our Past: Studies in Autobiographical Memory,* ed. D. C. Rubin, 244-267. Cambridge: Cambridge University Press.

Williams, J. M. G., J. D. Teasdale, Z. V. Segal, and J. Soulsby. 2000. Mindfulness-based cognitive therapy reduces overgeneral autobiographical memory in formerly depressed patients. *Journal of Abnormal Psychology* 109(1):150-55.

Williams, M. G., J. D. Teasdale, Z. V. Segal, and J. Kabat-Zinn. 2007. *The Mindful Way Through Depression: Freeing Yourself from Chronic Unhappiness.* New York: Guilford Press.

Zettle, R. D., and S. C. Hayes. 1987. Component and process analysis of cognitive therapy. *Psychological Reports* 61(3):939-53.

Zettle, R. D., and J. Rains. 1989. Group cognitive and contextual therapies in treatment of depression. *Journal of Clinical Psychology* 45(3):438-45.

Kirk D. Strosahl, Ph.D., is cofounder of acceptance and commitment therapy and an internationally known expert on managing depression and suicidal behavior. Strosahl has practiced as a psychologist for more than twenty-six years, working with depressed patients in both mental health and primary care settings. He is coauthor of several books, including *Acceptance and Commitment Therapy.* Strosahl currently lives in a vineyard in central Washington.

Patricia J. Robinson, Ph.D., is a long-time practitioner of acceptance and commitment therapy and an author of ACT publications concerning the treatment of medical patients and patients with chronic pain. Her career of twenty-six years includes conducting research about use of ACT and cognitive behavior therapy in primary-care settings and writing two books on treating depression.

Foreword writer **Steven C. Hayes, Ph.D.,** is Foundation Professor of Psychology at the University of Nevada, Reno. He is among the most influential figures in contemporary behaviorism and clinical psychology and the author of innumerable books and scientific articles, including the successful ACT workbook *Get Out of Your Mind and into Your Life.*

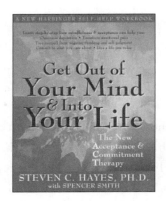
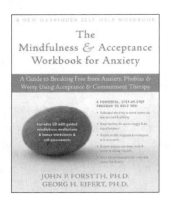

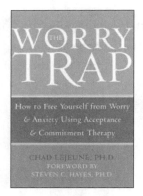
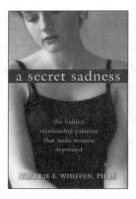